Praise f

"Josh Stephens is one of the best writers in city planning, and now he has written one of the best books on cities. Unlike academics who "theorize" about cities, Stephens observes cities and interprets them for us. What he says often seems obvious—after he has said it. I particularly admire his unfailing ability to summarize a big problem in the perfect phrase, like his disapproving description of Honolulu as "Houston with volcanoes." Every chapter of The Urban Mystique contains many similar gems of critical observation, and they add up to a genuinely enlightening and thoroughly enjoyable book."

—**Donald Shoup, Distinguished Research Professor, UCLA Luskin School of Public Affairs; Author,** *The High Cost of Free Parking*

"On numerous occasions throughout my career, an essay or an article by Josh Stephens redirected my thinking and changed my understanding of the world for the better, and for good. Stephens's long career as a thoughtful and insightful observer of the professional field of urban planning reveals how fruitful a passion and interest in that subject can be for anyone searching for knowledge of the built and natural worlds. With this book, every reader has the chance to expand their understanding of the world through an improved understanding of the communities that call California home."

—**James Brasuell, Managing Editor, Planetizen**

"Cities are provocative, blunt and idiosyncratic creatures -- but too much writing about cities tends to be predictable and self-important. Not here. Josh Stephens uses his perch in Los Angeles to take stock of, and take aim at, everything from housing policy and gentrification to the histrionics of NIMBYISM. In short, *The Urban Mystique* is a bracing look at the way we live now."

—**John King, Urban Design Critic,** *San Francisco Chronicle*

"*The Urban Mystique* is a lively and wry collection of essays and reflections on the past decade of urban politics and trends, from Los Angeles to cities around the world.

In the tradition of Joan Didion, Stephens roots many of the stories in his personal history and travels. At this moment of both promise and crisis for cities, Stephens chronicles key events from the rise of the Tea Party and pro-housing YIMBYs to sports stadia and ballot box controversies. For those who care about cities and their effect on our culture and politics, it's an engaging and worthwhile read."

—**Ethan Elkind, Author,** *Railtown: The Fight for the Los Angeles Metro Rail and the Future of the City*

"Josh Stephens is a bit of a magician. His trick? Taking often convoluted, context-dependent strands of thought and action—about zoning, floor-to-air ratios, density, NIMBY-ism, YIMBY-ism, all manner of arcane, acronym-laden planning ideas—and then weaving them into intensely human, compulsively readable stories. It's a contradiction worthy of the city that he writes so evocatively about. His insights are deep and informed, but also witty and elegant. The voice is singular. Josh's stories shouldn't be as much pure fun to read as they are, but there you go—that's the magic I'm talking about."

—**Martin C. Pedersen, Editor, Common Edge Collaborative; Editor Emeritus,** *Metropolis Magazine*

"Josh Stephens is an astute observer and interpreter of the idiosyncratic built and spatio- political environment of Southern California, writing with both the fondness of a native and the critical perspective of an outsider. His provocative choice of subjects and penetrating- yet-pragmatic style make his work a pleasure to read, for both the practicing Los Angeles planner and thoughtful urbanist."

—**Ashley Atkinson, President-Elect, California Chapter of the American Planning Association**

The Urban Mystique: Notes on California, Los Angeles, and Beyond

By Josh Stephens

Solimar Books
Ventura, California

Copyright © 2020 by Josh Stephens

All rights reserved. No part of this publication may be reproduced, stored in a retrieval system, or transmitted, in any form or by any means, electronic, mechanical, photocopying, recording, or otherwise, without the prior written approval of the author and the publisher.

Solimar Books
P.O. Box 24618
Ventura, California 93002
http://www.solimarbooks.com/
admin@cp-dr.com
805.652.0695

"What part of the Middle West?"

"San Francisco."

"I see."

> — F. Scott Fitzgerald, *The Great Gatsby*

Table of Contents

Foreword by Bill Fulton i

Introduction v

1. A Sense of Place
Dispatches from the heart of Los Angeles 1

2. NIMBYism and Its Discontents
The mess that is the California housing crisis 41

3. Density Scolds
Taking on Kotkin, Cox and friends 89

4. Politics of the Local
Commentary on the squabbles
that are the lifeblood of planning... 125

5. Matters of Taste
Musings on architecture and design 163

6. Everywhere is Florida
Urban Economics in the Age of the "Creative Class" 213

7. Developer-in-Chief
A different kind of "urban" president 255

8. The Culture of Planning
Ideas, trends, and personalities behind the profession..........293

Sources 329

Photo Credits 333

Acknowledgments.. 339

Foreword
by Bill Fulton

Sometimes these days, I have to admit, I don't quite get Los Angeles. It's better than it used to be, but also worse, and even though both the good and the bad are kind of predictable and understandable, I don't always see how they fit together inside the city so many of us have spent our lifetimes trying to understand. That's when I realize I need to start looking at L.A. through Josh Stephens's eyes.

Josh is not quite a millennial, but he is a late Gen Xer; indeed, it's pretty startling to me when he points out that the world I described in *The Reluctant Metropolis*—essentially, Los Angeles as it evolved when I was in my 30s—was the world he grew up in.

In writing that book—and, later, as a local politician—I had to navigate the NIMBYs very gently, calling them to account without quite dismissing them altogether. Josh, on the other hand, is an unabashed YIMBY, to cite one of the more significant developments that have arisen in planning on Josh's watch. He's not insensitive to neighborhood character, but he believes neighborhood bars are more important than building setbacks, and isn't afraid to point out that if you have to spend most of your money on housing—for rent, not a mortgage—your definition of neighborhood character might be a little different.

And he's unabashedly a *Los Angeles* YIMBY. The pieces in this book aren't exclusively about Los Angeles. But *The Urban Mystique* is a book with an L.A. sensibility. Also—and this is a reflection of both the times and Josh himself—it's a book that unapologetically treats Los Angeles as a great city worthy of serious consideration by a serious urbanist writer. Back in the '80s and '90s—when L.A. was emerging as a great city but not quite sure of itself—that was an almost impossible trick to turn. In his always-graceful way, what Josh has succeeded in doing in this book—and, indeed, in all his writing—is conveying the zeitgeist of what might be called the Not-So-Reluctant Metropolis. Now that Los Angeles is undeniably a great city, Josh wants it to be greater still—and to be accessible to as many people as possible.

The other thing Josh has done, almost single-handedly, is revive the art of the urban book review. There surely have to be more books about cities being published these days than at any time in recent history—maybe ever. And yet the discussion of these books often takes place without much context—not so much a pro- or anti-urban slant, but a context devoid of much true understanding about cities and their history. Josh, having been trained in literature at Princeton and urban planning at Harvard, has a deep understanding of both and a strong appreciation of how they fit together. His book reviews reflect this appreciation (as do his occasional movie reviews, such as his take on *Blade Runner 2049*, which has to be one of the most heavily read stories ever posted by *California Planning & Development Report*).

Indeed, when I am reading his book reviews, I am often reminded of something that Ray Bradbury used to say. Though Bradbury was best known as a science fiction novelist, he was also a perceptive, if quirky, urbanist, especially knowledgeable about his hometown of L.A. Bradbury used to say that movie theaters and bookstores should go together in the urban environment because "seeing a good movie makes you want to read a good book." It's true that bookstores and movie theaters are pretty much obsolete in the Amazon/Netflix world we live in these days, but Bradbury was hinting at a larger point that Josh intuitively understands: good cities and good stories go together, so we can best understand a city as a kind of story, and you have to critique a book on cities from that perspective. Incidentally, Josh has also written about how good cities and good *stores* go together, with a Gen Xer's anxiety about the rise of online commerce and culture.

Of course, one of the things Josh is best at—and clearly has a lot of fun doing—is the takedown of people who disagree with him about cities. Admittedly, it is not all that difficult to do an effective takedown of Joel Kotkin or Donald Trump—both of whom seem to have become caricatures of themselves as they have gotten older—but nevertheless, Josh does it with gusto and style.

But even when he's taking people down, he doesn't take himself too seriously, and you can feel his underlying joy about cities. You always get the impression that, as much fun as he is having taking them down, he'd much rather be sitting around having a beer with them, swapping great stories about great cities. At a neighborhood bar. In a building with no setback. And, most likely, electric scooters scattered all over the sidewalk. In some L.A. neighborhood that has just a little bit of urban mystique.

The truth is, I can't imagine anything more fun than that. Except maybe reading this book.

Introduction

To use a phrase not normally found in the Southern California lexicon, my childhood neighborhood was neither fish nor fowl. I grew up on the Westside of Los Angeles in the 1980s and 1990s, back when the Westside was not fashionable but merely ... fine. It was then, as now, a weaker version of the Upper East Side or the Inner Richmond, desirable but utterly characterless, with very little backstory of its own. What struck me even then was the in-betweenness of it all.

The Westside is middle everything: middle density, moderately attractive, some walkable places, but not many. It offered none of the suburban amusements—backyard swimming pools, empty streets for skateboarding and stickball, neighborhood friends close at hand—of the city's outer sprawlscape. But it also offered none of the excitement and freedom of a true metropolis. It's dense enough, but not in an exciting way. When I got to college and met kids who'd grown up in Manhattan, with everything from the Metropolitan Museum to Broadway to, well, less wholesome destinations at their disposal for the cost of a subway token, I realized what a bumpkin I was.

I was in college when Bill Fulton—publisher of *CP&DR* and my boss of many years—published *The Reluctant Metropolis*, his landmark analysis of the political economy of land use in Southern California. Bill focuses on the last quarter of the 20th century, meaning that, unbeknownst to me, I had grown up in the Reluctant Metropolis. For all that has changed about the world and about Los Angeles, Bill's analysis still rings true. *The Reluctant Metropolis* calmly explains how financial concerns—of real estate developers, city boosters, and public officials—shaped Southern California more than any other influences, in a process that Bill calls "the fiscalization of land use."

I am, therefore, a product not just of the palm trees, beaches, and mountains, but also of the growth machine, riots, the stodgy Proposition 13, the (semiracist) fight against the subway, institutionalized segregation, and strip malls, strip malls, strip malls. I grew up feeling the reluctance: the lack of neighborliness, the lack of civic pride. I grew up in a functional but uninspiring neighborhood where I don't think I knew a single neighbor. My Los Angeles was still one where it was fashionable to praise New York City, if only to cut down L.A.

Fiscalization of land use means that decisions often depend more on fiscal impacts than on aesthetics, livability, or social harmony. That's how we get auto malls and tract housing rather than main streets and row houses. That's how we remain stuck alone in cars rather than riding the rails with our neighbors. It's how we perpetuate the feminine mystique among homemakers marooned in the suburbs, and it's how we get the urban mystique among all of us who grew up in the city but knew that there had to be something more.

***

The notion of a childhood origin story remains relevant to anyone who lives in cities because, in many ways, everyone who lives in a city is still a child. Whether we live in Beacon Hill or Greenwich Village, Livermore or Santa Clarita, or Richmond or Compton, we are all passive subjects to the decisions made by planners and developers years and generations ago. Too many Americans are resigned to living and working in mediocre places. Too many of them, like the homemakers invoked by the title of this book, live in quiet desperation, unaware of the impact their environments have on them and unable to do anything about it.

Therein lies the urban mystique.

I borrow the phrase from Betty Freidan, who plays a prominent role in one of these essays. Rachel Carson, Jane Jacobs, and Freidan all published enduring, revolutionary books in, miraculously, the very same year (1963). In *The Feminine Mystique*, Freidan described the unsung plight of American suburban housewives of the 1950s. They were meant to have "perfect lives," lived out in deliberately nonurban places. But, predictably, isolation, uninspired architecture, unchecked sexism, and the impulse to believe in "perfection" itself became a recipe for despair. The suburban dream was one foisted upon women (and men) of the era and not necessarily one that they chose for themselves.

Cities are wonderful places, but they can be terrible places too—sometimes all at once. Cities' mystique lies in the idea that their value is not necessarily evident or definable. The urban mystique is different for everyone. But, as Freidan implies, we must at least acknowledge that it exists. We must acknowledge that cities can be special places and that they must not simply be a collection of demographic data, economic output, and real estate transactions. Why are they special? Because people are special. And more people live in cities than anywhere else. Cities are where some people go to survive and where some people go to chase, and sometimes achieve, their highest ambitions. Cities will never be "perfect" the way the suburbs have been rumored to be. They can be better than perfect, though, as long as we don't pretend that perfection should be the goal. And, ideally, they require everyone to contribute to their evolution. Urban life should center on inspiration and improvement, not passivity and resignation.

The subjectivity of the urban experience unites this collection of essays, written roughly over the course of the past decade for the *California Planning & Development Report*, Planetizen, and other city-focused publications. I use "unite" loosely, though. I've covered a collection of themes and topics that are, I think, every bit as jumbled as city life itself. They range from grave issues like crime and housing to aesthetic niceties of starchitecture and setbacks. I hope it will all—through praise, criticism, or something in between—lead to provocation, consideration, and, ultimately, action to create better cities, especially here in California, where I still—for reasons I can't always explain—reside.

I've been lucky enough to write during a fascinating decade. Cities have grown more quickly in other decades (1980s). And they have suffered more problems in still others (1970s). But, I'd argue, the 2010s have been about as interesting it gets. Much of the stuff about which I am most cranky has been improving. Many of my fellow members of Gen X feel just as I did about their upbringing and have been working like crazy to reclaim the urban experience for themselves and the next generation (and their parents' generations, in some cases). Principles of smart growth, new urbanism, and environmentalism have permeated the mainstream so fully that we rarely even refer to them as such anymore.

What makes Los Angeles frustrating and unpleasant is the very same thing that makes it fascinating: it was built imperfectly, at an imperfect time. Now, Los Angeles—along with the rest of California—is trying to reinvent itself. That's a difficult process: to shoehorn a new city into the old. In a 2015 *CP&DR* article on Los Angeles's new mobility plan, I equated the process of urban redevelopment to the infusion of adamantium into the bones of Wolverine. It's the geekiest thing I've ever written (and I don't even like comic books), but it's apt because, well, they are both unspeakably painful processes. This evolution stretches all the way back to Frederick Jackson Turner's Frontier Thesis, on which I wrote my undergraduate thesis. He described the continent's endless tracts of empty land as America's escape valve and the thing that made America uniquely American. Turner pronounced the Frontier "closed" in 1890. By then, San Francisco had a population of 300,000 and Los Angeles 50,000. But the Frontier found new life in the suburbs, as cities expanded and conquered their own hinterlands. That lasted for another century.

This process is what *Los Angeles Times* architecture critic Christopher Hawthorne refers to as the "Third L.A."—the pioneer city and the post-World War II boom town being the first two. I've called it "the backwash of sprawl." The unseemly metaphor is deliberate. We've built some heinous stuff: cheap, low-density development from the coast to the mountains to the desert. Now this form of urbanism faces a reckoning.

The political element of these challenges has gotten more contentious and more colorful of late. Several of these pieces refer to the rise of the YIMBY ("yes in my backyard") movement and its venerable predecessor and antagonist, the NIMBY movement. Both have gotten more active with the rise of the housing crisis in the early 2010s, as the recession wore off and young Californians with disposable incomes—and penchants for urban living—found themselves with far too many homes to choose from.

This debate also includes the social justice community, which rightfully fears for low-income residents who are being displaced, and it includes what I call the "radical left," which is more outspoken, more militant, and reviles for-profit development. That's why, for every great new development, be it a renovated loft building, light rail line, affordable housing complex, or community garden, there are countless others who cherish (or at least tolerate) the 20th century model of urbanism. And there are discontents who, either out of spite or genuine concern for their livelihood, resist the changes that many of us believe cities need.

In that sense, the title of Bill Fulton's book is as apt as ever. Any place housing 15 million people is nothing if not a metropolis. But many of Los Angeles's citizens still resist metropolitan life. They didn't buy into it 50 years ago—when center cities were genuinely unpleasant (and when white people were more overtly racist)—and they don't want to buy into it today. Sometimes, the best thing you can say about Californians is that we couldn't care less about one another: you do your thing, I'll do mine. That attitude might be great if, say, you want to become a Hollywood star or just put food on the table as a day laborer, but it is not a recipe for a great city.

In Los Angeles and across the state, we do some things really well and some things really badly—sometimes at the same time. We protect some environmental treasures while bulldozing others. We preserve historic architecture while putting up crap left and right. Most notably, I think, we have ourselves one of the most spectacular natural environments in the developed world, and, excepting some gems, we delight in sullying it with utterly mediocre cityscapes. On the days when Los Angeles gets me down, I find some solace in looking up at the Santa Monica Mountains.

To its credit, Los Angeles gets better year by year—in some ways. I get excited about new transit lines and many of the new developments. Sure, I try to stay balanced and objective in my news reporting, but I'm still a human being and a resident. The city is different enough now to keep me interested. I realize, of course, that the things I love aren't universally loved. Much of the backlash against so-called gentrification and hipster-fication is understandable (if not always warranted). My fear, which I imply in several of these pieces, is that these rivalries are going to lead to stagnation, at best. I hope they will not. Our greatest challenge is to make sure that urban life serves everyone so that rich and poor, marginalized and powerful are all enriched by one another.

***

Though I majored in English, I took a class entitled The American City my senior spring in college. I read Kenneth Turner Jackson, William Julius Wilson, Yi-Fu Tuan, and Jane Jacobs for the first time. I discovered that, indeed, cities result from choices. They do not arise by the forces of nature. And they cannot be dreamed up whole like the plot of a novel.

I'm not a planner as such. I was not trained to write precise ordinances or ensure that things were up to code. The literature student in me was, and still is, accustomed to ambiguity, interpretation, and argument. Walt Whitman even taught me to be OK with contradiction—and to appreciate multitudes. And what has more multitudes than a city?

The essays in this book, spanning 2007 to 2018, do not hold the solutions to California's or America's urban challenges. Again, I'm in the storytelling business, not the solutions business. Taken together, I hope they convey equal parts outrage and hope. They cover the big issues, like housing and gentrification. They cover fun issues like transit and design. They comment on urban-related art and on the culture of urban planning. They comment on, of all people, Donald Trump.

Many of these pieces may come off as critical or combative, and I pick my share of fights. I realize that it's easy to criticize, but I do so in the hope that cities can be marketplaces not only of goods but also of ideas. I am not a planner, a developer, a policymaker, or an architect. I am, for lack of a better description, an informed consumer of cities. I hope that my observations inspire practitioners to do their best work and envision the best possible projects and policies. I believe that anyone who works in the public realm deserves at least the potential for admiration, but they also must be held to account. Their work deserves as much scrutiny as any movie, artwork, or, indeed, book. I hope, of course, for every critique to include a glimmer of hope or a constructive suggestion. I do not want to wallow in quiet desperation.

There's another reason for negativity. In many ways, we already know everything we need to know about what constitutes great cities. We don't need a book for that. We can experience urban greatness in places all over the world, from Kyoto to Istanbul to Munich to Paris to New York to Vancouver, to name just a few. These places are not flawless, but their success proves that great urbanism can transcend cultures and centuries. Indeed, though every city has its own streetscape and its own style, great cities have a lot in common with one another no matter what continent they're on.

Any time I think long enough about California, I come back to Joan Didion's exquisite description: "here ... is where we run out of continent." Didion captures California's essential ambivalence: an intense bipolarity that, in many ways, cancels itself out. California is the triumph of American ingenuity and the culmination of the great American experiment in land use: that of Manifest Destiny, in all its heroism and horror. It represents the celebration of conquering the American landmass as well as the melancholy that sets in when a great mission is finished, leaving uncertainty in its wake. It speaks to California's sometimes naive fixation on the future and its often perilous disregard for the past.

California's cities were established almost as afterthoughts once the pioneers and rancheros faded away. Far be it for California to build cities like its East Coast forerunners. Indeed, how can a society built on forward movement ever seek to contain itself? To build lovely, lovable cities—of the type where you really want to settle down—would be to contradict the American spirit. And yet, as Didion tells us, that spirit became outdated a long time ago. As Freidan tells us, we cannot settle for desperation, quiet or otherwise. This book is, as best I can put it, my attempt to reckon with the urban mystique.

    Los Angeles
    February 2020

1 A Sense of Place
Dispatches from the heart of Los Angeles

As a journalist, I'm not supposed to be biased, but I sometimes grow weak when I write about Los Angeles.

I think of it this way: journalists are supposed to approach stories objectively, but that doesn't mean they can't have underlying convictions. Crime reporters probably should be opposed to murder. Business reporters probably should want a healthy economy. Restaurant critics probably should enjoy food. I don't love everything about Los Angeles. But, to the extent that I am a resident and an observer alike, I do always want it to become a better city.

When I say I don't always love everything about Los Angeles, that's an understatement. I share many of the usual, wearisome complaints that everyone shares (traffic), and some that probably require a more seasoned eye (the government-imposed shortage of bars). But, really, being invested in a city is not about loving it all the time. Cities are not amusement parks. They are complex, conflicted, conflicting places. Indeed, they are not unlike people. And, like people, they have personalities, styles, and, yes, souls.

Cities' souls depend in part on how they look, of course. Los Angeles has dingbats and the beach and San Francisco has Victorians and the bay. Cities have histories and crucibles, be they shared tragedies (like the Chicago fire or Superstorm Sandy), shared cultures (like Berkeley's free speech movement or New York City's support for the arts), or shared values (like those of the military in San Diego or the entertainment industry in Los Angeles).

Two pieces in this chapter warrant updates: I gently opposed Los Angeles's Olympics bid, but the city has been awarded the 2028 games. I also cheered the arrival of downtown Los Angeles's first full-service supermarket, a Ralphs. It has since been joined by a Whole Foods. A long-awaited Trader Joe's remains elusive. As it did with the Olympics, Los Angeles pursued NFL football against my advice.

Cities' personalities often reinforce themselves. We can't choose where we're born. But many of us—even, and sometimes especially, the most disadvantaged—make our way to places where we feel at home. Migrants, be they aspiring movie stars or exhausted refugees, arrive every day because of some attractive quality about a city. Then they go about, in their own small ways, realizing and contributing to that quality. That's how we end up with places that are distinctive even in the midst of a national culture that is, sometimes, bland in the aggregate. And then, sometimes, cities experience shocks—economic changes, natural disasters, political upheaval—that set them on new courses.

These processes and ineffable characteristics fascinate me, beyond whatever the built environment looks like. They are, I hope, the same things that fascinate planners and everyone else involved in the evolution of cities. In the case of Los Angeles, they've created something not always loveable, but fascinating nonetheless.

A SENSE OF PLACE

Where Nobody Knows Your Name
2015

The dear, departed Smog Cutter, in East Hollywood.

London has pubs. Munich has beer halls. Houston has outdoor honky-tonks. Denver has brewpubs. Paris and Rome have sidewalk cafés. In Brussels, bars pour 300 beers. San Francisco has its mixology labs.

The drinking scene in Los Angeles is less easy to characterize. Like so much else in this city, it's diffuse, fragmented and characterized by extremes: achingly cool lounges like the rooftop of the Ace Hotel, raucous destination bars like Saddle Ranch on the Sunset Strip, and windowless dive bars that often seem anything but inviting. We have bars that are beauty salons, video game arcades, and one that thinks it's an airport terminal. Skybar, the original luxury bar and one of two places where I saw Cindy Crawford (the other being Blockbuster Video), is still going strong. I'm not cool enough to know what trend is coming next. Like Angelenos themselves, the city's bars are fascinating, unique, individualistic—and mutually indifferent to one another.

As an urban experience, the scene is mediocre, unbecoming of a great metropolis. Los Angeles does not take pride in its bars the way many other cities do. Many neighborhoods revile them entirely.

Homeowners, especially those on the Westside, strain to keep bars out of any neighborhood with even a whiff of domesticity. Take Westwood, for example. Home to 43,000 UCLA students, it has exactly two bar-restaurants and zero true bars. In Pacific Palisades, the No. 1 hit on Yelp for "bars" is a Chinese restaurant that happens to have a liquor license; No. 2 is Juice Crafters. The specific plan for San Vicente Boulevard, the main commercial street in Brentwood, outlaws stand-alone bars. (I sit on the Brentwood Community Council, which is known to have interminable discussions over tastings at wine shops—as if anyone would become a public nuisance after a few sips from an $80 bottle.)

Many Los Angeles residents have no place within walking distance to share a pitcher of beer or a bottle of wine with friends. Consenting, responsible adults can't just "get a drink." They have to "go out," which often means driving to an area where large numbers of true bars are tolerated, like Downtown, Koreatown, Hollywood or Venice. In those places, kids drink their fill, have frighteningly few meaningful conversations, and create just the sort of fraternistic haze that strikes fear in the hearts of homeowners. They, in turn, are unlikely to approve, or even conceive of, a bar that genuinely wants to be a good neighbor. The fear of bars is a self-fulfilling prophecy.

The situation may be about to get worse.

In late 2015, council member Mike Bonin introduced a motion that, if passed, would, according to the Los Angeles Area Chamber of Commerce, add $2,484 to the already astronomical cost of opening a bar or liquor-serving restaurant in Los Angeles. (A bar license alone is $13,800.) That's to say nothing of the costs that bars must pay consultants and public relations firms to conduct outreach and expedite the permitting process. Every dollar spent on these expenses is a dollar that can't be invested in ambiance, aesthetics, and good cheer.

Bonin's proposed fee would pay for enforcement of development agreements. Bars and "bona fide eating places" (that is, restaurants that are supposed to serve booze only incidentally) operate under conditional use permits, called CUBs. CUBs often are based on rules imposed by neighbors, usually homeowners with political clout. Restrictions can include crowd-control measures, limitations on operating hours, and agreements to serve a certain ratio of food to alcohol.

Restaurants break these rules because, in short, demand for night life far exceeds supply. A restaurant that rolls away the tables and turns into a de facto club at 10 p.m. stands to make a killing on alcohol sales. Bonin wants to hold restaurants to their agreements—which is fine, as far as it goes. But doing so ignores the outdated policies and provincial attitudes that lead to these neighborhood efforts in the first place and that restrain our bar culture.

However louche Los Angeles's image may be, it remains a puritanical city in a puritanical state. California caps the number of bar licenses (not to be confused with restaurants that serve alcohol) at one for every 2,000 residents. That number hasn't changed since 1939, six years after the repeal of Prohibition.

According to a recent survey of "bar density," California ranks 35th in the nation, at around 12,000 residents per bar. The national median is 7,000. Who's drier than California? The Bible Belt. And Utah.

Although alcohol permitting is a state matter, cities issue the CUBs, meaning that they control exactly where bars can locate. Want a demure wine bar on your corner? The approvals process in Los Angeles is so convoluted—often involving consultants, license lotteries, stakeholder outreach, inspections, and more—that it can take a year and more than $100,000. And that's only if your neighbors are on board—which of course requires them to grasp that there's a difference between a wine bar and a packed, rowdy club for twentysomethings reliving their college days.

Obviously drinking is associated with its share of social ills. But like it or not, drinking is part of the culture of every city this side of Saudi Arabia. Los Angeles being what it is—a city full of transplants, often reliant on their cars—neighbors seldom bump into one another over casual drinks. Folks can rarely stroll down the street to a local watering hole. A healthy bar culture can bring people together. A whole universe of collaborations and relationships—business, creative, romantic—can be forged over a drink or two. Mingling is, ultimately, what cities are for. In Los Angeles, though, a "relationship" too often means cutting someone off on the freeway. This in a city whose lifeblood is creativity.

The city's urban planners are working feverishly to create more walkable, intimate neighborhoods. Those neighborhoods need destinations worth walking to, and they can't always be Starbucks. The answer is not fewer bars, but more of them; not tighter, costlier regulations, but looser ones; not suspicious neighbors, but friendlier ones.

We need our megabars, our dives, and our weird places that are trying just a little too hard. We also need as many muted wine bars, creative gastropubs, friendly holes-in-the wall, and festive beer gardens as we can get—and more.

We need to learn to drink responsibly in places to which we feel attached. We need to not be so afraid of drinking and not so afraid of one another. We need to break the vicious cycle of distrust. When you share a drink with your neighbors, you might not compose symphonies with them, but you at least become less afraid that they'll vomit on your lawn.

I'd love to chat more about it over a martini. Just not at Skybar. I'm still not cool enough to get in.

In the Market for a Supermarket
2007

Ralphs supermarket opened in downtown Los Angeles in 2007.

Babylon was a market town, and so was Jericho. Civilization tumbled from their bins and sprouted from their gardens. Then grew cities, empires, and states. The process continued, and then came Los Angeles.

It took 10,000 years to reach this point. Add another month, maybe two, and Los Angeles too will have a market.

When I was a few years out of college I was teaching a journalism class not far from the ocean, and I used a *Los Angeles Times* article to demonstrate that even a seemingly insignificant piece of news could be of deep importance—the proverbial first draft of history. The headline that day, April 21, 2003: "Downtown L.A. Could See a Ralphs Market in 2005."

Two years later, I accepted the editorship of a publication covering urban planning. I had hoped to immerse myself in the new life of a great city and maybe pick up some groceries on the way home. Instead, I arrived in the wholly functional Financial District, which devolved into something nondescript to the south, full of remnants of the neglect that was fashionable in the '70s.

In light of this void, no venture in the world makes more sense than a market Downtown.

Los Angeles of course does not want for markets—super-, mini-, farmers, ethnic, and otherwise. Surely no other radius in the world has ever encircled a greater variety of food. That bounty only makes more ridiculous the barrenness of its center, from which the mystique of "downtown"—top hats, champagne, Petula Clark—long ago departed. Ralphs, part of the Market Lofts on Ninth between Hope and Flower Streets, may not usher back elegance, but at least it will bring something nice. It may be a typical outpost of a familiar chain, but its location, and the diverse masses it will serve, makes it extraordinary.

So eager is the local anticipation that Ralphs has, since that first mention, found its way into countless articles, each one revising the date of its debut. So dear is the prospect of more markets that mere speculation—otherwise known as hope—makes the front page of this very publication, and rightfully so. Downtown has been holding out an empty plate for too long.

I cling to the notion that the universal pleasantries of procuring food, whether by trap, bow, basket, or credit card, still lift the human spirit. And so they must. Week in and week out we have, since forever ago, dug at roots and slain prey and pushed trolleys down aisles. If it did not please us, humanity would have starved. Even today, blackberries still matter more than BlackBerrys. Ordinary as it is, Ralphs will, in many ways, serve its neighborhood far better than Disney Hall, the Ace Hotel, or the next loft conversion.

Despite the clamor, Market Lofts did not, of course, open as planned. When I arrived in the summer of 2005, I found a hole where it was supposed to be. Since then I have walked past the site from my parking lot to my office every day for two years and literally watched concrete harden, but I can wait no longer. I am taking leave of my job and of Downtown Los Angeles at the end of this month, at the very moment when the building stands nearly ready for the stocking.

Those of us who prefer peace like to note that America's current foray has outlasted world wars. What, then, of a supermarket that takes just as long?

Surely economics, in the classical sense, did not keep Ralphs at bay. As Maslow reminds us, the demand for housing is second only to that for food, and Downtown has a half-million customers. (Commerce is never so palatable as when supply rises to meet demand.) The developers, Lee Homes and CIM, are accomplished and credible, and any financier who dawdled on Market Lofts shouldn't be trusted with other people's money. But these dreams still depend on the cold logistics upon which a city is really built.

In L.A., four years from murmur to reality is not so long. Los Angeles's planning and permitting process—with its innumerable strata of approvals and bureaucratic gymnastics—notoriously spins days into months and months into years. Between the Planning Commission, the City Council and its committees, bureaus, agencies, departments, and personages that weigh in on projects in Los Angeles, the average shopper could hardly fathom the labor required to put a roof over their heads. But while bureaucracies—however necessary and well-intentioned—perform their civic duties, frustration mounts, and people go hungry.

The built environment that envelops us today is like the light of a nearby star, which shot forth many years ago and crossed the heavens in due time. These are the forces that defer dreams in Los Angeles and that stand in the way of the countless good ideas—rail, transit-oriented development, walkable neighborhoods, design guidelines, and all the rest—that are blossoming but will have to wait to become real. In a city of so much power, wealth, creativity, and ambition, patience has emerged as the cardinal virtue. I wish I had enough of it to finally reap the harvest.

Soon grains, cheeses, elixirs, sweets, and fruits of all kinds will burst forth, and perhaps the "renaissance"—spoken of so gingerly since Tom Gilmore waved in the first new Downtowners—will evolve into more than just a slogan. I imagine bankers emerging from their glass corners, janitors laying down their mops, artists checking out the scene, and junior associates setting aside their briefs.

With a place for all of them to gather, otherwise anonymous shoppers might strike up conversations in the freezer aisle. A bell pepper might drop to the floor, and a stranger's hand might reach down for it. Across a heap of sweet potatoes, gazes may meet, hearts may race, and then…

When future civilizations dive down to the wreck of our city, those archeologists should take pause when they arrive at Ninth and Flower. The strata will tell them that it was built sometime in the early 2000s, but by then, today's precious increments will have long ceased to matter. Whatever number they assign it and whatever they serve at their own tables, they should conclude that it was, indeed, a special year.

Beating Boston at Its Own Games
2015

A better choice than Fenway Park.

Are there any two American cities more different from each other than Boston and Los Angeles? History vs. modernity, compactness vs. sprawl, chowder vs. kale, snow vs. sun, modesty vs. flash, intellect vs. entertainment.

Back in January, Boston beat out Los Angeles, San Francisco, and Washington, D.C., to become the United States Olympic Committee's official pick to bid for the 2024 Summer Olympics. Since then, civic leaders in Los Angeles have been nearly salivating with every hint of disaffection on the part of the Beantown faithful. Concerns were legion: Boston doesn't have room; Boston's transit system can't handle the crowds; Boston doesn't have the facilities; Boston doesn't want to spend billions; Boston, to be characteristically blunt, has better things to do.

Even Boston's hometown newspaper, the *Globe*, called the bid "improbable."

Boston bailed out not long after being awarded the nomination, with Mayor Marty Walsh refusing to put taxpayer money at risk. All of two weeks after Boston's surrender, Los Angeles Mayor Eric Garcetti issued his first public statement about turning Boston's loss his city's gain, acknowledging "very positive discussions with the United States Olympic Committee" and claiming, "the L.A. Olympics would inspire the world and are right for our city." Garcetti's attitude thus adds to the list of distinctions between the two cities. Whereas Boston wants nothing to do with the world's premier global event, Los Angeles considers it its birthright. According to one poll, an insane 81 percent of Angelenos support an Olympics bid. We are either supremely enthusiastic or supremely blasé.

(The group that backed the San Francisco bid is mildly interested in a joint bid but seems otherwise content to let L.A. do its thing.)

Los Angeles deservedly gets a lot of mileage out of its Olympic history. Both the 1932 games and 1984 games were rousing successes, the latter turning a small profit (as compared with billions, and tens of billions, spent in Beijing and Sochi). Of course, no one involved with the 1932 games is still around, but, amazingly, the most important venue is: the Los Angeles Memorial Coliseum. Los Angeles takes the Olympics in stride because, as an urban behemoth dedicated to spectacle, it needs hardly lay a single brick.

Garcetti's message to the USOC: "Want to have an Olympics here? No problem, let's check the calendar!"

By 2024, Los Angeles will have even more to offer the world, with miles of new light rail lines completed, more housing (we hope), more transportation options, and more vibrant neighborhoods. In fact, the development and planning efforts underway in Los Angeles constitute the best reasons not to seek the 2024 games.

I lived two years in Boston that were among the most miserable of my life. So, as a native Angeleno, I never thought I'd say this, but Los Angeles could stand to be more like Boston.

I don't mean that we should give up our pressed juice for Dunkin' Donuts or that we should start wearing boat shoes without socks. We could, however, stand to let some other city realize its Olympics dreams. As fun as the Olympics would be—and there's no doubt that Los Angeles could pull it off well—Los Angeles too has better things to do. In fact, we're already doing better things. Downtown and its surroundings are booming. Formerly anonymous neighborhoods, from Highland Park to Culver City, are on the rise. The City Council just adopted a revolutionary new mobility plan, and a revamp of the zoning code is underway. We have new museums and concert halls. We might have a river someday.

If you think about it, Los Angeles's built environment is becoming ever so slightly more similar to that of—wait for it—Boston.

Meanwhile, dire problems remain. We're short tens of thousands of housing units, with production only beginning to pick up. Gentrification is leading to displacement (anecdotally, at least). Traffic remains unbearable. LAUSD schools and others throughout the county remain shameful. Neighborhoods that were war zones in 1984 are more peaceful, but they're scarcely healthier, with pollution and none of the Technicolor bounty of the farmers markets and Whole Foods that serve L.A.'s haves.

These positive developments, and these dire problems, all deserve our full attention, not just this year, but for many years to come.

I know the argument goes that an Olympics will be a catalytic event, bringing prosperity to the city. That's probably true for some Angelenos, but not for everyone. Ask residents of South Central, circa 1992, how much good the 1984 games did them. Ask the same of the aerospace workers whose plants closed and the generations of high school kids who have graduated hardly knowing how to write.

The fact is, Los Angeles needs to keep doing what it's doing and not distract itself with a global mega-event. (Interestingly, a private group is promoting an odd sort of transit-oriented world's fair for the early 2020s.)

We've proven that we can be our own catalysts: 2008's Measure R sales tax measure is having a bigger impact on the city than any sporting event could. We don't need stadiums around those new transit stops. We need housing. We need mobility hubs and wayfinding. We need thriving small businesses, not huge stadiums and not ads for corporate sponsors.

And let's face it, the reason why Los Angeles can hold an Olympics is the very reason why it doesn't need to hold an Olympics: Los Angeles already knows how to amuse itself. We have two of pretty much everything, including big-time football teams (the kind that doesn't pay their players). As I've written before, Los Angeles can thrive without the NFL. We can thrive without an Olympics too. And if we want to "beat" Boston at something, we can't rely on the Lakers anymore, but we still have the Clippers.

In even my darkest days living in Boston, I could never deny the city's charms. Crooked streets, red bricks, wrought iron, leafy blocks, neighborhood pubs, and handsome public spaces are what cities are supposed to be about. It's no accident that Bostonians are willing to endure those awful winters. Boston has places that many Southern Californians, trapped on freeways and consigned to strip malls, can't even imagine. And yet, Los Angeles could have its own versions of Boston's delights. It just has to keep its eye on the ball.

Searching for Los Angeles in Blade Runner 2049

2017

The seas rise and replicants discover their feelings in Los Angeles of the 2040s.

If ever a movie made a star out of a building, the movie was *Blade Runner* and the star was the Bradbury Building. Rumor has it that it was restored in part because of the fame director Ridley Scott conferred on it by making it the setting for the death of Roy Batty, the emotional undoing of Deckard, and one of the more potent testimonies to the fragility of humanity.

The real Los Angeles is thus better off for what happened in the fictional Los Angeles. Then again, 2019 is still two years away.

Blade Runner created a dystopian vision of Los Angeles that remains as culturally potent today—if not more so—than it was when it came out in 1982. It shows up in books, articles, and offhand remarks with astounding regularity. It's a testament to the arresting visuals of hyperdense polyglot streets illuminated by sparkling advertisements and the possibility, however slim, that our sunny, spread-out paradise could someday become one of the dark places of the earth. After all, perhaps the biggest fantasy to come out of Los Angeles is Los Angeles itself.

For all the theorizing about *Blade Runner*, it's worth asking not what Scott was saying about the future of Los Angeles (or of cities in general), but rather why he chose Los Angeles in the first place.

If *Blade Runner* had taken place in an older, more endearing city—say, San Francisco or London—we'd be sad to witness its demise. If it had taken place someplace more generic, like Phoenix, Denver, or Gotham City, we might not care. Los Angeles hit the sweet spot between lamentation and acceptance, and, as Mike Davis says, between sunshine and noir. Director Ridley Scott, like his fellow Briton Reyner Banham, approached Los Angeles with equal parts dread and fascination. His choice was not so much a commentary on the Los Angeles of the future but rather on the Los Angeles of the present.

The challenge that speculative fiction faces, of course, is that eventually the future catches up with it.

***

Blade Runner 2049 takes place 30 years later, in an even bleaker world. An apparent combination of nuclear war, climate change, and technological sabotage has rendered the planet even less habitable than it was before. The dove that Batty released years ago has left no offspring.

J. F. Sebastian, the sad-eyed toymaker in the first film, jokes, "No housing shortage around here. Plenty of room for everybody," since everyone who can has moved Off-World. That's how he can afford an entire office building for his dolls and marionettes and how Deckard can afford to live in an architectural masterpiece on a cop's salary. In the intervening years, though, the housing shortage has returned with a vengeance, not necessarily because the world has more inhabitants, but because it has less land. The moral question, of course, is whether the city should accept all who need safe haven.

That's the same question that today's Los Angeles is asking itself—or should be asking itself, at any rate.

In 2049, untold numbers of stragglers, humans, and replicants alike are forced into cities, where they subsist on synthetic food and artificial light. In fact, there may be no cities—plural. From the looks of things, there may be nothing else left besides Los Angeles, with all of humanity and nonhumanity crammed into a piece of land whose chief virtue is that it is not radioactive. K, the new blade runner designed to hunt his own kind, searches among tens—or maybe hundreds—of millions of Los Angeles residents, all waiting for their time to die.

Aerial shots depict the city's familiar endless rows of boulevards and residential streets. The houses that dot Reyner Banham's Plains of Id are replaced by high-rise shantytowns, made up of apartment buildings, each many stories tall, each more dilapidated than the last. Mere dingbats they are not. In this *Blade Runner*, the billboards walk the street, as 80-foot-tall interactive holograms that shake their asses just for you. (We've come a long way from Angelyne.) Skyscrapers rise into the ocher fog, and all is overshadowed by the new citadel of the Wallace Corporation, the corporation that rose from the ashes of Tyrell.

There's a popular Angeleno parlor game in which you try to spot real-life locations in movies, whether they're playing themselves or standing in for other places. The original *Blade Runner* was not all fantasy. Somewhere beneath the gas flares, the billboards, and Tyrell's pyramid are the Ennis House, Union Station, and, of course, the Bradbury Building. These locations give Blade Runner a sense of reality, at least to those of us who live in L.A.—a chilling reminder that the future may be closer at hand than we think.

That game brings few rewards with *Blade Runner 2049*.

Director Denis Villeneuve wisely avoided the Bradbury Building, which, in the world of *Blade Runner*, is as fraught and freighted as Calvary. But it was far from his only omission.

In fact, not a single structure or landscape connects fiction to reality. Villeneuve offers no ruins or repurposed vestiges of the old city. The camera catches no glimpses of a ruined Dodger Stadium, a looted Getty Center, or even a lifeless palm tree. The Wilshire Grand does not stand next to the fictional police station. We know *Blade Runner 2049* takes place in Los Angeles only because of arbitrary signifiers, like the LAPD, and because of its cosmetic resemblance to the city in the previous film, not to the one that lives and breathes, evolving before our eyes.

In only a single, fleeting sequence does the cityscape of Los Angeles become legible. K flies his Spinner police cruiser over a recognizable, but altered, expanse of the Los Angeles Basin toward what used to be the ports of Los Angeles and Long Beach. Tendrils of ocean creep into what used to be Venice and the other coastal communities. A metal seawall the height of the Hoover Dam and width of the coastline itself protects the city from the bloated Pacific.

***

Neither edition of *Blade Runner* is a prescription for urbanism. And yet, some among us appreciate the original *Blade Runner* for its urbanity: the density, the diversity, and the grit. By avoiding Los Angeles entirely, the sequel lacks that exquisite ambivalence, making Los Angeles seem less human—it is a replicant of itself. Los Angeles does not so much play itself as it stands in for the entire world, obliterated beyond recognition. Villeneuve's vision conveys more about the future of cities in general than it does about Los Angeles specifically. (Las Vegas makes a cameo, however.)

Interestingly, of all the reasons that Scott might have envisioned for the demise of the world, climate change surely was not one of them. *Blade Runner* came out in 1982, after all. If anything, he probably had in mind the Cold War, signified by passing references to our then-communist antagonists, Russia and China. So while the fictional city hasn't changed much, its allegorical power has changed dramatically, as the real threats to humanity have evolved (and, arguably, worsened).

So *Blade Runner* may yet turn out to be a prediction. If the Los Angeles of the original *Blade Runner* was, as Ridley Scott put it, "Hong Kong on a bad day," the updated version is closer to Mumbai or Lagos. The misery and squalor of K's Los Angeles of the future prevails today in plenty of real places on our own planet. Add rising seas or an unthinkable human tragedy, and more people may have to cram into smaller areas. Urban planners are going to have to be ready for that—maybe not in California, but in plenty of other places—and we're going to need compassion, cooperation, and emotional resilience just as dearly as we're going to need planning wisdom and technological advances.

We're all going to have to be ready to find out how human we really are.

A SENSE OF PLACE

Shared Hardship and the Souls of Cities
2012

Superstorm Sandy tested New York City's mettle.

I can't remember the last time I left my apartment and gave a moment's thought to whether I'd be warm enough, or whether I needed to bring an umbrella. Meanwhile, half the East Coast is underwater right now, thanks to Superstorm Sandy. Friends on Facebook have posted status updates about "hurricane envy," and the tales of destruction, disruption, heroism, and all-night parties gush in like tidal surges.

Sandy will give urban planners pause for many reasons, not the least of which is how to build in low-lying areas in the age of climate change. But seawalls and shoreline setbacks don't interest me nearly as much as the little things:

- Extension cords and power strips with signs inviting passersby

- to charge their phones.
- Fireside gatherings.
- Huddled walks through dark, quiet streets.
- Searches for the old and infirm, and efforts to shuttle them to higher ground, in what has become America's corner of the postapocalypse.
- The elation of making it out alive, and of beholding so much of the city that still stands.

Those are the subjects of some of the photos posted on social media and on news sites during Sandy. I imagined eight million New Yorkers all with their own images of the storm.

The day Sandy hit, a friend of mine sent me an email describing how he walked three miles, over the Brooklyn Bridge, from one borough to another to seek safe haven. How many multitudes must he have passed? How much like Whitman must he have felt?

Planners define cities by their form: the curve of their streets and the massing of their buildings. But we all know that the character of a city—its values, culture, and, yes, personality—however ineffable it may seem, matters as much as does the built environment. Usually the two are complementary, of course. Certain places breed certain people.

But places do not breed people so much as they do events.

Most people move to places because of things they like about it. Most planners want to plan places that they think people will like. No one moves to a place with a worst-case scenario in mind. But sometimes the worst-case scenarios are what define cities—and, paradoxically, perversely, sometimes for the better.

You don't have to be a psychologist to know that hate is a stronger emotion than love, and that fear is stronger than elation. You don't have to have fought in a war to know that trauma can bind people. As New York has demonstrated in the days after Sandy hit—as it has so many other times—the true character of a city lies in shared hardship.

I wish we shared more things, these days. I wish we shared more cups of sugar and bottles of wine. I wish we shared more jokes and stories. I wish we still had mixtapes. But America is usually too busy for those things. Even the greatest American cities are too frantic, to be sure.

I conceive of shared hardship from a position of envy, a position which I know I ought not have. And yet, Los Angeles, my hometown, exists to avoid hardship. We gripe when the temperature drops below 60. All of the real hardships—inconveniences, really—are of our own making. They are generally not the kind that ennobles civic character.

Nothing pains Angelenos as much as traffic does. But we are not in traffic. We are not fighting, together, against a common current. We are traffic. We are all one another's enemies. There is no beast to slay. And traffic, much as we might like to commiserate, drives us apart from one another by definition. We are at our most miserable and our most alone at the very same time.

Earthquakes are a special kind of disaster. Nothing in this world strikes with so little announcement. The earthquake proclaims itself, without time for us, the jolted, to summon our inner tenderness. The worst of them entail endless seconds of terror followed by an indefinite period of being pissed off, jumpy, and anxious. Holding each other closely does no good; it just heightens the chance that you'll be crushed by the same chunk of ceiling. Our signature weather event is the Santa Ana winds, which yield nothing but sleeplessness, irritability, and dry skin.

Los Angeles wears its indifference like a Prada label. I'm a pretty friendly guy, and I don't know a single neighbor's name. In Los Angeles, we complain a lot. But we do not suffer.

Consider so many other places and how they cope. In the Twin Cities, you can't help but be "Minnesota nice" when you know that six months of frigidity and five-foot snowdrifts are in the offing. The Cajun spirit was forged in New Orleans in part by decades of hurricanes, of which Katrina is only the latest example. The chill of Denver pushes twentysomethings into bars and brewpubs; same for the rain in Seattle and Portland. Civic pride in San Francisco and Chicago both arose in part from those cities' ashes. Across the Great Plains, tornadoes, hail, and even a good thunderstorm will do.

And there's always New York: blackouts, blizzards, hurricanes, and other acts to which no God would ever lay claim.

In each of these cases, disaster and discomfort have raised civic spirits. They inspire little gestures, like shoveling a neighbor's sidewalk or letting her borrow your cell phone. They create heroes. They wash away dreams and force residents to rebuild. They force people to congregate on street corners, forget about their phones and computers, and share some stories. If the corner bar or café stays open, that's where the neighborhood rides out the storm. Sometimes, when the lights go out, they lead to even more residents.

One Facebook friend wrote, with the raw eloquence that can only come from intense experience:

> People lying prostrate next to outlets at banks and restaurants; putting makeup on in public restrooms; cheering when Linksys is a wi-fi option; trucking a suitcase around with you everywhere; drinking at all times of the day; endless delays—and thus more drinking; New York City literally has become one giant airport.

Meanwhile, people out here in California—no matter how strong our feelings of sympathy and support may be—are selling scripts and doing Pilates.

Nobody would wish Superstorm Sandy on anyone. And yet, there's that envy. The envy derives from our fascination with the power of nature, to be sure. But it is, I think, also an envy of human contact. It's an envy of how we feel, about ourselves and about one another, when we collectively face something more awesome than we are. It's an envy that comes from the conviction that something good must come of this.

As the post-Sandy days wear on, I dearly hope that spiritedness does not give way to frustration, with so much to rebuild and so much drying-out left. I don't know what the threshold is for despair or when frayed nerves will overwhelm the cooperative instinct.

The next time a Sandy—or a Harvey, or a Big One—arrives, I hope we don't find out. In Los Angeles, as in so many other places forged in the name of comfort, I know we will never find out. In a perfect world, one that looks superficially like Los Angeles and not at all like Atlantic City, everyone would always work to make life better. The brawn needed to sump basements and haul debris would go toward noble buildings and flat sidewalks. The momentary cooperation would be spread into daily nods and smiles.

As the people of the East Coast undergo these trials involuntarily, may the rest of us, who have the luxury of light, power, and mobility, show our mettle in ways of our own choosing so that no one and no place needs to be the object of envy.

The Real Problem with Carmageddon
2011

The opposite of Carmageddon.

If you haven't heard, we're expecting a little traffic here in west Los Angeles this weekend. Actually, we're expecting it all over the city. No, wait. All over the county.

Forget it. The entire state is going to be paralyzed. Now everybody freak out!

I am writing, of course, about the two-day closure of Interstate 405 between the 101 and 10 freeways, otherwise known as "Carmageddon." This weekend, LA Metro turns off the busiest freeway in the country, like Niagara Falls running dry.

The stanching of the flow of 500,000 cars daily will be a grand experiment in transportation planning and public relations, and as far as I'm concerned, there's not a single credible hypothesis. I'd like to think that I have special insight into what's going to happen because I live a two-minute drive from Ground Zero—the Sunset exit of the 405, where the cascade of cars from the Valley splashes down into the pool of gridlock that is the Westside—but I don't have a clue about whether this will be a blessing or a curse.

It's quite likely the parallel routes to the 405 will be stuffed. I wouldn't drive Topanga, Coldwater, or Laurel canyons for all the oil in Saudi Arabia. The 101 and the 5 are likely to absorb traffic well beyond their carrying capacity.

But it's the broader network effects that are going to be most interesting. For instance, if drivers want to get to Century City but take the 101, does that mean that all the east-west streets between Hollywood and Century City are going to be clogged? Will through-traffic—from, say, Santa Clarita to LAX, or even San Francisco to San Diego—have to make massive detours, thus backing up the entire statewide freeway system?

Or will most people just stay home and fire up the grill?

Carmageddon has elicited some hopeful proclamations from folks who say that it presents a great opportunity to stay home, hang out with local friends, smoke a few joints, and contemplate the lamentable role of the automobile in modern life. I'm all for it. But I'm not sure that people who have to work Saturday and Sunday feel the same way.

However fun or inconvenient it may be, all the speculation about Carmageddon weekend ignores important questions that policymakers may have missed in their original cost-benefit analyses. For sure, the improved freeway will be better than the old freeway. But you can't compare the new and the old. You also have to consider the costs that we have incurred in between.

If you haven't seen the construction site, you'd be amazed at what's already been going on for two years. This isn't Texas, where another lane just requires laying down another strip of asphalt. And it's not even the San Francisco Bay, where you can build a new bridge right next to the old one.

We're talking about demolishing houses. We're talking about

cutting 200-foot-high chunks off hillsides and replacing them with retaining walls. They're tearing bridges down one half at a time, so traffic can squeeze past until they rebuild them whole (that's what they're doing this weekend). On- and off-ramps have been jury-rigged. Lanes on surface streets have disappeared.

In short, Carmageddon may be arriving this weekend, but we've been on a highway to hell for as long as this project has been underway.

Everyone, save a few transportation planners, is familiar by now with the arguments about induced demand. Once the lanes are added, they could fill up almost instantly. But that's only half the problem with freeway construction.

The other half—which is never mentioned or measured, as far as I know—is the time and money lost to drivers while the freeway is being improved. Even if the 405 doesn't clog up instantly and does flow freely for a few years after the project is finished, I find it hard to believe that the time savings will compensate for all the time lost during its construction.

To wit, a one-and-a-half-mile drive from my apartment to Westwood, via Wilshire Boulevard, that can take five minutes can now take over a half hour. Walking is literally faster. Multiply that by the tens of thousands of other drivers who take that route daily. Then multiply it by the other choke points. We'd all need Bugattis and open roads for years in order to make up for what we're now enduring.

Then there's the pollution. One of the arguments in favor of carpool lanes is that commuters consolidate their vehicles and that they'll pollute less because they're flowing freely. But the cars stuck on Wilshire are now polluting more. Again, unless every car stuck in traffic on the new 405 runs on hydrogen and fairy dust, the construction alone will have caused a net increase in pollution.

In other words, by the time this thing has a chance to reduce pollution and traffic—if it ever does—it will already have generated plenty of pollution and traffic.

So who benefits from this feat of engineering? I know that a certain construction firm is reaping $1 billion in revenue. But I'll get something more sublime. On Saturday evening, perhaps near sundown, I get to stroll across the Sunset Boulevard bridge, peer into the twilight, and see, for once, what an empty freeway looks like.

How Much Is that Joint in the Window?
2018

Hide the children.

Five decades and six months after the Summer of Love, the age of legalized cannabis has arrived in California. As of January 1, cities may officially permit the sale and commercial production of smokable marijuana and other wacky products to consenting adults, not just those who have back pain or faint appetites. Once confined to crowds of peaceniks in Golden Gate Park, marijuana is finally free.

Within limits, of course.

California's marijuana regulations, as ordered by Proposition 64, which passed comfortably in 2016 after many prior defeats, defines minimum standards for locating cannabis-related facilities. It includes sensible restrictions like minimum distances to schools and types of signage allowed (neon green crosses, and punny names have become the signifiers of choice). The regulations also permit cities and counties to impose stricter regulations—or to ban commercial activities entirely. Jurisdictions must decide whether they want to satisfy their residents' demands and reap sales tax revenue—or whether marijuana is too unseemly for their fair cities.

This discussion came up in a meeting of the land use committee of my local Neighborhood Council in West Los Angeles, on which I sit. One of my colleagues, clearly unnerved by the whole notion of legalized marijuana—and by the conflict between federal and state law—encouraged us to resist any form of commercial marijuana on "ethical" grounds.

I'm not about to predict Jeff Sessions's inclinations on this matter. But let's talk about "ethics."

Let us not doubt that every decision concerning the built environment includes ethical components. Every publicly useable or visible building, whether large or small, ugly or fair, imposes itself on other people. Every imposition is, by definition, an ethical choice. When, for instance, Apple's Jonathan Ive says "We didn't make Apple Park for other people"—referring to the company's new intergalactic doughnut in Cupertino—he's making an ethical statement, whether he likes (or knows) it or not. That's because, of course, "other people" have to look at it, contend with traffic generated by it, etc.

In autocracies like, say, Turkmenistan or Apple Inc., ethical considerations—for better or worse—might not matter a whit. But in democracies, they matter quite a bit. And they naturally apply to storefronts that sell marijuana. My colleague was right to raise the issue.

I, personally, do not have an ethical problem with selling or using cannabis. If, though, we're going to condemn one form of legal commerce on ethical grounds, we might as well take a look at all the others while we're at it.

The neighborhood in question is not exactly Haight-Ashbury. It's a predictable upscale collection of hair salons, restaurants, juice bars, and fitness studios. How many of my neighbors smoke a bowl after doing downward-facing dog is anyone's guess.

If we care about ethics, though, a few of our existing, perfectly legal establishments may warrant scrutiny:
- Starting with the obvious, what about the bars, wine stores, and grocery stores? The antisocial effects of alcohol are exhaustively documented. For every stoner who has stubbed his toe while high, someone has lost a life to drunk driving.
- What about the dry cleaners, desoiling $200 business shirts and $2,000 evening gowns with chemicals that would peel your skin off?
- What about vacant lots, growing uglier by the day, offending passersby and denying would-be residents the chance to live there?
- What about the chain restaurants, clogging arteries and paying scarcely minimum wage in the expectation that diners will show their largesse?
- What about the hair salons, where the cost of a blow-dry could feed a homeless person for a week?
- What about the homeless themselves, camping on our sidewalks rather than being housed with dignity?
- What about the former redlining, blockbusting, HOA covenants, and discriminatory lending practices whose echoes still resound in neighborhoods rich and poor?
- What about the gas stations, dispensing a product that has swallowed more money, instigated more wars, supported more dictators, and blackened more lungs than probably any other in human history?

What, indeed, about the "ethics" of selling marijuana?

We need not condemn every land use decision humanity has ever made. We have arrived at this point largely through convention, inertia, rational analysis, and good faith. In some cases, we have inherited, and perpetuated, landscapes created by coercion and acculturation that took place before any of us were born and, in many cases, before our cities were ever built. We need not have ethical crises with every step we take or every mile we drive. And yet, we should not apply asymmetrical standards just because something is new. The appeal of "grandfathering" depends entirely on who your grandfather is.

Surely it's reasonable not to want our children to be tempted by cannabinoid fantasies. But do we want them buying gasoline? Do we want them spending all of their allowance on hair care? Do we want them to shrug as they pass the destitute veteran on the sidewalk? Do we really want them to grow up in neighborhoods scarcely less segregated than those in which we grew up and which instilled our values in us?

These questions do not yield easy answers, whether you're discussing them stone-cold sober at a community meeting or drawing deep thoughts out of a tight, fat, and—finally—legal joint.

A Sense of Place

The Oklahoman Who Figured Out California
2016

Ed Ruscha gets L.A. (even in New York).

Several of the smallest pieces in the de Young Museum's extraordinary retrospective of California artist Ed Ruscha depict abnormally vast Western landscapes. Thin strips of prairie stretch just above the bottom edge of the frame. Attenuated horizons separate starry skies from a dark continent. Extreme horizontality makes even Ruscha's tiniest images appear immense, capturing the grandeur and loneliness of earth and sky.

Upon this template, telephone poles recede achingly into a blue-black dusk (*Let's Keep in Touch*). Two oil derricks stand at attention on opposite sides of a canvas (*Well, Well*). Clusters of tiny lights huddle close under a starry sky (*Two Similar Cities*). In *America's Future*, an empty horizon at dusk extends forever with every hue between yellow and taupe looming above. These are the pieces that gave the exhibit its title: *Ed Ruscha and the Great American West.*

Though Ruscha depicts landscapes, he is not a landscape painter. For him, the Western landscape turns into a symbol of itself, representing all the Americanisms—individualism, freedom, expansion, commercialism—that derive from having so much space on our hands. It also gave rise to a particular type of urbanism, of which Ruscha is a remarkably astute critic.

Even Ruscha's emptiest landscapes are foils for the peculiar type of city that arose in the West. Raised in Nebraska, he migrated to Los Angeles in the 1960s to discover the beauties and ironies of this corner of America. He looks with bemusement upon the place to which so many Midwesterners escaped. At age 78, he continues to work there.

***

Ruscha is to painting what the team of Robert Venturi and Denise Scott Brown are to architecture. Both were inspired by roadside landscapes of the West and fascinated by signage. Both balance aesthetic appeal with visual and verbal irony. Not coincidentally, humor for both of them comes in the form of unexpected use of text.

The Great American West traces Ruscha's interest in unexpectedly diverse subject matter while keeping a firm gaze on the ties that bind his works: from monumental paintings of gas stations, to silhouettes of coyotes, to raw words, to photographs of the entire Sunset Strip. The work of humans—power poles, warehouses, streets, and, of course, written language—inhabits every Ruscha image.

But humanity is deliberately absent.

Buildings are rendered sterile and ironic, curious interlopers on God's creation. His Standard Oil stations recede so perfectly into the vanishing point that they look more like architectural renderings than they do actual structures. Ruscha's trademark words are disembodied too, appearing as if stenciled onto the canvas by God, every bit as inscrutable as the landscape itself. This effect reaches its apotheosis in Ruscha's series of the Hollywood Sign, in which words and landscape really do intersect.

Even Ruscha's photos are vacant. They reveal not architectural beauty but rather its banality. (The de Young itself, an earnest work of starchitecture by Herzog and de Mueron, is the opposite of all which fascinates Ruscha.) He captures empty parking lots and backyard pools with undisturbed surfaces. The same goes for his conventional cityscapes and his Sunset Strip photos, which look as if they've been evacuated by an atomic blast or an urgent Sunday morning sermon.

Ruscha's West is not a place for people.

The second room of the exhibit includes pieces from Ruscha's most deliberately urban series of paintings. Ruscha's "city" paintings are not paintings of cities at all but rather are works of abstract expressionism that ostensibly refer to Los Angeles. Ruscha depicts the city as a gray plain of static, like an untuned television, interrupted by lines representing streets, with names that mean something only to veteran Angelenos: Oxford, Beverly, Western; Laurel Canyon/Ventura Boulevard; Sunset, Coronado. In *Sunset-Gardner Cross*, the entire Los Angeles Basin extends up the canvas to meet with a bonfire of yellows, oranges, and reds.

His most haunting cityscapes depict Los Angeles from above at night, with beads of light forming straight lines and right angles on the "Plains of Id," as Reyner Banham called the working-class flats of the Los Angeles basin. His most nonsensical: the words "La Brea," "Sunset," "Orange," and "De Longpre" arrayed in their proper geographic arrangement against the backdrop of what appears to be Mount Everest.

Ruscha reduces the city to cartographic signifiers: lines and names. This is the bureaucratic vision, familiar to thoughtful planners, that has sapped so many American cities of their would-be texture, soul, and joy. Those implacable white dots on the prairie connote our cities in their entirety—they signify locations, but they are not places. Ruscha offers a chance for planners to step away from the trappings of bureaucracy and literally envision cities and landscapes in new ways.

***

You cannot think about cities without thinking about the

landscapes atop and within which they sit. Too often the quality of California cities, especially their pedestrian environments, is inversely proportional with the grandeur of landscape. Los Angeles is not warm, and not always humane, because it was not designed to be warm and humane. The sterile, empty, vacuous Los Angeles that Ruscha depicts is a place of our own making. (The lone exception is San Francisco, which Ruscha has not, as far as I know, ever depicted.)

Too many planners of past generations approached Western cities the way Ruscha does—but without the humor and without the harmlessness of paint and canvas. They created real places that are inhuman and hew more toward commerce and automobiles than to joy and communion. Ruscha's lines are the placeless thoroughfares down which we drive.

Unlike the abstruse, theory-based creations of many of Ruscha's late 20th century contemporaries (particularly abstract expressionists), his images are aesthetically gorgeous, with the precision of a graphic designer, sense of proportion on par with Renaissance masters, and command of color rivaling Mark Rothko. These renderings deliberately belie what many of our cities are like.

Viewing the West through Ruscha's eyes offers planners the opportunity to think about the opposite of roadside America: the vibrancy of center cities so often dismissed as "crowds"; the pedestrian environments so ripe for redesign; the public spaces that we forgot to build as we expanded; and, most of all, the zoning laws, street patterns, and real estate typologies that pretend as if we can expand infinitely, all the way to that long horizon.

2 NIMBYism and Its Discontents
The mess that is the California housing crisis

A community leader in Los Angeles who generally espouses, shall we say, skeptical attitudes toward development once scolded me for referring to someone (not herself) as a NIMBY in a piece I'd written. Point taken.

No matter how fitting a label may seem, it's never appropriate to impose one on someone else or to force individuals into broad categories. Lately, the YIMBYs have arisen, but that's different—many of them refer to themselves as such. But, interestingly, almost no one refers to him- or herself as a NIMBY, no matter how blisteringly they may rail against that new apartment building or homeless shelter. Fair is fair. I have retired that label when I'm writing about people.

While NIMBYs may not exist, NIMBYism most certainly does. It is surely one of the most powerful forces in land use today. It's one that planners, and planning, are often ill-equipped to address. NIMBYism thrives because of fundamental flaws in urban political systems and in the tools of planning.

In most cities, homeowners wield shockingly disproportionate degrees of political power compared to renters. Less development means that their property values rise (because of scarcity) and the lifestyles that they paid for remain unchanged. Planning works most effectively on empty land. Planners envision brand-new places, write the appropriate regulations, and then those places grow.

Typically, new places are the types that have generous backyards. But when the backyard is already there and you want to—literally or metaphorically—build in it, on top of it, next to it, or around the corner from it, that's an infinitely more complex matter. Finally, zoning, which is the fundamental tool of planning, itself is sublimely equipped to divide cities (by land uses and, by extension, by race and class) but falls short when cities need unity, diversity, and complexity.

These challenges lie at the heart of America's, and especially California's, next era of urban development. California's cities are no longer being built. They are being rebuilt. As a friend of planning and an urban resident, I support this rebuilding. Planners by nature cannot support the status quo; indeed, that may be a fundamental failing of planning sometimes. Though we should keep an open mind about exactly what, and how much, should be built in our proverbial backyards, it surely cannot be nothing.

I've tried to do my part to tip the scales away from NIMBYism and toward a more productive discussion not of growth vs. no growth but rather about what kind of growth our cities should pursue. Indeed, I hope that if we get rid of the labels—and the combative thinking they represent—we may find that we are all biased in favor of better cities.

Dispatches from the Country's Worst Rental Market
2014

A bygone solution to the housing crisis: the dingbat.

Some years ago I spent a day canvassing on behalf of a city council candidate with whom I was friendly. At dusk, I traded my leftover door hangers for an armload of lawn signs. I brought them home and quite pathetically propped one up in the courtyard of my building, next to my front door.

My shortage of lawn was only mildly absurd. What really troubled me, despite my fondness for the candidate, was the message: "Another Family for Flora."

And there you have almost everything you need to know about land use politics in Los Angeles.

***

I didn't exactly qualify as a "family." Like hundreds of thousands of other Angelenos, I lived alone, with occasional flatmates. I routinely equated dinner with Trader Joe's frozen burritos and the inattentive company of Tom Brokaw. I cared about schools only as a general public good and would have welcomed a few more bars, and a few fewer hair salons, in my neighborhood. But what the neighborhood—and all of West Los Angeles—really needed were apartments. Lots of them.

As an editor of *The Planning Report*, I regularly ran across a harrowing claim: Los Angeles County was short 280,000 housing units. That statistic was propagated, on a nearly weekly basis, by the local Building Industry Association (whose director we interviewed). So, it's to be taken with some skepticism. But not 280,000 units of skepticism.

This was back in the mid-2000s. Of those two city council candidates, neither discussed this shortage and neither seemed too eager to promote the production of rental housing. The candidate who won, Bill Rosendahl, championed the preservation of rental stock. Once in office, he supported rent control and legislated against the conversion of rental apartments to condominiums. Rosendahl was avuncular to a fault, and renters were "his people." But he apparently had all the "people" he needed.

A full 10 years after that election, the residents of Los Angeles—families and otherwise—have even fewer suitable places to rest their heads. That's because a city whose politics is dominated by homeowners is often incapable of promoting housing for renters.

***

A UCLA study released this summer contends—probably to the astonishment of baristas in San Francisco and assistants at publishing houses in New York City—that Los Angeles is the least affordable rental market in the country. The study calculates affordability as a function of average incomes, average rents, and the percentage of the former consumed by the latter.

The numbers are enough to make you want to move someplace easier and cheaper. Like Monaco, Montecito, or Tokyo, maybe. It found the following:

- As of 2013, on average, renters in Los Angeles are paying 47 percent of their income for rent (median rents in the county are $1,473).
- Los Angeles has the highest median rent burden in the nation—at 47 percent.
- Burdens among the bottom quintile have "gone from bad to worse."
- Los Angeles has relatively fewer publicly subsidized units and weaker rent control.
- Finally, "Los Angeles is the metro area with the largest share of renters vs. homeowners: While U.S. rentership has fluctuated around 35 percent, Los Angeles is at 52 percent."

Distressingly, the study notes that the extreme rent burden is as much a function of incomes as of housing supply: "Los Angeles has a lower median household income than comparable cities such as New York or San Francisco." But, make no mistake, housing supply is in crisis every bit as much as wages are.

The study contends, "The city needs to produce roughly 5,300 units per year that are affordable to moderate-incomes or below. Los Angeles has instead averaged roughly 1,100 units per year since 2006." Those 5,300 annual units square all too well with the 280,000 that we were short countywide in the mid-2000s.

(Los Angeles Mayor Eric Garcetti subsequently announced an initiative to promote the development of over 100,000 housing units in the city by 2021. This blog was drafted prior to that announcement. We will see how it goes.)

The UCLA study does a lot of data-crunching. It does not, however, try to explain the underlying reasons for this crisis. I don't blame the authors. It's a mess.

***

Los Angeles isn't short of housing because of the names on those lawn signs, regardless of who won or lost. The signs don't divide this city. The lawns do.

You don't have to be Howard Zinn to know that homeowners hold political clout in cities. Politicians appeal to homeowners, of detached

homes and condos alike, for a few major reasons:
- Stability: they'll be there to vote, year-in and year-out.
- Engagement: homeowners know who their public officials are.
- Unity: homeowners define their interests, and often vote as blocs, because of their homeowners' associations.
- Wealth: duh.

Meanwhile, renters are transient, politically naive, disparate, and often poor. In Los Angeles, we're talking about a disastrous constituency that includes, among others, would-be starlets, undocumented immigrants, the chronically poor, and the chronically overworked. In the March 2012 primary election, Rosendahl's successor (and former chief of staff) Mike Bonin won with just over 22,000 votes—in a council district with 283,000 residents.

The Los Angeles turnout crisis is making headlines and inspiring studies. One of the findings of the Pat Brown Institute's 2013 election postmortem: "Older voters and homeowners are disproportionately represented in mayoral voting." Imagine how few show up for a mere council seat.

So, the politicians have every reason to appeal to, and appease, homeowners. But that's just one half of the equation. The other half entails the particular bidding that they are asked to do.

***

In the second half of the 20th century, Los Angeles's single-family homes gave way to small "dingbat" apartment buildings by the thousands, thus creating our awful pattern of high-density living on streets and in neighborhoods that were designed to be suburban. But at least we had housing.

The stucco dried on the last dingbat decades ago. Today, houses get converted to multifamily (usually condos) only where long-standing zoning laws allow it. High-rises that you'd trip over in Sao Paulo or Shanghai draw lavish ribbon-cuttings and excited blog posts here, but that's because they're few and costly.

Typical reasons for opposing high-density housing center on notions of "neighborhood character." Whatever the neighbors' particular concerns are, the message they send to politicians and planners is

"Do not upzone. Do not grant that variance. Do not promote the use of density bonuses, and find any loopholes you can to resist them. Parking, parking, parking."

And then there are scholars, such as Joel Kotkin, who promote single-family suburbia and have deemed high densities to be "unbecoming" of Los Angeles. I can think of a lot of things that are a lot more "unbecoming." Spending every last dime for a roof over my head is one of them.

Whether they like it or not, the politicians and planners comply all too often. How else would you account for such a profound shortage of units, amid rising prices, in a country that considers itself a free-market economy? Especially when rental housing is the hottest typology in the country right now.

Here are a few examples of high-density projects (both for rental and for sale) that have been scuttled or constrained with a few miles of where I live:

- A rental building that was supposed to have been 20-plus stories was just completed with eight stories.
- Hundreds of units of housing were quietly proposed for the site of a car dealership, which currently generates plenty of traffic. I haven't heard a peep from it in months.
- Homeowners' groups in Santa Monica have routinely supported policies and even ballot measures to stifle growth, even though much of the city's traffic comes from workers who drive in from elsewhere because they can't find housing near their jobs.

***

Surely, homeowners are entitled to worry about traffic, sight lines, city services, and all the rest. What I suspect, though, is that many homeowners really want to do what any rational, self-interested actor would want when they own valuable assets: they want to constrain supply.

Arguments over neighborhood character play well at public hearings. No one will ever admit to being motivated by the crudest manifestation of microeconomics, but here are the facts:

- In a desirable, geographically constrained jurisdiction, the less supply there is, the more valuable each unit becomes.

That's it. Just one fact.

For all the macroeconomic benefits they would bring, the more units renters have to choose from, the less they pay. The less they pay, the less likely they are to ever want to buy a home. The less they want to buy a home, the less each home is worth, on the margin. So, homeowners have every reason to oppose the addition of rental properties. At the very least, they have no incentive to support them.

Homeowners need not worry so much about competition from new for-sale homes. The only new homes in Los Angeles get built on top of, and usually improve upon, old ones. Condos that displace rental units tend to be relatively more expensive, and less dense. And, of course, apartments hold no intrinsic appeal for homeowners, since no one ever wants to trade down.

This pattern is rare on the national level. Plenty of other cities are building like crazy. Most of those cities, like Denver and Houston, enjoy abundant vacant land.

Among its built-out, high-priced peers, New York City is already hyperdense, so it's harder to build anything. San Francisco and D.C. are more geographically constrained than Los Angeles is. All three are significantly denser than Los Angeles. Los Angeles could easily up its game in appropriate places, especially major boulevards and transit corridors, but for this perverse economic rivalry between owners and renters.

**

I wish I knew how to solve this problem.

Public housing and subsidies are crucial, for sure. But they are costly, complex, and solve only a fraction of the problem. This city needs greater supply, period. And it needs it from the source that has always created housing here: private developers. Those developments need to be built responsibly, of course, but they deserve far more support than they're getting.

If all renters got off the futon and out of the second bedroom to donate their tip money to candidates who served their interests and to cast their votes accordingly, our city would look radically different—

and for the better. People who rent apartments aren't setting up drug empires or plotting to abduct children. They want to work. They want to get a beer. They want to buy stuff at stores down the block and fall in love with the girl or guy around the corner.

They just don't want to buy your house. But your house, though, is going to be fine, as long as it's appreciated with inflation and given you a nice roof over your head. What's not fine: four people in a two-bedroom apartment, each paying half a month's wages for a bed. Imagine how Los Angeles would prosper if even a fraction of that 47 percent rent burden was liberated to be spent on other things.

That's why if everyone in Los Angeles had a decent place to live, those home values would still do all right. If a city economy does well and all residents prosper, some of those residents might make enough money to—guess what?—buy houses. We just have to see cities as the vast, amazing entities that they are, and not enemy territories that start just the other side of a homeowner's property line. That's the message of that UCLA study.

Now is as good a time as any to acknowledge this truth—and to start working toward a grander vision of how we live and prosper in Los Angeles. I don't mind it when a cranky homeowner tells some kids to get off his lawn. But I do mind it when that same homeowner would, however unwittingly, deny them—singles and families alike—decent places to live.

We need hundreds of thousands of units. And anyway, we're in a drought. There's never been a better time to stop caring so much about our lawns and start caring more about one another.

Los Angeles Reaches Capacity
2015

Go home. We're sold out.

Los Angeles's housing crisis has been building for long enough that just about anyone who rents an apartment here could have told you about it years ago. But it wasn't until last summer that UCLA released a report confirming what many of us already know: as a function of average rents (high) and average incomes (low, especially compared to those in San Francisco and New York), Los Angeles is the least-affordable rental market in the country.

Circulating around the blogosphere now is a single graph that illustrates why.

This graph comes from a dissertation by then-UCLA Ph.D. student Greg Morrow, posted on the blog of Professor Richard Green of USC. Green showed it to me at the Urban Land Institute's Urban Marketplace conference. I'd like to say that it sparked a lively

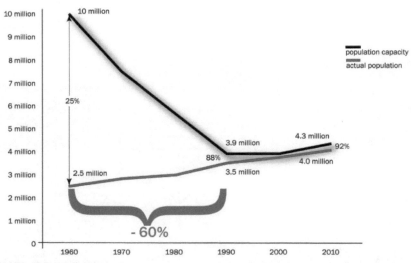

Fig. 1-1: Down-Zoning versus Population Growth. Data Sources: Census and all 104 Community Plans (cumulative population capacity)

discussion (which we had, on other topics), but instead we shared a moment of mutual speechless bewilderment. The graph mostly speaks for itself: Los Angeles's population is, after 100 or so years of development, just about equal with the city's maximum allowable population.

As Henry Grabar puts it in *Salon*, Los Angeles has "reached capacity."

The difference between those two lines is affordability. It's also opportunity for developers. Constrained supply and ever-increasing demand equals insane housing prices. In a typical industry, supply would never become this constrained. Firms would produce more, or consumers would seek substitutes. Equilibrium would be restored. But this is real estate, and those rules don't apply.

Usually "constrained" is used as a passive verb, as if it's something that just happens. But the "hand" here is very much visible. When we think of "capacity," Los Angeles didn't lose 60 percent of its landmass en route from 10 million to 4 million, and it didn't lose 60 percent of its water, power, food, or sewage capacity either (though the first one remains to be seen).

Those six million men, women, and children were zoned, voted, and legislated off the island.

That downward slope tells a fascinating tale for anyone who's not currently struggling to make rent. The greatest irony is that Los Angeles's peak population of 10 million was allowed at a time when its population was a fraction of what it is today. Either the city's public officials were thinking big prior to 1960, or they figured that even a number like four million was unthinkable, so what difference did a few more million make?

What happened, though, was a revolt by homeowners. The 1960s were heady times for the conversion of single-family homes into multifamily dingbat apartments, leading residents to fret about the loss of "neighborhood character." This usually equates with a fear of poor people and/or minorities. They were, at the same time, horrible times for public transit, as the trolley system clanged its last bell. The freeways ran smoothly for a while, but then they filled up, leading to more fears about growth.

Los Angeles has always been a "reluctant metropolis," to borrow *CP&DR* publisher Bill Fulton's phrase, and the dream of the single-family home has held sway. Worries about "Manhattanization" have persisted for years, never mind that even at 10 million people, Los Angeles would be about as dense as New York City as a whole, but still nowhere near as dense as Manhattan.

So, homeowners pushed through antigrowth legislation, advocated by residents who wanted to keep Los Angeles all to themselves. As Grabar catalogs in his *Salon* piece, small measures to keep Manhattan out of California included silly, unjustifiable requirements like setbacks, which do nothing but waste land, and parking requirements, which also waste land and jack up developers' costs.

On the more monumental scale, these sentiments culminated in 1986's Prop. U.

Prop. U, which is where that top graph bottoms out, was the mother of all slow-growth measures, downzoning much of the city's commercial areas. (According to its framers, Prop. U itself was crafted not to directly impact housing supply.) It passed by a 2:1 ratio. What you can bet is that the actual sentiments among Los Angeles residents were probably flipped; however, owners of single-family homes control 80 percent of L.A.'s residential land while representing a far smaller proportion of the population, so they dominate elections. A 2013 poll by the Pat Brown Institute found that "older voters and homeowners are disproportionately represented in mayoral voting."

Half measures and creeping protectionism that had satisfied antigrowth activists during the 1960s and 1970s were no longer enough once they saw the city hitting 3.5 million. (Not coincidentally, the city's public transit system was in a world of hurt at the time, thus favoring lower densities and people who could afford cars and places to park them.) The implications of movements like Prop. U were largely invisible for a while—you can't see what you can't build—until they started showing up in astronomical rents.

Today, many of Los Angeles's planners are trying to wring as much density out of the city as they possibly can. Developers are too. But, contrary to the stereotype of the marauding capitalist, they know as well as anyone that they build only at the pleasure of city policy and the public officials who can grant variances to it.

Los Angeles's planners are also working on re:code LA, a comprehensive and much-needed overhaul of the city's zoning code. You can bet that they're going to go for more density, especially around the city's new transit nodes. If the effort fails, though, that thin line on the graph might one day overtake the thick one. People are going to keep coming to L.A. whether the slow-growthers of 1986 like it or not. Then we'll really have a crisis on our hands.

Housing Crisis, Meet Transit Crisis
2018

If you lived here, you'd be home now.

The low point in my occasional career as a rider of public transit came a few months ago when I looked down the center aisle of an Expo Line car to discover that the (apparently) homeless guy at the front of the car was not merely homeless but also drinking gin straight from a plastic bottle.

Rest assured, this incident has not scared me away from public transit. According to a recent report by the UCLA Institute for Transportation Studies, incidents like this haven't dissuaded other riders either—they're dissuaded for other reasons. Across the Southern California Association of Governments region, annual transit trips per capita have fallen from a high of 42 in 2007 to 34 in 2016. The biggest enemy of transit these days, as it has been for the past 100 or so years, is the automobile.

I've never bought the idea that Angelenos have a "love affair with cars." They just have the misfortune of living in a city where driving a car makes it a lot easier to do other things—like, say, hold down a job. Under the right circumstances, Angelenos would be just as happy to walk, bike, or take transit as they are to drive. Unfortunately, the circumstances are far from right.

UCLA reports that between 2000 and 2015, private vehicle ownership increased from 1.7 to 2.4 vehicles per household. This dramatic increase stems largely from increased car ownership among newcomers to the region, who tend, by and large, to be low-income immigrants. The share of foreign-born households without a car dropped by 42 percent between 2000 and 2015.

These tend to be the very same people who comprise the vast majority of transit riders in the region: the often-pitied class known as "transit-dependent riders." The average resident of the SCAG region made about 35 transit trips in 2016, but the median resident made none. That's because less than three percent of the region's commuters ride "frequently," meaning that a small number of individuals take hundreds of rides per year, compared to none for most residents. When one of those high-frequency riders gets a car, ridership drops accordingly.

That's a virtuous cycle, of a sort. What's not so virtuous is the region's housing crisis. Low-income residents essentially cannot choose where to live—meaning they can't choose housing close to work, and they can't choose housing that makes transit convenient.

Really, the transit crisis results from the housing crisis.

Los Angeles's shortage of housing and shortage of high-density transit-friendly neighborhoods has run headlong into the obscene, bacchanalian overabundance of automobiles. They might not be making any more land, but we produce cars as if in an Ayn Rand fantasy (only to drive them in a drab, Gosling-less version of *La La Land*). And for each new Tesla that rolls off the assembly line, that's one more used Ford, Chevy, or Toyota to hit the market for cheap.

Meanwhile, the apartment equivalent of a 2001 Corolla is impossible to find. The housing shortage means that every time a unit is vacated—especially if it's rent-controlled—rents keep going up. That's because we don't produce enough units—be they market-rate or subsidized—to keep up with demand.

In other words, people with a little more change in their pocket can buy cars. But it takes a lot more than pocket change to find an optimal place to live.

In fairness, the UCLA report cites the effects of ridesharing, gas prices, and, yes, the occasional wino who makes transit unpleasant. And some new rail lines are doing well, often beating ridership projections. But none of these factors compare with the increase in driving, and, I reckon, no factor fuels the increase in driving more so than the shortage of well located, fairly priced housing.

Transit-heavy areas are those that are either dense enough to support transit or poor enough to require transit. The UCLA report notes that 60 percent of the region's commuters live in neighborhoods covering 0.9 percent of the region's land area. Increasing that number will require development of new transit-oriented neighborhoods. It requires fancy new apartments for the would-be Tesla drivers. And it requires the equivalents of those 2001 Corollas—older apartments that trickle down to new tenants without somehow becoming more expensive with each passing year.

The report also holds out hope for the elusive but tantalizing discretionary rider. Whether enough do-gooders and millennial urbanists can jump on board to compensate for the loss of the transit-dependents is anyone's guess. Indeed, that too depends on having enough transit-oriented housing that the hipsters and the transit-dependent can live, and ride, side by side.

That's why, regardless of what this means for Metro's fare box, the bigger issue here concerns the physical and social fabric of California's cities and, indeed, of the California Dream. For decades, the California Dream and the American Dream were one and the same: suburban-style homeownership (at least for folks of the correct skin color). Today, that dream is either inaccessible or unappealing to many Californians, and other dreams are in short supply. And so, the Automobile Dream—which used to be a complement to, rather than a replacement for, the American Dream—persists.

   I don't know exactly where this dream is driving everyone. I know, though, that it's almost enough to drive me to drink. Just not while I'm riding a train.

Renters vs. Tenants: A Distinction with a Difference
2016

Good luck with that...

Like 45 percent of other Californians and 52 percent of other Angelenos, I live in a home owned by a stranger. It's not quite the American Dream. Nationwide, 65 percent of households own the units they occupy. But it suits me fine.

The question I've asked myself lately, though, is: am I a renter or am I a tenant? I happen to be both, so the point is moot. For renters who aren't yet tenants, or who want to be a tenant someplace else, the difference is more important than you might think.

A while back, I spoke on a panel on affordable housing, sponsored by Enterprise Community Partners. The panel included Larry Gross, the executive director of the grimly named Coalition for Economic Survival (CES) and longtime Los Angeles-area housing advocate.

I contended, based on study and anecdote, that relief from the city's crushing rental rates will come only from increased housing production—for residents of all socioeconomic strata.

I recalled this discussion as I did my reporting for a 2016 *CP&DR* article on rent control in the Bay Area.

CES primarily lobbies not necessarily for more housing but rather for housing policies like, among others, rent control, which is Gross's signature issue. As he stated his case for rent control, I found us speaking different languages. They aren't mutually unintelligible. But they reveal fundamentally different ways to approach the problem of housing affordability.

I think of renters expansively, as more than just parties who signed a piece of paper. Renters are a demographic group, and an enormous one at that. They are people who, by necessity or choice, are committed to the lifestyle that renting connotes. Renters might be new in town. They might be inherently transient. They might like low-maintenance situations. They might not be able to afford to purchase a home, or they might simply have better things to do with their money.

The renter demographic has notable subsets. All those millennials we hear about who are repopulating center cities? Almost all of them are renters. Seniors who want to downsize? They might be renters too. Minimum wage workers? Surely renters. Same with young families and many others. Whatever their reasons, they approach the housing market as customers. In theory, the more choices they have, and the lower the cost for their choices—at any given level of quality, location, and amenities—the healthier a city's economy and urban environment will be.

A tenant is defined by a contractual relationship. They are people who live in someone else's property and pay rent. Policies that support them, such as those advocated by CES, are crucial. But they confer narrow, isolated benefits. Legal protections generally serve only the tenants in question and then only when disputes arise (though they surely deter malfeasance).

Many tenant protections, including rent control, reflect philosopher

John Rawls's maxim of the "veil of ignorance," by which any action must serve those who are least well-off. And they generally uphold negative rights: they prevent bad things from happening; they do not cause good things to happen. I've rarely heard from an economist who didn't argue that rent control drags down an urban economy. Those arguments are well known. Granted, they mean little when a family is faced with an unfair eviction.

I am pretty much the poster child for the perverse effects of tenant protections. I live in a rent-controlled apartment in a part of Los Angeles where rents are, to use the technical term, bonkers. I can afford more. I'd be glad to try a different part of town. But I can't afford that much more, and I'm not that eager to move. So I stay put. I get to enjoy my market distortion as a tenant and yet I feel trapped as a renter.

The dire, immediate perils that tenants face have given rise to organizations like the Coalition for Economic Survival. As well they should. They do crucial work. But make no mistake: groups like CES, and rent control itself, are necessary primarily because housing, both market-rate and affordable, has been unnaturally suppressed for decades. The slow-moving renters' crisis, because it is enormous and amorphous, has had no such advocates. Until recently.

Groups like the San Francisco Bay Area Renters Federation (with everyone's favorite schoolyard acronym, SF-BARF) have enthusiastically taken up the cause up north. Similar groups are quietly forming in Los Angeles (disclosure: I am involved with one of them), and there's even going to be the first-ever YIMBY—"yes in my backyard"—conference in Boulder, Colorado in June 2016.

As rent control spreads like wildfire across the Bay Area, even its advocates admit that it's not a complete solution. It is a solution for tenants, of course. But it will only create a game of musical chairs in which many of the state's renters end up without a seat. (Literally—once you've paid your deposit and first month's rent, how can you afford furniture?)

As the renters' movement grows, I hope renters and tenants will ultimately find themselves on the same page and speaking with a common voice. Ideally, that page is a brand-new lease, listing a rent that everyone can afford.

Minimum Wage? How about Minimum Housing?
2016

Housing shortages are not sexy.

Sexy-sporty clothing brand American Apparel has long been one of Los Angeles's most beloved, and most controversial, corporate citizens. It is known for paying decent wages and treating its workers well.

When it easily could have outsourced jobs to Asia, it has also resolutely kept its main factory in Los Angeles, occupying a muscular, seven-story industrial building on the southeast edge of downtown since 2000. American Apparel has proudly championed social justice causes, including immigration reform and gay rights, and assured consumers that they are buying "sweatshop-free" garments made by well treated workers.

They're just the sort of workers who might—*might*—benefit from the forthcoming increase in California's minimum wage. If only they—and every other low-wage worker in Los Angeles—had decent roofs over their heads.

Unfortunately, American Apparel, which has suffered through jittery balance sheets and the checkered reputation of founder and former CEO Dov Charney, hasn't made a profit since 2009. The *Los Angeles Times* distressingly, if unsurprisingly, reports that American Apparel now intends to shed 500 of its roughly 4,000 Los Angeles-area jobs.

This downsizing may be due to a social justice cause that the company surely would have supported in better days: the recent approval by the state legislature and Governor Jerry Brown to raise the state's minimum wage to $15 per hour (from $10) by 2022 (it comes on the heels of Mayor Eric Garcetti's decision to pursue a $15 citywide minimum wage). One economist told the *Times*, "The exodus has begun."

Of course, everyone deserves to make a living wage. Brown and Garcetti surely hope that the city and state are attractive enough to avoid the "exodus." Really, though, the social justice triumph of the minimum wage movement means nothing so long as it's not accompanied by a revolution in workforce housing.

Los Angeles is the country's least affordable city not just because of high rents. As an often cited 2014 UCLA report found, low-wage workers in Los Angeles dedicate a scandalous amount of their incomes to rent. At best, raising the new minimum wage will compensate for the difference between the 50 percent of income that many low-wage Angelenos pay and the 25 or 30 percent that economists consider reasonable.

A 2016 USC report reached one of the more predictable conclusions in the history of scholarship: rents in Los Angeles are continuing to rise. At the rate things are going, most of the increase in the minimum wage will end up getting sucked up by rents anyway. Employees will make more money, but they'll enjoy no net increase in quality of life.

Consider what would happen, though, if Los Angeles increased its housing supply at the same time that it increased wages. Regardless of the mix of subsidized and market-rate units (ideally with a generous number of subsidized), there is some number of units that will, based on the laws of supply and demand, stem the increase in rents. There's a greater number out there that will actually decrease rental rates. The 2013 Regional Housing Needs Assessment calls for 82,000 more units by 2021.

Rather than making $15 per hour only to tread water, Los Angeles's workers would find themselves better off by not having to spend so much on rent. They would enjoy a real increase in wealth and a real increase in quality of life. A multiplier effect, fueled by disposable income, would further stoke the local economy.

Even better, consider what increased housing productions mean in the short-term: jobs, jobs, jobs. I'm wary of economies that rely too heavily on real estate speculation (cf. Phoenix, San Bernardino, circa 2007) and on short-term job production. But at this point, who cares? A housing revolution in Los Angeles would hardly qualify as speculation, and any stimulus is welcome.

That's why we don't just need a minimum wage. We need minimum housing.

You would think that the same interest groups that have lobbied so passionately;, and successfully, for the minimum wage increase would be equally enthusiastic about a housing increase. And they are. Sort of.

As anyone who has been following Los Angeles's housing mess already knows, voters may soon consider not one but two ballot measures that could determine the fate of planning and development for years to come. The Neighborhood Integrity Initiative (NII) entails a partial development moratorium and a massive overhaul of the city's plans; it is roundly opposed by housing advocates. The Build Better L.A. initiative, which sort of competes against the NII, would essentially require inclusionary zoning in certain types of projects. Whether it would actually stimulate housing production is unclear.

The initiative is, interestingly, backed by powerful labor organizations, including the L.A. County Federation of Labor (which has a mixed approach to the minimum wage hike). Their interests are clear and probably reasonable. But rather than nibble at the edges, what labor should be doing, though, is what essentially no one in Los Angeles is doing: advocating for wholesale increase in housing production. Period. Their members have the most to gain. But really, everyone stands to gain if Angelenos have less expensive roofs over their heads. Everyone except slumlords, I suppose.

I hope American Apparel figures its way out of Chapter 11, and I hope it can keep its workforce right where it is, minus the sexual harassment. If American Apparel goes away, though, that big factory would make for some gorgeous lofts.

Death by Gentrification
2017

Not long after the publication of his book *The New Urban Crisis*, Richard Florida assured me and a roomful of other journalists that, contrary to appearances, "not everything is a neoliberal plot." Tell it to Peter Moskowitz.

Florida's ideas about attracting the "creative class" may have been overhyped. But Moskowitz, a freelance political journalist and avowed opponent of pretty much everything Florida stands for, is dangerous. He's not dangerous in the cool way, as an idealistic guy who wants to stick it to The Man. He's actually dangerous. If his new book-cum-conspiracy theory, *How to Kill a City*, wields any influence, people are going to suffer. They are the very people whom Moskowitz champions.

Gentrification, by which Moskowitz refers to a range of urban crises that he considers, not unreasonably, to be violent, discriminatory, and unjust, is the most vivid and surely most emotionally fraught of the great urban challenges that American cities face. Moskowitz discusses the issue passionately and urgently—and totally disingenuously.

***

It would be hard to write about gentrification without discussing San Francisco or New York City, which Moskowitz does. Moskowitz could have told similar, generic stories from many other cities—including pretty much every city in coastal California. His big insight in what is, admittedly, a readable, provocative rant, was to include two poignant counterpoints: New Orleans and Detroit.

Gentrification in San Francisco and New York has been discussed many times, as Latino residents in the Mission have been pushed out by tech workers and as hipsters and yuppies have taken over Brooklyn. Moskowitz brings nothing new to these stories. His descriptions of gentrification are often parodies of themselves: "upscale food co-op and art spaces; there're also new queer bars, organic juice joints, and expensive coffee shops and brunch spots," he writes, referring to New Orleans.

Things get interesting in the sections covering New Orleans and Detroit. How can economically depressed cities whose populations have cratered also be gentrified?

Moskowitz posits that even the apparent successes of post-bankruptcy Detroit and post-Katrina New Orleans come with heavy prices. Tens of thousands of native New Orleanians, many of them African American, fled after Hurricane Katrina and never came back. New, inauthentic businesses serving a bourgeois clientele have sprung up. "Restaurants and rents many can't afford...and even pothole repair become signposts for displacement and cultural loss," he writes.

Detroit, he contends, has effectively shed 142 of its 150 square miles. City government, aided and directed by billionaire Dan Snyder, has decided to focus on the city's most promising 7.2 square miles clustered around downtown. That's where the proverbial yoga studios are going in. Otherwise, a vast plain of vacant lots, dark streetlamps, and abject poverty fans out in all directions.

***

In each of these cases, Moskowitz trolls the streets looking for villains. Sometimes it's Snyder. Sometimes it's New Orleans developer Pres Kabacoff. Sometimes it's tech, and sometimes it's finance. Sometimes, Moskowitz indicts himself and his fellow urban twentysomethings for being "pioneers" in places where people have lived contentedly for generations.

But, over and over again, Moskowitz blames capital. Capital wants to boot grandmothers out of their homes. Capital wants four-dollar coffees. Capital wants exposed brick. Capital runs roughshod over communities on its endless quest for profit. Capital sent white people to the suburbs, and capital is reeling them back in.

Moskowitz seems astonished by the most basic principles of economics. Referring to economist Neil Smith, he writes, "Smith realized that … if you wanted to find a neighborhood that would gentrify next, all you have to do was figure out … the place where buildings could be bought cheap and made more expensive."

In other words, "buy low, sell high."

Things get particularly weird when Moskowitz, who unapologetically favors a welfare state, tries to discuss municipal finance. He rightly decries white flight, which decimated cities' coffers. And yet, he excoriates Detroit and New Orleans for daring to reattract high-income, taxpaying residents.

And he chides San Francisco, writing, "The city doesn't need to keep attracting rich people," as if anyone needs prodding to move to San Francisco. In fact, San Francisco's prosperity is about as organic as it gets. In studying San Francisco, Michael Storper found that deliberate economic development policies generally amount to absolutely nothing. Young people move to San Francisco because they like it.

***

Most astoundingly, Moskowitz does not—as far as I could tell—make a single mention in his 200-plus pages of jobs. He implies that low-income residents must not, under any circumstances, try to glean the prosperity that surrounds them. Moskowitz cannot conceive—or refuses to admit—that the growth he so decries could benefit the very people whom he champions.

In fact, that's exactly what happens. Enrico Moretti's research, among others, suggests that incomes rise at all levels when anchor industries prosper in an urban area. Plenty of other research shows that people of modest means are typically better off in prospering neighborhoods. Obviously gentrification is a function of wealth. But that doesn't mean that only the newcomers can reap the benefits. Yet Moskowitz implies that incumbent residents ought to simply sneer at Apple and revile the coffee shop rather than, maybe, submit a job application to them.

Meanwhile, rents keep rising.

He mentions housing scarcely more often than he does jobs, and only then to promote subsidized affordable housing. Never mind the fact that, at least in New York and the Bay Area, it's the lack of housing supply (both market rate and subsidized) that drives up prices and drives out residents who can't afford those prices. Capital salivates when restrictive zoning, which typically has little to do with Goldman Sachs and much to do with incumbent homeowners, drives up real estate values.

And if you really want to talk about capital, maybe you want to talk about the $27 trillion embedded in homeownership. You'd also have to talk about the market distortions of $134 billion annual mortgage tax write-offs (as Pulitzer Prize winner Matthew Desmond is doing) and, in some cases, inequitable tax burdens that favor wealthier homeowners (looking at you, Prop. 13).

(Even so, Venice Beach, Silver Lake, and most of San Francisco did not gentrify because of building booms. Those neighborhoods are built out and have very little new development. Meanwhile, in the most capital-heavy neighborhood in Los Angeles, South Park, almost no one has been directly displaced because most of the new construction is taking place on parking lots.)

***

It would be one thing if *How to Kill a City* was merely an ideological rant. The problem is, it's an ideological rant in the guise of journalism. And it's a lousy piece of journalism.

Whenever Moskowitz wants to make a point about the hardships faced by urban residents, he calls up an anecdote or a firsthand observation. That's fine. But whenever he wants to demonize a developer, a company, or a city government, he unleashes conjecture and half-baked assertions.

I speak to public officials—mayors, planning directors, city council members—almost every day; they're pretty accessible. And yet, he doesn't even try to empathize with the challenge of, say, operating a city when 39 percent of its residents live in poverty. He never asks developers what their margins are or why they want to build high-priced "luxury" housing. He never assesses the challenges of running a city in the face of onerous and antiurban state and federal regulations.

Moskowitz's apparent refusal to interview his opponents speaks to his entirely unappealing tendency to not merely disagree with his opponents but rather to dehumanize them. I submit that dismissing developers as "capital" and public officials as toadies rather than collaborating with them is just as insidious as "capital's" supposed disregard for people. If Moskowitz cannot acknowledge that there are people behind these financial decisions and that they might— however unenlightened they may be—have autonomy and even good intentions, he cheapens his discourse and undermines his claim to the moral high ground.

Meanwhile, he makes claims like, "Gentrification...is today most often sponsored by the state and other powerful institutions," or he says that it's a "strategy"—meaning a purposeful, coordinated effort. He even goes so far as to imply that cities deliberately destroyed themselves so that, 40 years later, they could be gentrified: "Truly equitable geographies would be largely un-gentrifiable ones. So first, geographies have to be made unequal."

For such a grand plan, you'd think there'd be plenty of evidence that an eager crusader could dig up. And yet, Moskowitz presents little more than conjecture, supposition, and righteous indignation.

How to Kill a City has moments of clarity. Moskowitz isn't wrong about the effects of gentrification, even if he misunderstands the causes. He cogently describes the ravages of suburbanization in the latter half of the 20th century. He puts blame more or less where it belongs: on federal policies that promoted suburbanization while obliterating cities through urban renewal. And he expresses solidarity with people who grew up in the suburbs and roundabout sympathy with their desire to be "gentrifiers":

> This desire to escape the suburbs is not in and of itself a bad thing. The suburbs are a terrible way to house Americans. From a progressive urban planner's perspective, an ideal world wouldn't even contain American-style suburbs.... We cannot fault the children born into suburbs for abandoning an illogical, environmentally harmful historical anomaly in favor of something much better.

And yet, 150 pages prior, Moskowitz announces, with utter sincerity, "Those words—colonization, occupation, and genocide—do not feel sensational. They feel like what happened (in New Orleans)." He literally considers displacement in the wake of Hurricane Katrina on par with the Holocaust.

Sorry, dude. Not cool.

Moskowitz's outrage derives in part from some curious *a priori* assumptions about the purpose of cities. He writes:

> Gentrification...is really about reorienting the purpose of cities away from being spaces that provide for the poor and middle classes and toward being spaces that generate capital for the rich.... It is only in the last few decades that economic growth has become the driving force in the governing of cities, to the exclusion of every other metric of well-being.

Those things are nice, but when exactly did everyone agree on the "purpose" of cities? When were those "other metrics" agreed upon? Does he really mean that cities today exclude every other metric? Certainly cities can, and should, provide for the poor. But as an empirical, historic matter, it is the rare city that has explicitly pledged such a purpose. Moskowitz's outrage is thus based on a fiction of his own making.

(Meanwhile, he accurately acknowledges the history of urban development as an "age-old, racist process of subsidizing and privileging the ... the wealthy and white." I guess the good old days weren't so good?)

Then there's Moskowitz's hypocrisy. He admits that he is one of those suburbanites who have sought greener pastures in cities. Presumably, he does so with good intentions: he enjoys living in New York City and thinks he can do good work there. And yet, by his own standards, Moskowitz is himself committing genocide. I also hate to break it to him, but he's also committing capitalism. His publisher, Nation Books, is an imprint of publishing giant Hachette. I'm guessing that Moskowitz doesn't write for free.

***

I get it. Capitalism is ruthless. The United States is racist. Governments, especially the feds, have betrayed the poor. Moskowitz is more than entitled to illustrate those flaws. But you know what else is flawed? Disingenuously complaining about a deadly serious matter without offering constructive, viable solutions.

In his final chapter, Moskowitz pulls a few policy recommendations off the progressive stockpile like, "give people a say" (fine), "protect... public lands" (OK, if you have the money), "heavily regulate housing" (with what political capital?), and "implement a new New Deal" (with what funds? And in what political universe?). He generally wants "more taxes, more laws, more intervention from the federal government." Most of all, though, he exhorts residents in threatened communities to "fight." He doesn't mean they should fight for something, such as more housing or more job opportunities. He essentially recommends obstruction and conflict: stronger rent control, opposition to new development, rejection of newcomers, protection of incumbent tenants, and defense of the status quo.

Herein lies the danger of *How to Kill a City*: it is a deliberately antagonistic book. And there are millions of people across this country who might take it seriously. (As of this writing, it's the number-one seller in its category on Amazon.) Moskowitz clearly doesn't believe in collaboration, compromise, or common prosperity—meaning, he doesn't really believe in cities.

And, anyway, if you set up a "fight" between "capital" and poor people, how do you think that's going to turn out?

As Jane Jacobs, who is infuriatingly invoked by Moskowitz's title, told us two generations ago, "Cities have the capability of providing something for everybody, only because, and only when, they are created by everybody." Naturally, the poor deserve their voices, loud and numerous. But this is a choir, not a battle of the bands. Any attempt to segregate or pit groups against one another is counterproductive and inherently antiurban.

I hate to break it to Moskowitz, but "everybody" includes rich people—as it should. That's because the relationship between rich and poor in cities enables cities to thrive. Government needs to make sure that this relationship is equitable, productive, and symbiotic, partly by providing, and allowing, housing. This isn't voodoo economics—this is how life works.

And, anyhow, in a fight between "capital" and everyone else, who do you think is going to win?

Moskowitz's heart is undoubtedly in the right place. Every city in the world needs more equity and more justice. But fighting—that's a way to build walls, not cities. If the future of cities depends on it, then they are already dead. No conspiracy needed.

Radical Left Burns Bridges amid Quest to Build Housing
June 2017

Planners who tend to keep their heads down politically might have missed the firestorm that erupted a while back over a column about the "YIMBY" movement on the left-wing site Truthout. The grassroots, prodevelopment movement got savaged in a quasi-article by Toshio Meronek and Andrew Szeto originally entitled "YIMBYs: The 'Alt-Right' Darlings of the Real Estate Industry."

The headline was eventually changed to omit "alt-right" so as to seem less inflammatory, if still inaccurate. When culture-war terminology like "alt-right" gets thrown around in land-use circles, you know something is up.

For the uninitiated, the "Y" in YIMBY stands for "yes," and the "yes" refers to development—mainly to housing. By filing comments, testifying at hearings, and otherwise inserting themselves into public discourse, YIMBYs try to provide a counterweight to antidevelopment forces. They generally support market-rate and affordable housing developments alike.

The unofficial leader of the YIMBY movement—and prime target of Meronek and Szeto—is Oakland-based Sonja Trauss, who founded the San Francisco Bay Area Renters' Federation, delightfully abbreviated SF-BARF. They accuse her of being the powerful leader of "an army with soldiers around the world, from Boulder to Bratislava, while dominating the dialogue on how to deal with the very real problem of housing inequality." I think any planner would be surprised to find that prodevelopment activists are "dominating" much of anything.

In reality, Trauss considers SF-BARF an open-source grassroots organization, replete with a wiki website that irreverently uses Comic Sans font. ULI it is not. Trauss provides information and does her own rabble-rousing, but any concerned citizen can take up the cause at any time.

Trauss describes herself as an anarchist, with no love for political ideologies. Short of burning the whole place down, she has contented herself with supporting The Man (real estate developers) so as to stick it to The (other) Man (homeowners' associations and other antidevelopment forces). It's a compromise, to be sure. But even anarchists need someplace to live.

Meronek and Szeto have decided that Trauss and her colleagues are "progentrification," in league with "greedy" real estate developers. They equate support for market-rate housing with support for "luxury" housing. They also equate it with not just tolerance for but, it seems, approval of displacement. YIMBYism, they claim, is "rooted in the same classist, racist ideologies it supposedly seeks to disrupt," in line with redlining, slum clearance, urban renewal, and other explicitly discriminatory practices of decades past.

As a factual matter, their accusations are nonsense for all sorts of reasons. SF-BARF has routinely lobbied for projects with affordable units, with just as much enthusiasm as it has for projects with all market-rate units. Trauss famously "sued the suburbs"—or rather a suburb, Lafayette—for alleged violation of the Housing Accountability Act. The SF-BARF mission statement reads, in part, "Without an increase in overall yearly production of housing in the Bay Area, we will continue to suffer from displacement, crowding and exploitation from landlords." See? They don't like displacement, or exploitation.

Meronek and Szeto can't quite believe that anyone would want more housing, so they accuse Trauss of being in the pocket of just about everyone. This includes Jeremy Stoppelman, CEO of Yelp, and, presumably, an uncaring fan of "luxury" housing. Never mind the fact that no capitalist—other than a real estate developer—would ever want his or her employees to live in expensive housing.

Meronek and Szeto write of collaboration, "When asked about her organization's alliance with SPUR and realtors, she responds that the groups have 'a shared goal…so we work together.'" Collaboration—what a concept! They further accuse Trauss of "aligning" with controversial tech billionaire Peter Thiel simply for having breakfast with him—at his invitation.

Come on. They had *breakfast*. It's not like they shared a room at Davos.

Even after their story roused a slew of thoughtful—and frustrated—online chatter, Meronek and Szeto doubled down on many of their claims in an opinion piece in the *San Francisco Examiner*. They write that YIMBYs have

> co-opted social justice movements against gentrification toward a capitalist, pro-gentrification agenda. YIMBYism's long-standing affiliation with right-wing free-market, or neoclassical/neoliberal, economics is precisely what our article illuminated … . [T]heir politics are rooted in racist and anti-poor conservative neoliberal ideologies.

All righty then.

Notwithstanding the fact that it's pretty hard for a three-year-old movement to be "long-standing," tirades like this make it almost impossible to assign much credibility to the radical left. That's a shame. Many progressive mainstream planners and, I reckon, the majority of YIMBYs share 90 percent of the values of people like

Meronek and Szeto. They might have different priorities and favor different tactics, but I think we're all on the same team.

(That team is scoring points. In 2016, San Francisco voted for all sorts of funding for affordable housing, and the city is developing complementary ordinances.)

And yet, like children who've been so badly bullied that they won't let anyone be their friend, Meronek and Szeto make no attempt to persuade. They instead seem like they're spouting off only for personal satisfaction. They claim to support social justice and yet call fellow progressives "alt-right." If that's not otherization—which is, rightly, one of progressives' major bugbears—I don't know what is.

Enough, already.

I get it. I get resentment. I get fear. I get the fraught history surrounding the urban poor. But I don't get the vitriol, and I don't respect the dishonesty.

I submit that honesty and compromise remain admirable values and effective political tools—especially on the local level where policymakers, community members, and activists are literally rubbing elbows with one another.

Does YIMBYism have problems? Sure. No movement is perfect. But slander and willful misrepresentations are bigger problems. They create bitterness and fragmentation when there ought to be unity, cooperation, and respectful disagreement.

They may treat mainstream housing advocates like enemies, but, fortunately, we don't have to treat them in kind.

My best advice for YIMBYs and anyone else interested in building prosperous, inclusive cities is to embrace their causes—of social justice and affordable housing—more enthusiastically than ever. The equitable city depends on protections from displacement, social justice, and affordable (subsidized) housing just as much as it depends on market-rate development, place-making, and urban amenities. YIMBYs can wage those battles whether the far left likes it or not.

As for the planners quietly slaving over applications and zoning code rewrites: this debate is coming your way whether you like it or not. There's never been a better time to get fired up about housing, equity, density, and all the other fundamental challenges that make good planning—and good mediation—so important. I can't fathom who benefits from getting worked up over the 10 percent of disagreement rather than excited about the 90 percent of common ground.

That's not alt-right. That's just right.

It's Time to Stop Demonization of Developers
2017

A few years ago, Charlie Munger ended up with a piece of property in my neighborhood. He decided to develop an upscale retail center: restaurants, boutiques, nail salons, or whatever. His architect came up with an elegant design of an appropriate scale, and his development company set about getting approvals.

To make a long story short, neighbors bent over backwards to kill the project. Years later, the site consists of an empty lot and an abandoned building surrounded by chain link. It's probably the most valuable empty lot in Los Angeles.

I thought of Munger whenever I heard an activist rail about "greedy developers" during the recent battle over Measure S in Los Angeles. Munger insisted that he had no interest in profit and just wanted his project to be something "nice for the community," as he put it at a meeting I attended.

I believe him. See, Munger is Warren Buffet's business partner. He's over 90 years old and worth over $1.4 billion. The man literally has no use for greed.

Needless to say, not every developer is a Charlie Munger. Unfortunately, many people in Los Angeles talk about developers like they're all Charles Manson.

Among the grandiose promises, half-truths, and outright whoppers that sponsors of Measure S proffered, one of the most consistent messages concerned the depravity of real estate developers. They affixed "greedy" to the profession the way the president affixed "crooked" to his opponent. Perhaps most damningly, they referred to developers as "Trump's pals." (Munger, for one, isn't.)

To hear the Measure S coalition tell it, developers, be they individuals or companies, want to exploit the city, corrupt the politicians, and build the biggest, ugliest structures they can, everywhere and anywhere. They foist "luxury" apartments upon and invite gentrification into unsuspecting neighborhoods and drive up rents, as if gentrification depends purely on supply and has nothing to do with demand.

Left unchecked, Los Angeles would suffer "Manhattanization," as if resembling the most prosperous, most exciting city in the world would be a fate worse than death.

***

These accusations came from two angles. Traditional NIMBYs consider anything that blocks their view, slows their commute, or makes it easier for "those people" to live nearby to be a nefarious deed.

On the other end of the political spectrum, advocates for social justice implicate developers in all that is wrong with capitalism. To hear them tell it, every developer is, if not Charles Mason, at least Henry Potter, gleefully putting up shacks and gouging the good people of Bedford Falls at every turn. Of course, the greedy developer stereotype is grounded in reality. Like many other city-watchers in Los Angeles, I've taken my shots at people like Geoff Palmer. Mall developer Rick Caruso is an affable enough guy, but no one would accuse him of pursuing a modest lifestyle. Don't get me started on Donald Stirling.

Are developers aggressive? Many are. Do they come off as slick rather than earnest? Sometimes. Are they trying to make money? Of course. What I don't get is why their efforts are so much more nefarious than anyone else's.

Grocery stores don't sell food for free. Doctors don't perform surgery for free. Teachers don't go to class for their health. Movie stars don't act for free. Even staff members at charities are entitled to earn a competitive salary (more on that later).

Developers make money because they produce something that people are willing to pay for. Unless you built your own house, you are living someplace that was, by definition, built by a developer—or at least by someone willing to make that knotty leap from use value to exchange value. If you don't like developers, I'm sure A16 has a few tents they can sell you.

Developers get special attention—and special derision—for two related reasons. First, their products are literally visible. We see what they are doing, and we can decide immediately whether we approve or not. Second, their business inherently depends on the public trust and impacts the public realm. Land, sky, and infrastructure are public goods, in the strictest, Economics 101 sense of the term. They are not to be handed over wantonly. Developers who manipulate the public process—maybe, as the Yes on S coalition claimed, with the occasional campaign contribution or secret handshake—are classic rent-seekers. I get it: that's not cool.

And yet, if we're going to get all huffy about capitalists, I'd submit that real estate developers are the least of our worries. Sure, you might hate the Hollywood Palladium towers. But at least you see what you're getting. The very quality that makes real estate threatening is the same quality that limits the damage it can do. I'm far more concerned about, say, greedy drug companies, greedy food companies, greedy financiers, and greedy defense contractors than I am about greedy developers.

***

The Carusos and Palmers notwithstanding, many developers are more like regular white-collar professionals than they are captains of industry. They put in crazy hours—nay, years—partly to navigate our regulatory morass, often with uncertainty every step of the way. Many of them make good livings, but few of them make killings.

With that said, from a purely psychological standpoint, do we really expect developers to do good work and to want to cooperate with the city if we're berating them all the time? If you call people "evil" and "greedy" often enough, they're either going to get really uncooperative, or they're just going to say to hell with it and conform to the labels they're given.

In the middle of all of this, you have the pot calling the kettle black. If anyone has committed the sin of avarice, it's the AIDS Healthcare Foundation. They're the ones who created, sponsored, and overwhelmingly funded (if you consider 99 percent overwhelming) the Yes on S campaign. You have to wonder how a nonprofit company manages to sock away so much money that it can spend $6 million on billboards. (The answer: you can do it when you have annual revenue of $900 million, an annual budget of $160 million, and pay the executive director $380,000 per year. How many developers would love to have that kind of balance sheet?)

It's usually easy to claim the moral high ground when you're an AIDS charity. Until, of course, you stray so far from your mission that you start seeming like a plague on the city.

And let's not forget about the real power brokers in Los Angeles. In many ways, the Measure S campaign was a smoke screen for homeowners' own greed. Indirectly, their properties become more valuable as supply is constrained. There's rent-seeking capitalism at work yet again. More directly, homeowners' associations are pretty adept at extracting concessions from developers. Developers lop off a few stories from their buildings and add community amenities all the time. Sometimes they even cough up cash payments that fund HOA's own war chests, to be deployed the next time someone proposes 22 stories rather than 16.

***

Developers, like the grocery store and the doctor and plenty of other capitalists, serve crucial functions in society. In fact, planning and development are inextricably and symbiotically linked. Plans mean nothing without someone to build them.

Of course, a city's plans can be lousy. That's why Measure S was so potent. It called out Los Angeles's antiquated plans and rightfully highlighted the absurdity of "spot zoning." But, whether plans are outdated or enlightened, most developers are just trying to do their thing.

For too long in Los Angeles, developers have been the only ones actually advocating for more housing. The vast majority of Los Angeles's rent-burdened residents have sat by (probably because they're working three jobs) while slow-growth interests have lobbied against every additional unit. This situation has left developers to fend for themselves, pleading their cases before roomfuls of indignant homeowners, praying that planning commissioners and zoning administrators will see through their protests and acknowledge the greater good. And, yes, I'm sure they make occasional campaign contributions.

My point is, no one is entirely guilty in this mess, and no one is entirely innocent.

***

We who live in the new, ascendant, post-Measure S Los Angeles can choose how to understand one another and how to relate to one another. If we restrict development just because developers are "greedy" or fail to implement policies to reduce their temptations, then the joke's on us. As rents keep rising, it's the landlords—not the developers—who win big.

The way to prevent this is to reject the divisiveness of the Measure S campaign. We four million people live in close quarters on a small piece of this earth. We are neighbors, whether we like it or not. And, contrary to the city's history and culture, we're going to have to embrace one another a little bit more. We're going to have to stop the name-calling and tone down the distrust and put aside the rivalries so we can all work toward a better city, compromises and all.

No matter how high the towers of the future rise and no matter how dense certain neighborhoods get, it's the attitude—more so than any single development or any citywide policy—that will help Los Angeles put its past behind it and embrace a new era.

To paraphrase the president, some developers, I assume, are terrible people. But most are not. In this new era, developers deserve the benefit of the doubt. Charlie Munger certainly does. As for the Donalds—Stirling, Trump—and their ilk, not so much.

3 Density Scolds
Taking on Kotkin, Cox, and friends

Like avocado toast and kombucha, cities are trendy these days. Downtowns are lit up. Food scenes are cool. Art scenes are cool. Biking, walking, and even public transportation are cool. It's cool to say cities are cool, which makes me wonder if it's soon going to be not cool.

As we ponder that question, we can also acknowledge an axiom: there's almost nothing cool about the suburbs. The suburbs may be comfortable. They may be expedient. They may be affordable. They may foster "community." But they are not cool.

The thing is, our memories are short. The urban "trend" isn't exactly a passing fancy. Civilizations have organized themselves around cities for several thousand years. Before there were cities, there were camels and huts. Only in the past 70 or so years have automobiles, freeways, and obscene expanses of single-family homes dominated urban growth patterns. Those patterns didn't happen by accident. They had boosters, policies, moneyed interests, and racial tensions that wrested urban America away from the patterns and densities that civilizations around the world had developed for millennia—not just for millennials. These boosters went out of their way to influence government policy and consumer tastes. They encouraged at least two generations of Americans to forget about the pleasures and benefits of urban living.

Unfortunately, many suburban boosters are still around. They are still fighting a battle they won long ago.

Supporters of suburban development tend to profess libertarian theories, most importantly "property rights" and circular arguments about preferences. I say "circular" because these supporters often cite Americans' preferences for suburban living when, in fact, suburban living has often been the only viable option for many Americans.

Los Angeles maintains a particularly fraught relationship with suburbanization. I consider it the first suburban-dominated city. Yes, East Coast cities have sprawled to their hearts' content too. Levittown was on Long Island, of course. But New York, Philadelphia, Baltimore, and Boston had 200 years to mature before someone got the bright idea of eviscerating them. Los Angeles, while older than many people realize, was just getting started. It was in not quite its infancy but certainly its adolescence when its upward growth was cut off and its outward growth began. I often imagine wistfully how it would have developed had they waited even a decade to build the freeways and dig up the orange groves.

It would be one thing to defend the suburbs. People who want to live in suburbs should have that option, and people who appreciate them the way Joel Kotkin does deserve attention. But many of the thinkers whom I label here as "density scolds" often take it upon themselves to criticize and even mock the city. They treat the urban-suburban rivalry like a zero-sum game rather than a complex symbiosis. I'm not saying that urban living shouldn't be scrutinized. But there's a bitter sort of mockery that, as far as I'm concerned, undermines whatever worthwhile analyses they might offer. Finally, density scolds tend to be white and male. I can't fault them for that—I am too—but I can fault them for espousing lousy, self-serving views.

As this book's namesake, Betty Friedan, told us over 50 years ago, the suburbs were very much a product and reinforcement of the traditional American patriarchy. She's the one who told us that the suburbs are worse than merely "not cool"—they can be sickening and oppressive. I've taken it upon myself, one white guy to a few others, to stick up for the city.

Debunking, and Creating, Myths of Sprawl
2016

The American dream writ large.

Every movement—be it political, academic, or geographic—needs its points and counterpoints, and in a world that for the past few years has embraced all things denser, smaller, and "smarter," even smart growth can use a devil's advocate. In *Sprawl: A Compact History*, University of Illinois planning professor Robert Bruegmann takes on that role and offers a compelling array of claims contradicting now-conventional ideals of urban development.

Sprawl poses a series of provocative questions. Was redlining racist, or merely a prudent strategy by banks nervous about lending money in neighborhoods already on the wane? Does bulldozing virgin land reveal deeper flaws in capitalism than cramming immigrants into tenements? Does sprawl represent a uniquely American desire to conquer the wilderness, or does every culture seek more living space? Is waiting for the bus more fulfilling than piloting two tons of steel anywhere at any time?

With lively, pointed prose aimed at hipsters and homemakers alike, *Sprawl* is engaging enough to deserve a great many readers who like entertaining histories and enthusiastic arguments, even if their logic springs a few leaks. Those leaks arise in part because, as *Sprawl*'s subtitle implies, this is not a comprehensive history. It focuses on examples somewhat in isolation, and even if those examples are compelling in their own right, implied generalizations, wordplay, and strategically chosen statistics combine in arguments that ultimately are only momentarily tantalizing.

Sprawl includes three sections: a history of sprawl, an analysis of movements against it, and the "remedies" that those movements spawned. At each turn, Bruegmann accepts that the current American landscape is more than all right, and argues that Americans should have chosen sprawl because sprawl is good and that no movement toward density, no matter how fervent, should obscure suburbia's virtues.

Bruegmann first sets out to provide a fair, comprehensive definition of the concept of sprawl, because, he claims, interest groups and ideologies naturally pervert the definition of such a nebulous concept. He refers to sprawl as an "invented" concept, as if by any other name it would contain less asphalt and kill fewer trees. He explains, "sprawl, like the terms 'urban blight,' the 'slum,' and many of the other terms associated with urban development, is not so much an objective reality as a cultural concept, a term born at a specific time and place .... It has accumulated around it an entire body of ideas and assumptions." Never mind that he declines to provide similar explications of "community," "lifestyle," "front yard," and "American Dream"—but so far, so postmodern.

Bruegmann then attempts to define away that which makes sprawl—by any conventional definition—most troublesome. He ignores sprawl's inherently spatial component, preferring instead to depend on its more subjective cultural, demographic, and political implications. And he dismisses aesthetic concerns by way of mockery.

With as much snarkiness as has ever been applied to urban planning, he admits, "and, by the way, it is ugly." By the way, indeed. This is nearly the only mention of aesthetics, and the dismissal indicates more than that he probably would not enjoy carpooling with Peter Blake. Bruegmann does not actually deny the visual degradation of sprawl—he concedes it, in fact—but instead tries to imply that it does not warrant serious discussion, presumably because aesthetics do not lend themselves to objective measurement and therefore have no impact on people's lives.

One of the most pointless redefinitions of sprawl that Bruegmann posits is that sprawl is not uniquely American. He points to the expansion of Paris as proof that sprawl is a universal force of nature, and he notes that only a small fraction of Parisians live on picture-postcard streets. Yet he fails to prove that the proliferation of sprawl amounts to anything but a contagion, regardless of national origin. Sprawl might not be confined to America, but neither are cancer, AIDS, or the Backstreet Boys. That doesn't mean that it's not an American problem. Moreover, this claim still begs the question of whether all those dwellers on the fringe would jump at the chance to live in the 7th Arrondissement, if only it weren't already full.

With this "definition" in hand, part one of *Sprawl* marches chronologically through the 20th century to provide a history of sprawl, the basic tenets of which will be familiar to any student, or even casual observer, of the American urban form. Bruegmann's appealing thesis is that sprawl has resulted from conscious choices that Americans have made about where they want to live, what they want to live in, and what they are willing to do to get there. Bruegmann addresses many of the typical sprawl conspiracy theories (which variously blame developers, banks, oil and auto companies, white people, and a myriad of pro-sprawl laws and policies), and he offers some reasonable alternative explanations that do not hinge on greed, corruption, or racism. But even if sprawl is humanity's gift to itself, Bruegmann's unkind words for other urban forms and their attendant lifestyles betray his bias.

In an America by now well versed in the politics and geography of red and blue, snide references to anti-sprawl "elites" and "city-dwellers" provide unsubtle clues about Bruegmann's political agenda. Having already denigrated Paris, he turns to sprawl's bourgeois detractors, who cling to

> a specific set of assumptions about urbanity made by members of a small cultural elite ... in dense city centers that contain major highbrow cultural institutions. In these dense city centers, they believe, citizens are more tolerant and cosmopolitan because of their constant interaction with citizens unlike themselves.

In characterizing the goals of the urban left as hopelessly quaint, Bruegmann fails to explain exactly what's wrong with welcoming disenfranchised classes, giving them equal access to those institutions, and enabling them to escape the sort of bigotry that would prefer them to just shut up, spread out, and accept their "lowbrow" fate.

Bruegmann does not rely entirely on cultural arguments, however, and when taking the wider geographic and demographic view, his most self-satisfied (and publicized) assertion comes when he declares that the bazillion-square-mile Los Angeles region does not really qualify as sprawl. Depending how you bend the census data, Los Angeles has grown into the densest urban area in the country. This dubious observation leads Bruegmann to proclaim that sprawl simply does not exist in L.A. In fact, he adopts the argument of his opponents by implying that density makes it all OK, as if high density means that millions of acres of desert, beach, farmland, chaparral, mountain, and coastal plain were never bulldozed, never polluted, and never carved up by developers seeking easy, short-term profits. Again, it's convenient when your contrarian argument relies on a definition of your own making.

Sprawl's greatest strength lies in its final chapters, which discuss the problematic nature of policies and regulations, such as growth boundaries and transit subsidies, designed to combat sprawl. Bruegmann notes that these attempts have often worked poorly, raised real estate prices, and/or created backlashes. He effectively argues that forces more powerful than those of public policy and aesthetic sensibilities have complicated and even thwarted efforts to zone, greenbelt, and light rail our way out of rampant growth.

Indeed, modern public policy would surely benefit from honest accounts of when policies' effects have deviated from their intent. Bruegmann evokes the dangers posed by policymakers and bureaucrats so entranced by their work that they fail to notice, or care, how those policies affect people. But Bruegmann gives this conclusion a defeatist tone by implying that the persistence of sprawl in the face of flawed regulations means that America should simply succumb to the naturalistic fallacy, as if nature is telling us that the easiest path is the best and that the best choice is the one we have already made.

The proponents of New Urbanism, smart growth, and the like often weather criticism that they are idealists who have the nerve to prescribe a gossamer world detached from the realities of politics, economics, and culture. Yet even if these theories sometimes lack a commitment to balance, objectivity, and rigorous scholarship, so does *Sprawl*. Bruegmann deserves commendation for advancing strong, controversial conclusions that counterbalance those of his intellectual adversaries, such as James Howard Kunstler, Andres Duany, or the late Jane Jacobs. But in fighting fire with fire, Bruegmann often neglects to explain his logic or acknowledge even a glimmer of wisdom in the theories he attempts to combat. Just as they cannot all be wrong, it would be absurd to believe that he, despite his bluster, is all right.

The result is a cartoon version of scholarship that advocates little but the status quo. It is entertaining, and it may be partially true, but it ultimately reduces the debate to a shouting match. And until a new devil's advocate comes along with some more serious and balanced challenges to the ascendant wisdom, the battles against sprawl will, no doubt, continue to rewrite the ordinances, divert the capital, and slash the tires of the forces that promote it.

Wendell Cox's Version of Dune
2015

Just add sandworms. And tract homes.

Whenever I consider Wendell Cox's take on urban planning, I remind myself that I am taking in not just a series of ideas but rather a whole worldview. It's kind of like reading *Dune*, which takes place on the famously comprehensive desert planet Arrakis imagined by sci-fi novelist Frank Herbert.

Cox spoke recently to the Urban Land Institute's Los Angeles chapter along with University of Southern California demographer Dowell Myers. The two weren't exactly adversaries, but they were a study in forms of reasoning. Cox is all induction, beginning with theory and explaining how the facts match it. Meyers is deductive, presenting the facts and going from there.

Cox's worldview does not, I think, correspond well to reality—certainly not the reality of California—but it's a complete, mostly internally consistent view. It doesn't require personal water recyclers or rides on giant sandworms, but it's complete nonetheless. An analysis of Cox, then, relies on finding those moments where his world matches up with the real world just closely enough to make a comparison.

Cox's narrative is a familiar libertarian one—and it's fine, as far as it goes. Rather than belabor it, I'd like to pick out a few of Cox's claims, all of which are worth considering if only because they are provocative.

In no particular order (numbered for future reference):

1. The U.S. average home purchase price is three times annual household income. California is north of five times and climbing toward ten times.
2. On a ranking of average commute times in world megacities, Los Angeles ranks last, at a mere 28 minutes. The top city clocked in at one hour, 15 minutes.
3. It's sexy to tell stories about how millennials love living in center cities—but not nearly as much as everyone else loves living in suburbs, with 90 percent of new households forming on the fringes.
4. Anyway, even hipsters are going to move away once their kids are old enough to go to school.
5. The Los Angeles region has plenty of land on which to build.
6. The dispersion of employment centers in concert with the dispersion of residential areas has led, on average, to shorter commutes.
7. Construction costs are the same in center cities as they are on the urban fringe; land costs are lower on the fringe, and there's less opposition.
8. Cox says that he helped pass the funding legislation for the Los Angeles subway. He's not a fan of subways, but he'd do it again because otherwise the RTD (predecessor to LA Metro) would have squandered money on something else.
9. Senate Bill 375, California's prodensity law, will "force" developers to reduce suburban greenfield developments but will

not, because of "regulations," promote much infill.
10. Accounting for housing costs, the poverty rate in California rivals that of Mississippi.
11. Cities with regulations limiting land development have the worst ratios of purchase prices to annual incomes (Hong Kong is the worst globally).

(No offense to Myers, who had a great presentation on demographics, but, you know, if you're not willing to say that Mojave should become the next great L.A. suburb, then, well, you're not going to get as much press.)

Some responses—see which one of us you agree with:
1. If you compare California to the entire rest of the country, you end up comparing it with many places that aren't nearly as prosperous, not nearly as appealing, and, therefore, not nearly as expensive. With that said, yes, we have a housing crisis.
2. Rankings depend on the objects being ranked. The No. 1 city on Cox's list was Jakarta. Does anyone think that Jakarta is relevant to a policy discussion about Los Angeles?
3. True enough. It is a sexy story, and we shouldn't be seduced by anecdotes. But you know what's a salient, if less sexy, story? The story of all the people forced into the suburbs—not by choice but by necessity—because of lack of supply in the center cities.
4. We do need to fix the schools. Before we do that, we need to fix the funding schemes that hurt urban schools. Prop. 13, I'm looking at you.
5. Here's where Myers and Cox got into it. Myers helpfully pointed out that Los Angeles has some pretty significant barriers to development, one of which is called the Pacific Ocean. That's when Cox gestured toward the desert. I'm still having trouble figuring out why it's more preferable to build houses in Victorville and Palmdale, which have more meth labs than offices, than it is to build apartments in Santa Monica, which has twice as many jobs as it has bedrooms.
6. Surely Cox's claim about intrasuburban commuting is spot-on for some people. If you live in Upland and work in Claremont,

more power to you. If you live in El Monte and work in Century City, not so much ...
7. This got me thinking. It's true that land on the fringe follows different economic rules than land in the center. Land is dear in the center, so landowners can estimate highest and best uses and charge accordingly. The cagiest landlords effectively suck up all the economic rent. On the fringe, one parcel is a lot like the others; it's a buyer's market, and the buyers can bid land costs down. Oh, and there's Prop. 13 again, which encourages landlords to hang on to their properties, sans improvements, indefinitely.
8. One hundred fifty thousand daily riders thank him. So do the drivers aboveground on Wilshire Boulevard. (If only we had sandworms to dig the tunnels for us!)
9. Most of Cox's arguments are based on passionate readings of actual data and are supported by theories that carry some glimmer of truth. This one, however, nudges discomfortingly into Tea Party/Agenda 21 conspiracy theories.
10. This is a crime and a travesty. See responses to 1 and 11.
11. I've saved the richest one for last. Over and over and over we hear free-market advocates and/or fans of sprawl decry the constraints and distortions of regulations. I'm not unsympathetic, just as Cox isn't, to be fair, a raving maniac about it. But the effect of regulations depends in large part on where you stand: one person's restraint is another person's savior. I'm also tired of wholesale condemnations of "regulations." That does two things: first, it enables conservatives and aggressive developers to nod knowingly and self-satisfyingly without doing anything productive; second, it prevents us from actually enacting regulatory reform. See, "regulations" can mean anything you want it to mean—usually CEQA, sometimes AB 32, sometimes SB 375, lately AB 779. To Cox, Prop. 13 doesn't count as a "regulation," of course, because it's all about property rights and freedom.

I challenge Cox and his fellow travelers no longer to refer to "regulations" but instead to refer to the specific regulations that they want to change. That approach will force them to explain why the regulation is bad and maybe propose a solution. They also might consider whether regulations precede or follow the enormous demand that may have pushed up prices in the first place.

Interestingly, Cox aimed his critique largely at regulations that complicate the development of greenfields. I did not hear him express support for, say, looser restrictions on density in urban areas. He's implying, of course, that houses will solve our real estate crisis, but, somehow, apartments will not. Regulations that protect virgin land are bad, but regulations that constrain the highest and best use of infill parcels—be they height restrictions, density restrictions, or parking requirements—are, I guess, fine.

It's worth noting the location of this event: Century City. We were on the 22nd floor of an office building, 50 miles from the nearest desert, with westerly and northerly views of single-family homes, the Los Angeles Country Club, and the Santa Monica Mountains. The audience consisted of developers who have probably never heard of Victorville, much less been there. They're all trying mightily to develop in Los Angeles—higher, denser. The jobs are already here and the demand is already here, whether Cox likes it or not.

I left the presentation at 9:30 a.m. and crawled westward on Olympic Boulevard. I was caught in the morning traffic. Everyone at that hour is trying to get into Santa Monica, from the east. They can't come from the west. There's an ocean there.

Valet, please bring me my sandworm ...

Dumb Objections to Smart Growth
2012

Transit and housing — what a concept!

For whatever reason, *The Wall Street Journal* really has it in for California. Recently, Wendell Cox's opinion pieces in the *Journal* have been heralding the "war" that California's urban areas are launching on the suburbs. Joel Kotkin's new piece—which isn't actually an op-ed but rather a sycophantic quasi-interview by Allysia Finley—levies familiar criticisms of California's land use policies, but with even more strained logic and offensive biases than usual.

I'd rather not make a career out of responding to erroneous analyses of California's demise. But, as a loyal Californian and fan of truthfulness, I can't ignore this latest volley of claptrap.

Cox and Kotkin both claim that policies that discourage suburban development and/or encourage dense urban development are undermining the notion that California is the promised land. This myth of the California Dream is particularly powerful for Kotkin, who contends that California used to be "God's best moment."

This is the blithe vision that none but the most daft have ever believed. The only cliché about California that is more abiding than sunshine is that of noir (itself a ponderous metaphor, but we'll go with it). Everyone, from scholars like Mike Davis to novelists like Raymond Chandler, has illustrated the dark side of the California Dream. Disappointment will always complement idealization. For Chandler, it means murdered starlets. For Davis, it means natural disasters and civil unrest. In short, they covered that ground extensively, as has almost every other honest student of California. So, to base public policy on a myth, or, more accurately, one half of a myth, makes little sense.

Kotkin's central claim is that the four million people who have reportedly left California in the past 10 years because of restrictive local land use policies have made coastal areas unattainably expensive. Rather than consign themselves to miserable outer suburbs, families are up and moving to states like Texas and Nevada because of low taxes. This trend has rendered urban areas like San Francisco and West Los Angeles "boutique" cities that cater only to the wealthy.

I couldn't agree more with Kotkin's implication: a more diverse range of residents *should* be able to live in lovely places like San Francisco and Santa Monica, and many local laws *have* restricted the housing supply and made cities more expensive.

Kotkin should be overjoyed by laws like Senate Bill 375. If all goes as planned, it will enable more people to live in expensive places near the coasts while relieving pressure on single-family home prices.

Here's where things get weird. According to Kotkin, the policies that would promote housing—and de-boutiqueify these cities by a) enabling more people to live in them, and b) creating more places like them—carry the air of a Stalinist plot. "Things will only get worse in the coming years as Democratic Governor Jerry Brown and his green cadre implement their 'smart growth' plans to cram the proletariat into high-density housing," writes Finley.

Let's overlook the lamebrain rhetoric of socialist class struggle and focus on capitalist laws of supply and demand. If the coasts are such nice places, then it would stand to reason that, if offered sufficient housing stock, people would willingly live in them. Yes, densities might be higher, but the benefits of living in nice places would far outweigh the negative, and biased, connotations of "cramming."

Alternatively, if those cities don't increase their densities, then the only way to make them more diverse, and suitable for the middle class, is to kick out the rich and let working-class families squat in their mansions. Viva la revolución! And good luck figuring out the espresso machine.

It's clear, then, that Kotkin's objections to smart growth are not reasoned policy analyses. They are ad hominem attacks against a class of people whom he finds icky: that of apartment-dwellers. According to Kotkin, if you're not rich then "your chance of being able to buy a house or raise a family in the Bay Area or in most of coastal California is pretty weak."

You can't raise kids in multifamily dwelling in coastal California? Who does Kotkin think he is, Dr. Spock? I'd like him to tell his theory to my mother—and to the millions of other parents who have raised perfectly decent children in tight quarters.

On this point, it's worth quoting Kotkin in full:

What I find reprehensible beyond belief is that the people pushing [high-density housing] themselves live in single-family homes and often drive very fancy cars, but want everyone else to live like my grandmother did in Brownsville in Brooklyn in the 1920s.

(This is the moment when, if I were Jon Stewart and this was *The Daily Show*, I'd be looking plaintively into the camera and stuttering, "But ... he ... just ... said ...")

Let's make this clear: Kotkin is claiming that the "reprehensible" people who are unbelievably supporting SB 375 are the very same single-family-home dwellers whom he venerates. And he's criticizing them for *not* living in the very places that, with all due respect to his grandmother, he thinks aren't fit for raising children. This would be contradictory at best—but it also happens to be wrong.

In fact, the current governor (who had nothing to do with the passage of SB 375) famously lives in a multifamily building in Sacramento. Granted, the former governor lives on a property in—where else?—West Los Angeles that could comfortably fit several extra families. And that's just in his carriage house. Regardless, who's the one who's making land more expensive?

As for the legislature, I have no idea where they all live. Probably in one big houseboat on the American River. But I do know that SB 375's author, Sen. Darrel Steinberg, represents Sacramento, and Sacramento is a city, last time I checked. And I know that, on average, Democratic voters are more likely to be urban dwellers and that Republican voters are more likely to be suburbanites. Kotkin must know this, unless he has forgotten where Nancy Pelosi is from.

So the voters who have supported SB 375 are in fact more likely to already live in denser urban environments. They support SB 375 not because they want to make everyone else miserable but because they want more people to enjoy the urban experience alongside them. Most of us city folk don't give a rip about what happens in the suburbs; if they want to stay boring, homogenous, and sparely populated, that's fine by me.

Meanwhile, I've never met Kotkin's grandmother, but I'm sure she's a very nice lady and would not like her grandson to say mean things about her home. But that's beside the point. All the people who currently live in Brownsville—whether they're hipsters who dig the lifestyle or families who enjoy the inestimable financial benefits of participating in New York City's economy—would probably not like him to say mean things about their lifestyle either.

And yet, Kotkin offers up a notion that is both logically and grammatically nonsensical: "The new regime ... wants to destroy the essential reason why people move to California in order to protect their own lifestyles."

This is where it gets personal. I live in an apartment. So do most of the people I know. By and large, all of us are pleased with our lifestyles because we get to live in great cities and reap their estimable social and economic benefits even if we don't have vast backyards or fences to shield us from people who make us uncomfortable. I support more dense urban development not just because I think it's a fine way to live but also because it will, indirectly, reduce my cost of living if the supply of apartments—which are already in high demand—increases.

This is how land use economics works.

So let's recap: Kotkin disparages people like me for liking a lifestyle that he disagrees with. He thinks that more people should live where I live (i.e. near the coast), but he doesn't think that coastal areas should build more housing, and he definitely doesn't think that the state should promote that housing. Because then there'd be too much of a bad thing, even though people want that bad thing very badly if it's located in the right places.

And that's why, according to Kotkin, California shouldn't have passed SB 375 and instead should have maintained the status quo. Or something like that.

Kotkin also spews some nonsense about the evils of green energy, but, to be honest, I'm too exhausted to write any more. Something weird is going on here, and I'll be damned if I can figure it out.

If Kotkin wants to discuss any of this with me, I invite him to join me in my fourth-floor hovel and witness childless depravity firsthand. He can bring his own espresso.

Job Creators Need Not Fear Urban Planners
2013

Recently, economist and entrepreneurship expert Carl Schramm announced a discovery in the pages of Forbes.com: "the practice of city planning has escaped reality." Planners, he writes, don't see the big picture. They don't understand economic growth. They've unleashed upon us scourges like live-work lofts, fire stations, and bloated pensions.

Planning thus joins a small list of imperfect human endeavors that could benefit from self-analysis and reform. To my reckoning, that list includes finance, medicine, government, journalism, technology, religion, and everything else short of *Pet Sounds*.

You need only take a few glances at major American cities and suburbs to know that there have been lousy plans and, by extension, lousy planners for a very long time. Most every cul-de-sac and downtown surface parking lot indicates as much. Schramm's criticism, as that of an entrepreneurial evangelist looking for business-friendly policies, is undeniably valuable.

How critical is Schramm? Quite. In "It's Time for Business to Adapt [sic] a New Model," he accuses planners of being self-serving and of writing many general plans good only to line the wallets of planning firms and architects. In reading a handful of cities' plans, he and his graduate business students at Syracuse University concluded that planners are blind to the forces of demographics and macroeconomics. Which cities? We'll get to that in a minute.

Schramm writes:

... measures of city health are clearly more faddish than practical. None set a goal of full employment or even mentioned unemployment. Poverty was a missing word. What discussion existed regarding economics was confined to making a specific kind of neighborhood, often called an arts district, to provide propinquity for the city's "creative" population. If a link to the economy is mentioned it usually is a passing reference to new and small businesses that would grow up if, again, the physical environment was engineered in a specific way.

In short, planners who believe that their job is merely to create a functioning built environment are shirking their duties as captains of economic development and reduction of poverty. They "have no idea of how the complexities of dynamic economies actually are sparked to life." He also accuses planners of ignoring demographic projections; he writes, "None of the plans ever spoke of what the city's population might be at the end of the planning period!" Schramm would replace all of those arts districts with facilities for "scale production ... [which] is the only path to growth and urban futures that hold the potential to restore communities"—as if American cities will be saved by Chrysler and U.S. Steel.

**

As debatable as Schramm's conception of the 21st century economy may be, many of his concerns are so obvious as to be implicit in the work of many contemporary planners.

When, for instance, New Urbanists speak of vibrancy and street life, they're not assuming that everyone is lolling around because they're unemployed. When developers build dense mixed-use developments, they do so in the hope that thriving businesses will fill those ground floors (and that the residents above will have more disposable income because they're spending less on cars). When progressive planners talk of making cities "better," they do so with the conviction that improvements in quality of life lead to economic prosperity—and vice-versa.

Plenty of contemporary plans address exactly the concerns that Schramm raises. Take Santa Monica's relatively new, much-admired general plan, for instance: it's chock-full of rhetoric about stoking the local economy and supporting local businesses. Same for San Jose's new Envision 2040 plan. But those are just two examples from two cities. Planners certainly aren't enlightened enough to pursue that line of thinking on a really large scale, are they?

As it turns out, they are.

California's Senate Bill 375, for instance, requires cities to do exactly what Schramm and his students advise. A huge component of SB 375 is based on demographic projections, with the goal of reducing per-capita greenhouse gas emissions according to targets for the years 2030 and 2050. It addresses the relationship between the location of jobs and that of housing—a key factor in cultivating a healthy workforce. The models that the Air Resources Board and the state's "Big Four" metropolitan planning organizations are using to meet these targets incorporate piles of data to this effect. Under SB 375, every metropolitan planning organization (MPO) must publish and abide by a Sustainable Communities Strategy (SCS), and every city in those planning areas has to address the SCSs in their plans.

Granted, SB 375 isn't expressly intended to promote business—it has far more important goals—but it most certainly takes the state's economic climate into account.

Anyone worried about demography might also check out California's Regional Housing Needs Assessment program, designed to ensure that every city in the state absorbs its fair share of new low- and moderate-income housing. (Whether cities follow these rules usually depends on politics, with conservatives often opposing growth.) Most sensible cities not only plan housing accordingly; they also plan for amenities and services. So if a city expects a population increase in a certain neighborhood, it might also add a fire station or a park. Schramm, however, sees fire stations as symbols of cronyism and waste: "Every plan discusses the importance of new buildings for fire stations," he writes disapprovingly.

Maybe Schramm thinks the problem on the local level is that planners are fixated on the arts, to the detriment of other economic activities.

Well, in many places, these industries probably play a smaller role in today's urban economies than boosters like Richard Florida and Elizabeth Currid-Halkett would like to admit. Then again, "the arts" is often shorthand for much larger and vibrant creative industries, ranging from entertainment, to video games, to interior design—but not, alas, to "scale production." But the reason that the arts have become an avatar for a new wave of urban planning is that urban forms that are good for the arts and artists may also be good for all sorts of other industries and residents. What's good for Banksy may be good for America.

Schramm also lambasts these plans for not calculating the costs of cities' pensions, claiming "not one of the plans discussed...the unfunded costs of pensions for retired and current public servants." Why not tell planners to cure cancer too?

While pension obligations gravely threaten some cities, I'm not sure why they are planners' problems or how planners would solve them. Conflicting obligations within a city—between, say, building a nicer city and paying long-term debts—need to be worked out at the level of city government. Then again, Schramm isn't a big fan of any sort of government. If planners have their way, "government ...[will have] control over all aspects of the built environment." He doesn't mean that in a good way.

How did Schramm and his students reach these conclusions? Is the state of planning as bleak as they imply? Of course it is—if you base your conclusions on Syracuse, Stockton, and ... wait for it ... Detroit.

(Schramm does not name these cities in his Forbes piece, but he was candid enough to reveal them to me via e-mail.)

Anyone who knows anything about contemporary American urbanism already knows what I'm going to say. Judging the planning profession according to some of America's most famously destitute (and bankrupt) cities is like judging lending by Countrywide, finance by Lehman Brothers, international banking by the Libor scandal, and entrepreneurship by the shuttered frozen yogurt shop down the block. Schramm's students might as well have thrown Atlantis into their study too.

If Schramm had presented his Forbes piece explicitly as a study of cities that have run aground, and his Forbes editors had titled it as something like "Bad Planning and Urban Downfall," then he might have ended up with a compelling, nuanced commentary about the common traits that poorly planned cities share. The graduate course at Syracuse that gave rise to his article is called Fast Cities/Failed Cities, so Schramm can clearly distinguish between good and bad. His students, though, seem to have taken a cursory, one-week look at a complex, generational issue and then rendered a sweeping decision that vilifies an entire field.

Regarding Detroit in particular, Schramm presents a curious argument. He writes that Detroit's general plan is a failure because "Detroit remains hopeful that someday 2.3 million people will live there once again." First of all, a lousy land-use plan is the least of Detroit's worries. Secondly, even if Detroit's general plan does refer to a target population of two million, that just means that the document disagrees with literally every single member of the greater planning field. That's probably to be expected from a city that elected a criminal as its mayor. So, it's a bad plan. That doesn't mean that planning is bad.

Fortunately for Schramm, if he thinks that planners should figure out how to plan for a smaller Detroit, then he should delighted— that's exactly what planners are doing. (Whether they can pull off such a monumental task, and generate the political will and financial resources to implement it, is another story.)

***

I have no doubt that Schramm would give great advice to an entrepreneur, such as the mom and pop who are setting up a small business, whether on a Main Street, in a mini-mall, or in a coworking space in a converted flour mill. He would likely fight like crazy to help that business succeed. He seems like that type of guy.

I'm also willing to wager that the first thing he would tell clients is to be true to their vision no matter what impediments lie in the way.

Schramm surely knows that entrepreneurs never create their own competitive landscapes—nor their literal landscapes—no matter where they are. To imply that any plan or planning decision could undermine ingenuity, hard work, and guts is an insult to the spirit of entrepreneurship. The best entrepreneurs know how to read existing conditions, adapt to changing circumstances, and anticipate what lies ahead. The availability of one kind of office space or another should not dissuade them.

Of course, Schramm is right that to say that planning and business are interconnected. But it's a two-way street. Schramm overlooks the very real role that business plays in creating plans (and, often, in circumventing them). I can't imagine a city in which the business community does not have its fingerprints all over the general plan. Many chambers of commerce have lobbyists dedicated to planning and development. If a plan isn't business-friendly, whose fault is it?

These days, it takes a real lack of imagination to disregard the ways that a pleasant urban environment can stoke economic development. But if business groups are as skeptical as Schramm is, then there's a raft of literature—dating back at least to Jane Jacobs's *The Economy of Cities*—that suggests that cities built on the principles of smart growth will be friendlier to business. Density creates more interactions, makes labor and customers more accessible, and can make people infinitely happier and more energized. It's not a coincidence that some of the densest cities in the world are also some of the most prosperous cities in the world.

Of course, whether you're in Hong Kong, Tokyo, or San Francisco—or not to mention San Bernardino, Riverside, or Stockton—no one ever said that business was easy. And neither is planning.

Fetishizing Families
2016

Not necessarily everyone's American dream.

I would like to buy Joel Kotkin a beer. I vote we try a gastropub downtown. Or maybe a rooftop lounge. I'll take the subway, and he can take a taxi. That way, neither of us has to drive.

Wherever we'd go, I'd like to invite some of my urban planner friends along. That's because, judging by his new book, *The Human City: Urbanism for the Rest of Us*, Kotkin may never have met an urban planner before.

According to Kotkin, planners today are "largely in favor of cramming people into ever-denser spaces." Kotkin describes contemporary planning trends so you can smell the body odor: "People clustering in ever more crowded cities, living atop each other, may fulfill the ambitions of corporate leaders, urbanist visionaries, and planners."

Kotkin has long been a contrarian and critic of contemporary planning—sometimes a perceptive and welcome one, especially when urbanists, myself included, have gotten too cute or too smug. *The Human City* is probably his most comprehensive critique and surely his most off-putting.

Normally, provocative claims that form the basis of an entire book would warrant extensive citations, surveys, data, quotations, interviews, analysis, and literature reviews. Kotkin alludes to "scores of interviews and survey data" but cites none of it but for occasional factoids. By keeping them "anonymous," Kotkin gets to mischaracterize planners and crusade against nonexistent threats.

Kotkin digs at "creative class" theorist Richard Florida for being a "retro-urbanist" (whatever that means), and credits New Urbanists for favoring "a somewhat human scale." Most surreally, though, Kotkin suggests that the theories of early 20th century visionary Le Corbusier "are widely shared by many urban thinkers today," as if everyone still wants to bulldoze historic neighborhoods and build towers in parks. That's what they were doing in the 1960s. In fact, legions of planners have been working for decades, by promoting infill and the like, to undo the damage that the Corbusians did. That damage has little to do with density per se; it has to do with the evisceration of street life. If Kotkin hates Le Corbusier, then he is in good company with the vast majority of progressive planners.

***

The Human City mainly concerns American cities, though it takes an early one-chapter detour into "megacities" of the developing world. This enables Kotkin to introduce a terrifying statistic: Dharavi, the densest slum in Mumbai, has one million people per square mile. Kotkin presents this as a cautionary tale, never blinking in his accusation that planners in the United States view Dharavi as a model. Never mind that Dharavi is an illegal settlement on nobody's blueprint.

You'd have to be a serious antigovernment fanatic to think that any bureaucrat would favor that kind of cityscape. You'd also have to be terrible at math. If the entire population of the United States crammed within the city limits of Los Angeles, they still wouldn't achieve one million people per square mile (especially not with all the Botox). Interestingly, the density of Mumbai as a whole is roughly equal to that of New York City as a whole, at roughly 28,000 people per square kilometer.

And yet, Kotkin says that "planners" celebrate Dharavi's density. He includes Harvard's Ed Glaeser, who is actually not a planner but an economist and the kind of free-market thinker whom Kotkin ought to like. Kotkin doesn't actually quote Glaeser directly, though, so I e-mailed Glaeser. Glaeser confirmed that he believes in the economic potential of megacities. Kotkin just left out the part about how Glaeser "warn[s] of their dangers—the demons of density."

As a gradient and not an absolute, density is relative. It's not like we have to choose only between formless void and black hole. To favor greater density in, say, Kansas City (1,474 people per square mile, in the center city, or one-tenth of one percent of Dharavi), or Jacksonville (1,142) means favoring "greater than what is *already* in Kansas City or Jacksonville." It doesn't mean "greater than Mumbai."

(Kotkin proposes a breezy solution for India: it should develop its midsize cities. That's a swell plan, except that it ignores the ultracorrupt, hyperbureaucratic entity known as the Government of India.)

But enough of the developing world. *The Human City* mentions it mainly to scare the bejesus out of "us" and make us thankful for America's abundance of bedroom communities.

The "us" in Kotkin's divisive title refers to nuclear families: husbands and wives who dutifully bear sons and daughters. They are, claims Kotkin, the ones whom cities ought to serve. They have no use for monumental statements like towers and superblocks or for fripperies like parklets, bike lanes, street festivals, and loft conversions. And they certainly don't want their children having to share personal space with "them," whoever "they" may be. That's why Kotkin wants us to spread out and build more and bigger suburbs.

Families are people too, though. It's not unreasonable to claim that "the question of what families need and prefer should be central."

But Kotkin explores this question only as far as his preconceptions will let him.

In asserting the preferences of some 122 million people (including many children who probably had no say in the matter), Kotkin makes no effort to distinguish desire from resignation. The status quo does not tell us whether they "want" to live in suburbs or whether they are merely willing to do so because that's where most housing units have been built over the last century.

Kotkin's veneration of the suburbs centers on three reasons: typology, typology, typology. Kotkin insists that families inherently prefer a "small home in a modest neighborhood where children can be raised." Adorable, right? To hear Kotkin tell it, a house in bankrupt San Bernardino is always more family-friendly than an apartment in booming Koreatown. I'm sure that's true for some parents. Others are happy for their kids to have ready access to culture, mobility, astounding diversity, and neighbors who are less likely to be cooking meth in their garages.

Kotkin has always been at his most appealing and most convincing when he's describing the suburbs' hidden diversity or celebrating the small businesses that thrive there. He rightly points out that, with the dispersion of job centers, life in the suburbs does not necessarily entail hour-long commutes on clogged highways. Meanwhile, he has a legitimate critique of some progressive cities that "are actually becoming whiter and less ethnically diverse as the rest of the country, particularly suburbia, diversifies."

Kotkin undermines these observations by concocting a false rivalry between suburbs and center cities—going so far as to proclaim "the war against suburbia"—and by equating suburban living with families while equating center cities with hipsters, singles, the wealthy, and the foreign wealthy. (He scarcely mentions the urban poor, many of whom also are families.)

These are the inhabitants of cities that Kotkin calls, variously, consumer cities, legacy cities, elite cities, and, most damning of all, "luxury cities." Kotkin cites compelling demographic data indicating that in some of these cities—especially San Francisco and Manhattan—

children are disappearing from the census data. Luxury cities are too expensive for families and, of course, they're too darn crowded.

***

For a free-market guy, it's odd how Kotkin ignores the true meaning of high real estate prices: that demand is outstripping supply. Believe it or not, a great many people, families and singles alike, "want" to live in Los Angeles, Seattle, San Francisco, Washington, D.C., and New York City.

If high prices are bad and density is bad, we are in quite a pickle, aren't we?

Kotkin clearly thinks that cities shouldn't build more high-rises and other multifamily dwellings because, of course, they are bad and houses are good. Plenty of (mostly low-cost) cities can accommodate the suburban-style houses he wants, which is fine. But they aren't the cities that Kotkin is concerned about.

He willfully ignores the predicament that expensive, desirable cities like New York, San Francisco, and even Los Angeles are facing: they have basically no undeveloped land. Either they build multifamily or they build nothing at all. Kotkin imposes on them an impossible choice—and blames planners for failing to sort it out.

Planners in center cities focus on downtowns, multifamily housing, commercial pockets, and certain amenities because, well, that's what they have to work with. Density is what a city is—especially "luxury cities." Being for or against density is a silly question. Managing density and making it work, for families and everyone else, is the real question.

In truth, a suburban preference doesn't necessarily connote a preference for suburbs; it connotes a preference for things that suburbs tend to offer. No matter their densities, cities can, if they try hard enough, meet suburbs halfway, with better schools, affordability (per unit if not per square foot), safety (urban crime is generally down), and even "community"—as long as your definition of "community" doesn't equate only with "middle-class white people." Americans might prefer suburbs less if they had more great cities from which to choose.

By demonizing big-city planners, Kotkin ignores another crucial part of the housing story: they have nothing whatsoever to do with the production of suburban housing.

Kotkin writes, "Urbanists would be far better off if they considered taking a more human-city approach: improve life not only in the core, but in the extensive areas that have developed around them." First, there's a contradiction here: if the suburbs are so great in the first place—such that families should always choose them over cities—then what exactly would make them "better off"? Second, Kotkin is entertaining another fantasy: he implies that we need to eliminate jurisdictions, hire region-wide planning directors, and give each of them enormous magic wands.

Many center cities are dysfunctional precisely because they have been competing with suburbs for decades—for population, development, jobs, and, of course, tax dollars. The suburbs have been winning by a landslide. As Kotkin points out, "Between 2001 and 2011, detached houses accounted for 83 percent of the net additions to the occupied U.S. housing stock." Whether composed of palatial dream homes or acres of ticky-tacky, the suburbs have prevailed for decades. So what, exactly, is Kotkin complaining about?

Kotkin could be part of the solution rather than part of the problem. Instead, he has written a dog whistle to the supporters and consumers of sprawl. In fairness, Kotkin admits that "we need both geographies." It's just an odd thing to say at the end of a book largely bashing one of those geographies.

If Kotkin likes families so much, he should love urban cores. He should love shaded sidewalks where people can catch one another's eyes. He should love bars where they buy each other drinks and share Instagram handles. He should love small apartments to which they can stroll arm in arm. If, a few years later, those same couples need another bedroom—well, good for them.

And if those bars are too "crowded" with young singles for Kotkin's liking, I'll grab some friends and we'll drive out to Applebee's. The Diet Cokes are on me.

4 The Politics of the Local
On the squabbles that are the lifeblood of planning

For all the ridiculousness of the national political scene, I sometimes think local land use is infinitely more ridiculous. For better or worse, national politics tends to boil down to familiar (if sometimes unsatisfying) binaries: hawks and doves, pro-life and pro-choice, conservative and progressive, protectionism and globalism, nativism and tolerance, etc. If the United States wants to invade another country, most thoughtful Americans will know where they stand. If you try to use a small-lot subdivision ordinance to put six bungalows on the lot of a single-family Craftsman home, you get chaos.

I have my political inclinations, of course, but I generally consider myself to be fairly dispassionate. I spent years coaching high school debate, and I've been a journalist since college. I don't have moral qualms about respecting both sides of an issue, even if I feel strongly about one side. In land-use debates, the general public often seems pretty passionate. Or, rather, certain members of the general public seem pretty passionate. Whether those members express ideas that planners can use is another matter. Yelling at a city council meeting doesn't really help a planner decide whether a project deserves a zoning variance.

I wonder constantly about the silent majority. Planning has techniques for recording public comments and integrating them into their plans. Sometimes the results are limp or overly complex, reminding me of the proverbial camel that is a horse designed by committee. Other times, the public conversation leads to paralysis or even nonsensical decisions. I have observed these instances with equal parts concern and bemusement, and I have even weighed in on a few issues myself. One of them is the emergence of the Tea Party in the early 2010s and its bizarre take on land use. The Tea Party now seems like a relic, subsumed by MAGA. I include it in this chapter, and not the Trump chapter, mainly because it was a distinct movement at the time.

While I sympathize with the challenges planners face, I also fear what can happen when planning goes badly—when fringe voices get the most attention and when petty politics override the public good. I consider myself a friend of the profession but, as these essays demonstrate, I also try to show some tough love.

Let the Sun Set on Ballot Measures
2015

Stop the madness.

Allow me to laud something about California's state and local ballot initiative system. No, really.

Voting schemes for electing human beings to office are inevitably flawed. Whether a jurisdiction uses party primaries, open primaries, ranked choices, multiple votes, pluralities, majorities, voice votes, or pebbles placed in a fishbowl, no system can capture the true passions and preferences of all voters as they relate to all candidates.

The ballot initiative system cuts through these ambiguities by posing a binary choice: yes or no. However ill-conceived, ill-timed, poorly written, and disingenuously promoted (or opposed) a measure may be, at least the vote itself is clear and internally valid.

Ballot measures could, though, take at least one cue from their human counterparts: impermanence.

***

A while back, I tossed off a blog about Los Angeles's housing crisis. And I mean tossed off—I wrote it on a fleeting notion fueled as much by frustration as by scholarship. Clearly other people share my frustration, because it went seriously viral. It went so viral that it even reached one of the original backers of a ballot measure that I mentioned.

Passed in 1986, Proposition U was designed to limit commercial development on Los Angeles's major corridors. It passed on an insane two-to-one margin, which I characterized as a symbol of Los Angeles's slow-growth movement and a precursor to today's housing crisis. In a subsequent e-mail to me, a backer of Prop. U who took mild umbrage insisted that, over 30 years ago, Prop. U was crafted specifically so that it does not constrain development or preservation of housing.

I don't doubt the earnestness or the wisdom of the authors' approach. As such, my criticism may have been unfair—at least in the context of 1986. The trouble, of course, is that what may have been entirely reasonable in 1986 may not be reasonable in 2015. Legislators, voters, activists, planners, planning philosophies, political alliances, and issues have changed. So have the density, function, infrastructure, economic base, ethnic makeup, and total population of Los Angeles. Try as they might to have predicted Los Angeles's needs one-and-a-half generations into the future, Prop. U's supporters were living in a different world.

Naturally, we can only legislate based on what we know and what we can reasonably predict. The ballot initiative process ignores this truism. From Prop. U to Prop. 20 (precursor to the Coastal Act) to Prop. 99 (eminent domain), to, yes, Prop. 13, many of the state's and localities' measures are structured to remain in effect until the end of time. If Los Angeles sticks around half has long as Rome has, a land-use measure passed today could remain in play in the 35th century.

I'm not a fan of term limits, and I'm sometimes disappointed to see elected officials retire (notwithstanding the immortality of Jerry Brown). But, at the very least, even the most popular elected officials have to submit to reapproval every four years. Ballot measures need a similar temporal safeguard.

I don't have an ideal structure for what I'm thinking of. We surely don't want to create chaos by yanking laws away unceremoniously. But we have plenty of other options.

It could be a sunset clause. It could be a mandatory revote at a certain juncture. It could be a fail-safe, with clear thresholds for success, overturned only by a supermajority. It could require incremental approaches known as "design thinking," with beta tests and pilot projects. Who knows? The point is that no law should ever elude reasonable scrutiny, and no law should presume to remain relevant decades into the future purely because of its own inertia. Supporters of an original ballot measure may need opportunities to gracefully update or even disavow those laws as circumstances change.

While we're at it, conventional laws could benefit from the same. Imagine, for instance, how much progress California might make if the California Environmental Quality Act had to be affirmatively revised and renewed rather than interpreted ad nauseam by the courts like a tumor?

(Naturally, concerned citizens can mount campaigns to repeal ballot measures that they don't like. But the money, effort, and political will for that kind of thing makes it effectively infeasible.)

***

I hardly think Prop. U is the cause of all of Los Angeles's troubles, just as I don't think Prop. 13 is the cause of all of California's troubles. Maybe even I would have voted for Prop. U in 1986. We were building some pretty hideous stuff back then; some of it probably needed to be cut down. Our traffic wasn't nearly as bad, our rents weren't nearly as high (in real dollars), and planners didn't have many alternatives to our auto-oriented mix of residential neighborhoods and commercial strips.

Today, infill development, mixed-use buildings, walkability, transit-oriented development, environmental stewardship, transit use, design guidelines, and all the other trappings of smart growth are at play in Los Angeles. We need more development on commercial strips, because we need a better balance between jobs and housing, and we need more amenities that residents can walk to. We need opportunities to build a few levels of commercial space and then layer on a few levels of residential space. Whether development on boulevards is commercial or residential, we surely need to wean ourselves from single-story buildings, some of which are surrounded by surface parking, on our most valuable, important corridors. We need to accommodate 3.9 million people, not 3.2 million.

These are the goals that Los Angeles's planners are pursuing. Are they compatible with Prop. U? I hope so. If they are not, there should be a reasonable system by which the city can unburden itself.

If that were to happen, I, for one, think L.A. boulevards would turn out OK. They include Wilshire, Ventura, Western, and, yes, Sunset.

Billboards, Big Money, and (Political) Blight
2014

The ultimate Los Angeles celebrity.

The United States Supreme Court could take a cue from a billboard.

I don't mean a particular billboard. One reading, "Political Donations Undermine Democracy" might be nice, of course. But I mean any billboard.

Much like Citizens United before it, the recent McCutcheon v. Federal Election Commission decision, which effectively undid the dollar limits on donations to political parties, was principled in part on the notion that more speech equals more democracy. If many ideas are in the "marketplace of ideas," as described by political philosopher John Stuart Mill, then consumers—i.e. voters—can choose those that seem most sensible.

Mill presumably wrote *On Liberty* on paper. Despite the utter reasonableness of his ideas, he never had to consider what the marketplace looks like when it is outshined by a looming image of, say, LeBron James, T. J. Eckleburg, or Frank Underwood blaring across miles of the night sky.

Cities have long been wary of this sort of visual blight and have enacted regulations to combat it. Quaint refuges such as Aspen and Carmel hardly let stores proclaim their own names in their downtowns. Some places require hanging wood signs, to invoke images of an America long past. Large cities keep a close eye on the billboards and megagraphics that have turned vertical space into valuable real estate. Houston, of all places, bans billboards entirely.

Though American governments cannot regulate the content of speech, except in extreme circumstances (such as libel or profanity), the Supreme Court has held that they may regulate the "time, place, and manner" in which speech is conveyed. As well they should. Restrictions on advertising are usually justified so long as they "advance the public health, safety, peace, comfort or convenience" of a community. This ability dates back at least as far as the Euclid decision of 1926, which first codified cities' rights to control land use in order to promote general welfare. This includes, of course, the avoidance of visual blight in public spaces.

(It's worth noting that some groups contend that the First Amendment does protect "billboard speech"; they also contend that limitations on billboards constitute unfair takings, prohibited by the Fifth Amendment.)

Regulation of public advertising can go both ways, of course. In Times Square, New York City planners have deliberately embraced the idea that advertising can be a form of theater. On the West Coast, boosters of downtown Los Angeles are keeping an anxious eye on the Wilshire Grand. As part of a complex development deal with the city, it will be the first skyscraper in Los Angeles to have animation and illuminated graphics. L.A. City Council members justified the deal by referring to the planned illumination as "art."

Interestingly, the Wilshire Grand project broke ground soon after the city pulled the plug on some 82 digital billboards operated by Clear Channel Outdoor. In April 2013, a Superior Court judge agreed with the city when he ruled that the billboards had been converted to digital displays illegally. They went dark almost instantly.

Even the most ardent civil libertarian has to see the logic of these restrictions, including those that confine truly stentorian advertising to a single district. In a city, the skyline is the classic public good: something that should be equitably available to everyone under all circumstances. Coca-Cola may not tell me to "Enjoy" if doing so floods my apartment with light, distracts me from the road, or covers up an aesthetically pleasing view. There's a reason that there aren't any billboards in front of the White House, Old Faithful, or, um, the Hollywood Sign. We all have the right to those views.

All of this illustrates a truth that is obvious to any urban planner but that apparently has gotten lost in the post-Citizens and now post-McCutcheon world. The Constitution protects the ability of people to speak—literally—to convey the ideas, emotions, and information that they see fit. Naturally, "speaking" can't comprise only vocal expressions. With that said, it's useful to think like a planner here. Consider the role of the individual as he occupies public space: billionaires and beggars are each due only as much space as their bodies can claim. By extension, each is free to say whatever he wants but only at the volume and range that his voice can project. I imagine that the framers of the Constitution had in mind things like town hall meetings. Imagine if the Koch brothers had to wait for their turn at the podium.

The thing about free speech is that it's most free at modest volumes. Whatever the differences between political and commercial speech may be, this should not be one of them.

The marketplace cannot be so loud that we all run from it screaming, leaving the hawkers to bargain among only themselves. Not every block must blare like Times Square does. Likewise, I may not voice my support for an Ayn Rand-Ralph Nader ticket for the presidency by yelling out all 1,455 combined pages of *Atlas Shrugged* and *Unsafe at Any Speed*, drill sergeant-style, within three inches of my neighbor's ear.

What the Supreme Court seems not to understand is that money is not an idea, emotion, or piece of information. In the case of McCutcheon, what is money but a "manner" of speech? It certainly isn't content. It is volume, deafening. It is brightness, blinding.

To put it in planning terms: McCutcheon puts Times Square on every street corner.

Silicon Beach Could Use Less Coding, More Voting
2015

Many locals would like Snapchat to disappear.

For being the envy of entrepreneurs the world over and the vanguards of the global economy, the tech superstars of Silicon Beach are oddly oblivious to what goes on in their own backyards—assuming, of course, that they can ever afford backyards.

Like any other knowledge-based industry, Silicon Beach—like its bigger and more expensive cousin up north—can thrive only if it can attract qualified workers and if those workers can live within commuting distance without bankrupting themselves.

In a way, the choice of Santa Monica as the next great tech hub makes sense. The city's real estate prices—median apartment rents of $3,400, $1 million for a teardown in Ocean Park—fit perfectly with the code-'em-fast, disrupt-this-or-that, buy-Patrón-shots, and cash-out-with-VC-money attitude of the tech economy. Silicon Beachers might not yet be able to afford to live in Santa Monica, but they want to afford to live in Santa Monica. That's what counts.

Unfortunately for everyone who wasn't a founding employee of Snapchat, the dull indignity of pulling in a salary, paying rent, and trudging to work every day remains a reality. Last month, the Santa Monica City Council, with prodding from the slow-growth advocacy group Residocracy, made this situation a little less dignified. The council voted to downzone significant parts of the city such that it will be even more difficult to build housing that Santa Monicans and would-be Santa Monicans need.

Here's a little pre-Silicon Beach history: in 2010, the city adopted a Land Use and Circulation Element (LUCE) that called for higher-density residential and mixed-use development on the city's major boulevards. The LUCE was hailed as a model of so-called smart growth; it won the California Chapter of the American Planning Association's highest award.

The LUCE would have added nearly 5,000 housing units to the city's stock. Assuming that they weren't all turned into Airbnb rentals, that would have accommodated nearly 10,000 new residents—in a city that has grown by all of 4,000 residents since 1970. You don't have to be a computer scientist to do the math: constrained housing supply in a desirable area leads to skyrocketing rents; adding supply leads to lower rents (or at least a lower rate of increase).

If I'm a Santa Monica startup, a new resident, or, most importantly, an aspiring resident, the LUCE was a godsend. (Of course, Silicon Beach is bigger than just Santa Monica, referring amorphously to the entire Los Angeles tech scene.)

This April, the City Council considered the new zoning code that would have finally implemented the LUCE (think of the LUCE as a rendering and the code as a blueprint). The City Council got an earful from dozens of residents decrying "densification" and begging them to maintain the character of their "quiet beach city." How anyone considers Santa Monica a quiet beach city is beyond me. The former home of Douglas Aircraft and the Coney Island of the West, Santa

Monica has always been bustling. But there they were, and there went the votes.

The majority of the City Council bought into it. They voted, 4-3, to reduce densities from those envisioned by the LUCE.

Haven't heard about that vote? Then you're probably in tech.

I'd wager that, behind proclamations of who's disrupting whom, talk about rents is the No. 2 topic at Silicon Beach happy hours. As of that council vote, Silicon Beach can officially blame themselves for some of this housing crisis.

I recently published an article on the City Council's vote to implement a new zoning code. In researching my story, I attempted two forays into the Silicon Beach world. First, I e-mailed the administrator of the Silicon Beach Facebook group to ask him if he knew of any Silicon Beach firms or employees that had discussed the proposed zoning change. Getting no response, I then posted to the group's wall, politely asking for "someone from the Silicon Beach world who's involved with local politics and can comment on ... the new zoning code."

How many of the 1,958 members of that group—arguably the most social media-savvy people in Los Angeles—replied? Zero.

I got not a single comment or private message. I didn't even get a "like." Not that there's anything to like, if you're a young Westside renter. Meanwhile, Silicon Beach seemingly has social and networking events every night of the week, including, recently, a beer pong tournament. Apparently, they discuss local politics at none of them, much to their own detriment.

I understand that tech workers are busy. They live on their screens, changing the world one line of code at a time. Yet, they still have to go to bed somewhere. The branding of Silicon Beach shows that they are not shy about pegging their aspirations to a place. The trouble for them is, no matter how many tequila shots they take at Circle Bar or how many concerts they go to at the Pier, Silicon Beach is woefully out of touch with the crucial issues that make Santa Monica what it is. If tech firms are going to embrace Santa Monica as an idea, it might behoove them to embrace it as a municipality too.

The Urban Mystique

In short, houses are a lot harder to build than apps are. With $4,000 rents on the way, Silicon Beachers had better get politically active, or hope those stock options pan out.

A Lesson in Planning for Beverly Hills
2010

Maseratis welcome. Subways, not so much.

As its location suggests, Beverly Hills High School enjoys its share of amenities: a gym that converts to an indoor pool; a planetarium; a professional-quality theater. But, like most high schools, it does not have a class in urban planning or transportation. Now that the Los Angeles Metropolitan Transportation Authority has proposed extending the Purple Line subway under school grounds, Beverly High is getting a few lessons.

On its way from downtown Los Angeles to Westwood, the alignment that would pass under the high school would lead to a station in the middle of Century City, a location that Metro planners favor for its centrality. A less expensive alternative would follow Santa Monica Boulevard but arrive at a station that some contend would be less convenient for commuters. The debate over these two alignments has brought out an array of concerned citizens. Some of them express informed, nuanced opinions about cost, walkability, and local control. Others fear for high schoolers' lives.

The latest voice to pick up the children's crusade is Lisa Korbatov, the incoming president of the Beverly Hills Unified School District Board of Education. Incongruously, Korbatov said that her "first priority" as board president would be "fighting the MTA's plan to possibly tunnel under the high school."

"If the tunnel is built under the high school," Korbatov told the Beverly Hills Patch at the height of her fulminations in 2010, "there will be interruptions in education from noise, pollution, traffic and other factors, and both the quality of our education and our property values will suffer."

As if all that weren't enough, she nearly invites nefarious forces to marshal against Beverly Hills: "I am also very worried about the high school being the subject of a terrorist attack. Terrorists have bombed subway lines in Madrid and London. Our high school, with its reputation as having affluent and Jewish students, would make a good target." (I'm sure she didn't really mean to say "good.")

If this world hasn't figured out how to get along with itself in the 20 years that it will take for the subway to reach Beverly Hills, then we have a lot more to worry about than a subway route. Moreover, they would have to be some very patient terrorists who would wait that long rather than pack a van full of explosives and drive it onto campus tomorrow. I don't mean to scare anyone—I just mean to point out the absurdity of stoking unnecessary fears.

Where's steely-eyed Dylan McKay when we need him? He'd stare down the terrorists, peel out on his motorcycle, and leave Brenda wondering if his wild heart can ever be tamed.

As for those "other factors," presumably they include everything from underground vibrations to the possibility that the tunnel could collapse and swallow the school whole. If this comes to pass, it would be, as far as I know, the first such instance of a subway with such a large appetite for teenagers.

This gruesome, if incredibly unlikely, prospect must be what

Korbatov means when she says, "Everything I do will be for naught if there are subway tunnels under the high school." In other words, the mere presence of the subway could obliterate every new hire, every tough budget decision, every ounce of learning, every essay, every math problem, every drama production, every athletic contest, every eager freshman, and every proud graduate. Little will the straphangers of the 2030s know of the havoc they are causing up on the surface.

Good planning is supposed to be built on research and, whenever possible, on data and valid analysis. Plenty of that is right there in Metro's draft EIR/EIS. These methods have their limits, but planners have reasonably effective, though not foolproof, tools to quantify the danger posed by a subway. And they have other tools to determine the relative efficacy and cost effectiveness of one alignment over another.

I don't actually have a position on the subway alignment, but I do have a position on the uphill battles that planners have to fight despite, or perhaps because of, these quantitative methods. For better or worse, planning has embraced metrics and objective measurements of everything from walkability to regional planning. The principles that planners learn everywhere from Harvard and MIT to UCLA and Cal Poly somehow go out the window when they are pit against an emotional public figure like Korbatov—someone at the heart of this country's education crisis—and the public at large. So passion, not planning, still rules the day.

And yet, one of the very purposes of education is the containment of passion. We gain ideas and analytical methods from books and teachers so that we are not always held captive by our own whims.

Korbatov did not respond to repeated interview requests, so neither I nor her constituents may ever know the basis of her concerns. But in her published statements she cites no data, no studies, and no statistics. She does not even present discursive arguments to support her doomsday claims.

For a few years, I taught high school and coached debate not far from Beverly Hills High. As an educator, I know what grade I would have given to a student who presented an incendiary, hyperbolic argument with no research or analysis to back it up. But we all deserve a rewrite now and again. So I hope opponents of the high school alignment come out with more measured arguments to explain their opposition to the proposed alignment—if not for the gratification of planners and the elevation of public discourse, then at least to set an example for the very students whom they hope to save.

Lodi Gets Stuck on Agenda 21
2011

A bulwark against one-world government.

Probably too much has been written about the Tea Party movement already—which may be emerging as a distinctive voice in land-use politics—but sometimes the urge to comment is irresistible.

In a few short years the Tea Party movement has already proven itself as much a celebration of negativity as it is a political movement, no more so than when it dabbles in land-use policy. A prime example comes from Lodi, where Tea Party activists in 2011 convinced the city council to delay the acceptance of a $120,000 federal grant to help it implement SB 375. That's right: the Tea Party hates Washington so much that it won't accept its money, even when that money is free.

Why would they do such a thing? Because they do not want Lodi to come under the sway of nefarious undemocratic powers.

Somehow the ghosts of Hamilton, Adams, Franklin, and Hancock have convinced Tea Party activists that SB 375—and seemingly all other manifestations of smart growth—is a tentacle of the United Nations' "Agenda 21." I have to hand it to the Tea Party for a moment. "Agenda 21" does sound menacing. What it really should be called is "Some nice things that countries and cities can do to ensure that they don't starve to death, exhaust their energy supplies, or fall into the ocean—but only if they want to."

Be that as it may, the Tea Party seems to be confusing "conspiracy" with "something that's just a good idea." There are a lot of good ideas floating around out there. If the U.N. were to, say, promote nutrition, women's rights, education, and democracy, should we reject those things too? Oh yeah, it does.

I'd say that this kerfuffle about smart growth is the opposite of a conspiracy. The last time I checked, the road to global domination did not begin in Lodi. Crying about the U.N. in Lodi is like praying to Jesus that you'll sink the next putt. Jesus doesn't care about your handicap, and, well, I think it's safe to say that the U.N. cares even less about Lodi.

If the creation of compact cities is really a conspiracy, then we can find its influence in slightly less obscure places—maybe, New York, Tokyo, and London, for starters.

We can certainly debate the merits of smart growth. In fact, we can debate the merits of Senate Bill 375. In fact, it would be a lousy piece of conspiracy mainly because many people think that it's not strong enough. Rather than force residents into urban high-rises, it calls for eight percent reductions in per capita greenhouse gas emissions. Eight percent means carpooling to the NASCAR race instead of driving in a caravan.

Back to that $120,000. These funds aren't just for Lodi to conduct a grand experiment on an unwitting population. They're to fulfill a state mandate to implement SB 375, which assumes that managed growth is probably better than haphazard growth. That means that it's going to have to spend the money one way or another—and if Lodi is like the rest of the cities in California, then it doesn't have the money.

The reason it has to spend it is that a few years ago something called the democratic process wrapped its icy fingers around the State of California and caused the passage of SB 375. That process included open debates and votes by legislators (of both parties) and approval of the dude who was then the state's Republican governor.

But it's no wonder that none of this fazes the Tea Party. The website of the California Tea Party Patriots still features that same governor on its website. It even urges citizens to "tea bag" him. I hate to break it to the Patriots, but Arnold is no longer in office. And he has almost certainly been tea-bagged already.

And if they don't know what that means, well, they probably can't figure out what smart growth is either.

Los Angeles Learns to Play Ball
2016

For the former residents of Chavez Ravine, development of Dodger Stadium gives new meaning to "stealing home."

Football fans who suffered through umpteen stadium proposals and yearly false starts before being rewarded with the Rams can be forgiven for thinking theirs was the most anguished tale of relocation in the history of Los Angeles sports.

Not by a Hail Mary.

The all-time championship of uncertainty, politicking, and contentiousness surrounding a Los Angeles sports team goes to none other than the Dodgers. In *City of Dreams*, Jerald Podair, professor of history at Lawrence University, reveals that the most stalwart and, arguably, beloved L.A. franchise did not descend upon Chavez Ravine like a pop fly hit from Heaven. It is an encyclopedic, if not always engrossing, account.

Dodger owner Peter O'Malley's plight begins, as do many stories of 1950s urbanism, with New York City infrastructure czar Robert Moses. A careful steward of public funds, Moses refused to contribute to a stadium to replace the decrepit Ebbets Field. Though O'Malley wanted to stay in Brooklyn, he decided he had to accept an offer from the upstart city on the opposite coast. O'Malley had visited Los Angeles all of three times. With promises of 300 acres in Chavez Ravine, a fresh fan base, and dominion over a city on the rise, it seemed like the right move.

O'Malley's unfamiliarity with Los Angeles meant that he was also unfamiliar with Los Angeles politics. It's too bad O'Malley didn't have Podair to show him around.

According to what was, essentially, a handshake deal, O'Malley agreed to pay for Dodger Stadium's construction. But the city had to kick in some of the land and develop associated infrastructure—an expense some city council members refused to bear, to O'Malley's surprise and consternation.

The Dodgers' biggest fans were City Council Member Rosalind Wyman, a Democrat representing the Westside, and centrist Mayor Norris Paulson. Meanwhile, Republican John Holland and Democrat Edward Royal insisted that baseball was all well and good but that public funds should not support the team. They represented citizens whom Podair refers to as "The Folks"—conservative, suburban Angelenos who wanted nothing to do with the Dodgers' potential to put Los Angeles on the national or global map.

The formation of coalitions for and against public funding "defie[d] conventional urban narratives," according to Podair, because it dispensed with party rivalries in favor of factions based on worldview: "one group's dreams were local and limited, the other's national and global." This tension, argues Podair, gave birth to "modern Los Angeles": a provincial city with global impact, a diverse city with marginalized minorities and no single power base, and a bland, ahistorical cityscape with cosmopolitan assets. This analysis is Podair's greatest contribution to Los Angles's political history, as it could apply to any number of issues before and after the arrival of the Dodgers—including, most recently, the debate over Measure S, the slow-growth ballot measure that failed this March.

Unable to negotiate past the deadlock, the team and its allies sponsored a ballot measure, Proposition B, to call the question in 1958. It prevailed by a slim margin: 25,000 out of 675,000 votes. It got support from African American and Latino neighborhoods and indifference from the white, suburban San Fernando Valley. O'Malley was far from home free, though.

As every Angeleno knows, Dodger Stadium controversially displaced a small but thriving Latino community in the semiwild of Chavez Ravine. O'Malley settled lawsuits with stalwart residents of the ravine. Another lawsuit went to the California Supreme Court, and local debates continued about zoning changes and development of supporting infrastructure. O'Malley nearly ran out of money before convincing Union Oil to stake him $12 million worth of advertising revenue in advance. (The "76" globe hung undimmed over the outfield until only recently.)

Podair argues that political enthusiasm for the Dodgers ran parallel with enthusiasm for downtown Los Angeles. At the height of suburban migration, the development of the stadium coincided with plans to build the Music Center, redevelop Bunker Hill, and otherwise solidify downtown's cache of civic assets. But, as with everything in Los Angeles politics, the categories were not so tidy.

Podair roughly characterizes Dodger Stadium as a "downtown stadium." That's true, as far as it goes. Home plate is less than two miles from City Hall. And yet, for pedestrians, the Dodgers might as well still play in Brooklyn. Major boulevards, two freeways, landscaping, 16,000 parking spaces, and an empty hillside insulate the site. So, while Dodger Stadium certainly isn't suburban the way Anaheim Stadium is (built in 1966 for the Angels), it is nothing like the cozy retro/urban ballparks of the past 20 years. It has none of the intimate urban connections of its relatively new counterparts in San Diego and San Francisco.

Podair competently describes the innovations of Dodger Stadium, especially its nearly perfect sightlines and intimacy, created by cantilevered decks stacked neatly on top of one another, which "was probably the most important departure from the architecture of the traditional stadiums." Podair praises architect-engineer Emil Praeger but oddly neglects to identify the stadium's other architect, Los Angeles-based Edward Fickett (known mainly for designing massive tract housing developments).

Podair calls their creation "the nation's first truly modern ballpark," but he uses "modern" only superficially: "the stadium's look, operation, and culture were distinctively modern. Its lines were sleek and symmetrical." Though Podair does not claim to be an architectural historian, he misses some crucial points by ignoring the ideology of modernism and its historical context. This oversight elides the fact that Dodger Stadium is a prime example of auto-centric, functional modernist design that, arguably, represents the worst of 20th century American urbanism.

Indeed, Dodger Stadium is, in many ways, a microcosm of Los Angeles: modern and ambitious, but also neither fish nor fowl, neither urban nor suburban.

O'Malley insisted on such a spiffy stadium not because he wanted the stadium to delight only Brooklyn-style roughnecks but, indeed, everyone else: men, women, families, and fans of all ethnicities, backgrounds, and income levels. Dodger Stadium introduced many delights that fans take for granted today. It had better food and bathrooms. It had an organ. Inspired by master modernist-capitalist and fellow Southern Californian, Walt Disney, O'Malley insisted that "at Dodger Stadium, everything would be pleasantly predictable, except for the outcome of the game itself."

This approach, argues Podair, was O'Malley's stroke of genius: in a city without provincial rivalries like New York, he recognized that the Dodgers could be everyone's team. He even attracted ample numbers of Latino fans, despite the Chavez Ravine controversy.

City of Dreams adds an essential volume to the Los Angeles canon. And yet, in keeping with an unfortunate convention in scholarly writing—it is not a book for the fair-weather fan—Podair allows the present to fade into oblivion.

Even today, the Dodgers' impact on Los Angeles is debatable. Really, the "revitalization" of downtown didn't begin until the early 2000s. In fact, the assault of modernism, embodied by the 1955 clearing of Bunker Hill (which puts the destruction of Chavez Ravine to shame, in terms of sheer volume), was arguably the worst thing ever to happen to downtown Los Angeles. And Podair discusses none of the subsequent political battles that echo those that he so painstakingly describes—most recently Measure S, a slow-growth measure that appealed directly to "The Folks." Given that the Dodgers arrived only 59 years ago, some of those Folks might have been the same to vote against Proposition B.

Meanwhile, the original question of whether the Dodgers deserved public support remains unanswered. Maybe, as is often the case with Los Angeles, the city managed to strike such an exquisite, if unexciting, compromise that the question has become moot.

Podair even fails to mention a crucial piece of Dodger Stadium trivia: O'Malley's space age creation is now the third-oldest stadium in the country. And yet, with few recent upgrades, it's still going strong.

The Rams have a lot to live up to.

Why Cities Should Back Off of Setbacks
2017

This is basically illegal in California.

I can think of at least a few buildings in the world that are exquisite enough that they warrant a little elbow room. The Taj Mahal comes to mind. The Farnsworth House. Certain monasteries and castles. Most quotidian pieces of architecture, though, gain their value not from splendid isolation but rather from their relationships—with surrounding buildings and streetscapes.

Setbacks, which are perhaps the most ubiquitous way that planning imposes on architecture, are to these relationships what adultery is to romantic relationships.

For those residents of, say, Paris, Vienna, and New York City who are unfamiliar with setbacks: they are spaces that "set" buildings "back" a certain distance from the property line and, usually, the sidewalk. A distant but useless cousin of the front yard, they appear in, I reckon, the majority of properties developed nationwide since 1950 and nearly all properties developed in California.

For all their popularity, setbacks have little basis in engineering or architecture. They are simply regulatory whims.

Setback requirements come in all shapes and sizes. Some are minimal (a foot or two) while others are dramatic (ten feet, fifteen feet). Some make way for pleasant things like outdoor dining spaces; others turn into unwelcoming bollards. In each case, setbacks are mandated voids, either to be ignored or landscaped, usually in decidedly half-assed ways. Ferns for everyone!

(I refer mainly to setbacks that separate buildings from sidewalks, not to those that separate buildings from each other. I have slightly more sympathy for the latter type.)

Received wisdom holds that setbacks make urban spaces feel less crowded. They supposedly ensure that buildings do not overshadow streets and sidewalks. They create the illusion of less density and protect buildings' personal space. They create room for "green space," "light," and "parklike settings," which sound great in real estate listings. They assume that buildings are impositions on their cityscapes, to be contained so as not to offend delicate sensibilities.

This rationale is mostly nonsense, of course. Like so many other concoctions that come courtesy of regulators rather than designers, setbacks are a scourge on our cities. At best, setbacks persist because of habit. But, like elevator music and parsley, they are not actually as pleasant as we pretend they are. They confer psychological satisfaction even if they have nothing to do with aesthetics or economics.

To the proponents of setbacks, a few patches of grass might as well be Luxembourg Gardens. But think about the classic street in any of the cities I cited above. If you enjoy Paris or New York, you already know why you shouldn't like setbacks. Density in a city is good. And not just population density. The actual appearance of density (which may or may not have anything to do with population density, depending on the type of structure in question) is good too.

With scant exceptions, the most pleasant streets and

neighborhoods—from the Île de Saint Louis to Greenwich Village to Old Town Tucson to the row house neighborhoods of Philadelphia—are those not where buildings recede from their streets but indeed where they are closest together, working in harmony with streets to create a public realm. A sense of enclosure is one of the hallmarks of great streets, whereby space is created and defined by the intersection of vertical and horizontal planes. Pedestrians also benefit from the shade created by snug buildings and vertical facades (and awnings, if they're lucky). The no-man's-lands created by setbacks detract from streets and buildings alike, only scarcely less aggressively than do walls and cyclone fences.

From a developer's perspective, setbacks waste space and, therefore, money. Who would want to give precious square footage to ferns, ficuses, and snails rather than to people? Even worse, setbacks create lousy buildings. When a pedestrian's feet and eyes might travel mere inches from a facade, that facade ought to be at least somewhat attractive or inviting. Setbacks invite architects to pay that much less attention to detail. I enjoy dragging my fingers on a Parisian facade because, well, Parisian facades are attractive.

To fans of setbacks, a building nestled right up against a sidewalk is scary. A ten-foot "landscaped" setback? Just fine. Never mind those shrubs look like mighty attractive hiding places to aspiring muggers. There's a reason it's "eyes on the street" and not "eyes on the setback."

What about privacy? I'm sorry, but if your living room faces the street, you're going to need curtains no matter how far back you are. Setbacks don't create privacy. They create the illusion of privacy.

In short, there is no economic, aesthetic, or security reason for setbacks to exist. Cities have gotten along fine for centuries without them. So, what gives?

Let's think about who might lobby for setbacks, either in an individual project or in a zoning code. They're certainly not the tenants of buildings. Unbuilt buildings have no tenants. The people most likely to demand that a development be worse are those who don't like development in the first place and who object to density on principle.

Setbacks are the currency of antidevelopment activism. Homeowners who like their cities and their property values just fine don't care how far away a building is from a street. They're likely only to see those buildings at 35 miles per hour anyway, and probably from a lane or two away (plus a few feet if there's a devil strip). But they know how to push planners around.

For them, setbacks are just a bargaining chip—a palpable way to stick it to developers. Setbacks persist because they are quantifiable and negotiable. Once opponents have whittled down the number of units or the amount of floor space in a project, they can bring on the setbacks. The developer wants a setback of zero feet. Neighbors want a setback of 10 feet. When it gets settled at five feet, the neighbors chalk up a win.

Why is that a win? Because they don't care in the first place. They gain nothing, except for a five-foot pain in the ass for the developer and a lousy place to take a stroll. This isn't advocacy, and it's certainly not planning. This is urban trolling.

I bemoan setbacks not to redesign every condo building from Riverside to Santa Monica. Setback regulations and their proponents have already done their damage to the buildings that exist and the streets that they face. Fortunately, with a few deletions from zoning codes, and more tenacity from the planners who care about density, walkability, aesthetics, and fairness, cities can play with a full deck once again.

And when the next Shah Jahan comes along with a great idea for a mausoleum, then we can talk.

The Opposite of Gentrification
2018

This is where you solve a housing crisis.

Any planner with an ounce of awareness should support social justice and fight for anyone who feels excluded from the bounties of global capitalist urbanism. I try to count myself among those ranks.

And yet, as I reflect on the gentrification debates of 2017, I grow increasingly anxious for what the future holds. For at least the last two years, we have been running a race between the adoption of municipal and statewide policies to promote responsible housing development and the reactionary frustration of marginalized stakeholders and left-wing activists.

In places like Los Angeles's Boyle Heights and San Francisco's Mission, those frustrations have already erupted, into a combination of protests and combative – if not necessarily productive – political organizing. Even less productive: the indifference of many residents in static, wealthy neighborhoods.

I've issued my share of criticism of the current wave of anti-gentrification protests and rhetoric. They rightfully express anger, but they often misdirect it. They demonize market-rate development and consider anything new—even something as benign as a coffee house—to be a symptom of cultural erasure and capitalist exploitation. (Case in point: the passionately written but intellectually bankrupt book *How to Kill a City*.)

Most interestingly, these groups tend to protest the one thing that can solve a housing crisis: more housing. Housing in amounts that, barring a major and unlikely transformation of the industry, can be provided only by for-profit developers. They include the Los Angeles Tenants Union, Defend Boyle Heights, the Coalition to Preserve L.A., Our Mission No Eviction and many smaller groups.

Many of these groups and their supporters recently amassed at Los Angeles's first ever "Resist Gentrification Action Summit." I could not attend, and I'm sure the organizers were not crushed. They didn't exactly send me a gold-leaf invitation.

The upshot of the event, and many of these protests, is that new development must serve local populations and that the only good development is nonprofit development (or some related form of cooperative or subsidized development.) They often claim that market-rate development equals displacement or that new development raises housing costs community-wide. But that's only true a) if new development replaces existing housing; and b) if nearby housing isn't rent-controlled.

They're basically saying that they'll reflexively support anyone who currently lives in a rent-controlled unit but everyone else who seeks housing—no matter how wealthy or poor they might be—should just move along.

To a great extent, these communities deserve their grievances and their own solutions. Many disadvantaged communities in the United States, including plenty in California, were created by the segregationist policies of the 20th century. They were designed to be disenfranchised, separated from decent schools, decent jobs, and political power. I'm willing to give a degree of deference to residents who feel, accurately or not, that they've been exploited for generations.

And yet, Los Angeles still has a housing shortage. Like all housing shortages, it victimizes the poor more so than anyone else. And, like all crises, solving this one requires everyone's participation—lest the rich further marginalize the poor. That's not so much a moral position as it is an Archemedian reality. Human beings take up space. If they can't take up space in one place, they will take it up in another place. And if space is scarce, wealthy humans will pay for the space they need.

If these communities are going to, at the same time, decry the invasion of newcomers and oppose most development, then they face but one option: they must promote development elsewhere.

If gentrification is evil, then let's do the opposite. I challenge leaders in disadvantaged communities—and everyone else who believes in equity—to stop decrying the invasion of those communities and start promoting the development of other communities. Since they are, essentially, trying to keep capitalism out of their neighborhoods, they might as well go whole-hog and explain why other neighborhoods, where people have done very well by capitalism, should accept it. That strategy might sound hypocritical—because it is—but that doesn't make it unjust.

What if activists brought their passions and arguments to advantaged communities? They should speak to Neighborhood Councils and homeowners associations. They should lobby planners and elected officials. They should explain why their livelihood depends on development in places that might be five or even ten miles away from their own homes.

In Los Angeles, I'm thinking of places like West L.A., Hancock Park, Miracle Mile, and Westwood, among others. These are all neighborhoods that do just fine for themselves and that frequently oppose new development. They need to hear from outside voices. They need to understand the pain that their choices are causing. They need to be compelled, inspired, or, if needed, guilted into inviting more people to share in their prosperity. If gentrification threatens poor neighborhoods, then we have no choice but to welcome poor residents into rich neighborhoods.

Naturally, stakeholders in Hancock Park or Westwood will ask why they should support more housing and new residents when many of their counterparts in Boyle Heights or Leimert Park do not. The answer is that what appears to be unfair in the short term is actually entirely fair in the long term. The poor neighborhoods of urban America have been kept poor for a very long time, sometimes unintentionally, sometimes insidiously. Segregation has been imposed on them. Anti-gentrification attitudes may seem like just another version of segregation—and perhaps they are—but it would be on their own terms. In these cases, segregation might equal protection.

Likewise, activists in poorer communities might wonder why they have to be the ones to take action, spend time, and raise their voices against spatial injustice to educate people in wealthy communities. I have no satisfying answer for them, other than this: if they don't do it, no one else will. Ultimately, it's a worthy cause that will help Angelenos of all persuasions.

If the critics of gentrification simply want to fight, I cannot help them. If the opponents of development simply want to oppose, I cannot help them either. Cities are where people congregate, mingle, and help each other be the best they can be. If they are willing to see themselves as citizens and collaborators, they can walk proudly into unfamiliar—not enemy—territory and help their fellow citizens understand their concerns and work towards solutions.

That's a meeting I will gladly attend, no gold leaf necessary.

5 Matters of Taste
Musings on architecture and design

Brassbound technocrats who focus on demographic trends, traffic counts, fiscal impact studies, and other quantifiable ephemera might consider aesthetics to be a frivolity. I maintain that everyone else in the world considers aesthetics to be crucial, if subliminal. We don't *flaneur* about the city drafting mental treatises on every building we see. But the sum total of a city's design has a powerful effect on our collective well-being. Indeed, if we care about how our food tastes, how our music sounds, and how our clothes fit, we should have no less concern for how our cities look.

Urban aesthetics—which includes publicly visible architecture, infrastructure, sounds, and even minute details like lampposts and sidewalk paving—is especially important in light of its coercive nature. No one, least of all the government, forces me to eat a certain food or wear a certain outfit. But, unless I drive around Los Angeles with my eyes closed, participation in public life requires that I take in the city's appearance. And, by prescription or permission, governmental policy always dictates aesthetics.

Here too, the latter half of the 20th century was disappointing, if not disastrous. In many ways, architecture ceased to be a public art. The great modernist citadels like the Seagram Building by Mies van der Rohe or just about anything by L.A.'s homegrown corporate modernists like Welton Beckett, A.C. Martin, or Charles Luckman are meant to be seen but not engaged with. They are like sculptures, not to be touched by unauthorized hands. Some of California's best, most adventurous 20th century architecture applies to private homes, such as those designed by the Eameses and Frank Gehry.

The "starchitecture" phenomenon of the past 20 years has produced some fantastic buildings and, in some ways, inspired more public appreciation of design. But it still misses the mark: however impressive the Bilbao Guggenheim or Disney Hall may be, nobody gets to live in either of them. As for public urban design: 20th century planners typically imposed setbacks, height limits, and floor-to- area ratios and called it a day.

For better or worse, we have been living in the postmodern era. It's an improvement on modernism, because it has shed the dogmatism and arrogance of modernism. But, as its name implies, postmodernism can mean almost anything.

I have figured out what postmodernism is. Or was. It was the acknowledgment that modernism tapped out—its idealism was misguided and its stark aesthetics a dead-end. We spent the latter half of the 20th century fooling ourselves—and exhausting ourselves—with a racist, hyper-capitalist fake idealism that manifested itself in corporate modernism. The result was a debris field of glass and asphalt stretching from the Atlantic to the Pacific. The playful, experimental style of postmodernism, exemplified most acutely by the designs of Robert Venturi and Denise Scott Brown, was largely a temporary reaction to modernism's dead-end.

It has taken a little while to gather our wits, embrace the past, and rediscover our humanity. Humanity, of course, includes the instinct for innovation. It also includes the need for community. The true postmodern era, which has yet to emerge, is one that does not deride the latter as 'retro,' nor does it fetishize the former as "disruptive."

Postmodernism means that we acknowledge that many aspects of old cities are, to turn Robert Venturi on his head, more than just "all right." In embracing density, muting automobiles, considering scooters and flying cars, rejecting office parks and freeways, and respecting—rather than just riffing on—the past, we now have the privilege of choosing, with far clearer eyes than we've ever had before, what we want cities and their component buildings to look like.

I write about design not just because I get a kick out of it but also because I think planners—especially those working in California's more insipid urban environments—must pay attention to aesthetics, lest all of their other efforts be for naught.

In case aesthetics seem like a luxury about which only affluent communities should concern themselves, I submit that nothing is further from the truth. First, while good design can sometimes come at a premium, design principle need not. A setback requirement determined according to design principles is no more or less expensive than one imposed by impetuous stakeholders. Second, while I would never want to encourage the displacement that sometimes accompanies aesthetic upgrades, I have to believe that disadvantaged communities deserve places and spaces that are just as carefully thought out as those found in affluent areas.

Oddly, Donald Trump makes an appearance in this chapter, but mainly by accident. I happened to refer to one of his monstrosities in Chicago to illustrate that architects deserve a little more credit than they get. This was long before Trump started taking credit for everything.

A good architecture firm can work on only so many projects. Good design guidelines, though, can change the shape of entire cities. They can compel mediocre architects to be better, and they can counteract the worst tendencies of uncaring developers.

The Quiet Evils of America's "Favorite" Buildings
2007

No. 99.

The American Institute of Architects recently threw its authority behind a list of America's "favorite architecture," ranking three centuries of indigenous design one to 150 specimens. The resulting menu, culled by survey, of buildings, bridges, monuments, and other solid things amounts to a joyous celebration and a remarkable commentary on America's embrace of beauty. It also reinforces the desperation that arises when aesthetics and nationalism mix.

I have my opinions on the potency of the Empire State Building (1), the sublimity of the Vietnam Memorial (10), and the disappointment of Disney Hall (99), but no matter. Those we can argue over demitasse. Before we go romping through architecture's greatest hits, it's probably worth asking, why do we recognize individual architects and individual works? And why do it in a country so awash in mediocrity?

Surely individuality has its place. Yet the stark itemization in the AIA's list puts buildings at a remove that betrays architecture's twin obligations to function and place. Architecture surely involves artistry, and art naturally owes itself to heavy doses of genius—plus equal measures of determination, arrogance, and wherewithal (Daniel Burnham, anyone?). But even the newest shock relies no less on history, fashion, politics, and the countless footfalls of the everyday. In architecture, that relationship—between creativity and influence—is no academic matter. Any architect who pays no mind to the material and ecology that swaddle his buildings should learn to sculpt and be done with it. (Only churches deserve absolution for attending to only their own form. The others do so only at risk of sacrilege.)

Recognition of buildings—even in the form of something as intentionally vague as "national favorites"—is different from, say, honoring the Best Actress, whose recipient will live again in another film. The best structures are, in many ways, the least available to evaluation because each is wholly unique, if not in form then in location. Among all the arts, only architecture defies Walter Benjamin and his duel between aura and machine (more about him some other time). As long as the continents stay put, structures will always keep their auras close at hand and owe themselves to forces beyond their walls. Would Grand Central's (13) magnificence grow dim if it moved to the edge of Kansas? Hardly. Against the dark prairie it would be stunning beyond measure. But unless 200,000 stock brokers show up for the 17:50 to Emporia, its displaced grandeur might draw a few tourists, but it would not qualify as architecture.

Surely the voters did not disregard the buildings' relationship with their "context" (I tried to avoid that word, an abstraction so blank as to suck meaning from the others around it). I trust that their votes did in fact spring from experience and that many of their selections revel in the neighboring pavement, people, alleys, and structures, either by elegant blending or brash contrast. In fact, most of them—the Ahwahnee (26), Monticello (27), Wrigley Field (31), Fallingwater

(29), the Golden Gate Bridge (5), the Apple Store (53)—do just that. (The Williams Tower [139] and the Dolphin and Swan Hotels [70] are another story.)

But by venerating only isolated creations and creators, the list reads like the manifest of an overloaded civilization; no mind can scan it and continue to behold the infinite features of a full landscape. As the light of the imagination contracts, blinking on each name, one by one, the streets empty out, the background dissolves into corners of the evening, and only impressive hulks remain. No coziness in this land of big skies and broad shoulders.

However the AIA promotes its craft and serves its country, architecture ignores the larger world only at great peril. The critic or layperson who fawns at Calatrava's skeletal swoops (59), the Atlanta Hyatt's atrium (103), or the Chrysler Building's hat (9) without also deciding whether those buildings enliven the populace, debate history with its neighbors, or otherwise tug humanity forward perpetuates the cycle of obliviousness that has infected the pathetic array of buildings—office parks, tract developments, and other quasi-fascist clutter—whose designers commanded neither skill nor care nor intellect.

To reward only artistry, to the point where we assign it to so many lumps of contrived grandeur (12), denigrates the places in which people actually live and promotes a spirit of detached awe that undermines the chance to improve them. Lest anyone forget, the AIA is a professional organization (unlike the Project for Public Spaces, which, in libertarian fashion, represents no one in particular), and most of its members, dream though they might, will fall far short of any future iteration of its list. The average architect, professional or otherwise, stands a better chance of improving the world by looking to the anonymous bricks of Paris (or even downtown Emporia) than by striving for immortality a hundred stories in the air. Even if great (or even good) works are in short supply, at least irony is not.

If the fans and practitioners of architecture are true to demographics, most of the people who read, voted for, and daydream about those 150 live nowhere near the structures that so warm their hearts. The median will sit at their computers and scroll down the page in flat jurisdictions like Riverside, Plano, Cary, Littleton, Gilbert, Shaker Heights, or West Chester, with not a landmark, or even a Main Street, in sight. To them, the list lends inspiration and perhaps comfort, as if just knowing that they are out there somewhere within America's bounds makes it all right.

Indeed, it is easier to marvel at something unique than long for something common that you simply don't have.

Cities and the End of History
2017

Krakow was Poland's capital as recently as 1596.

I sometimes travel furiously and write slowly.

I began this piece in 2007, a full decade before its publication, in Krakow, the capital of a forgotten version of Poland. Since then, it has traveled with me to Venice, Vilnius, Lviv, Bratislava, Ljubljana, and Rome. Later, to Beijing, Bangkok, Mexico City, Dubai, Tokyo, Toledo (Spain), Istanbul, and Washington, D.C. In each of these places, power has ebbed and flowed through city gates and beneath spires according to the writhing of borders.

In his 1989 essay, Francis Fukuyama proclaimed that the "end of history" was at hand. With the demise of the Soviet Union, he argued that free-market democracy would emerge atop the dustbin and mark "the end point of mankind's ideological evolution and the universalization of Western liberal democracy." Monarchy, empire, dictatorship, feudalism, socialism, and all the other isms would give way.

The triumph of democracy was always going to be an untidy process. But for a while—11 years, to be precise—Fukuyama seemed to be onto something. In 1989, democracy's two biggest modern rivals, fascism and communism, appeared to be surrendering. While established democracies still tinkered with the finer points of freedom (gay marriage? universal health care? invade Iraq?), the architecture of democracy was settling into place in so many places where it had been absent. The world was buoyant.

The trouble is, recent history suggests that Fukuyama's theory faces peril, if not outright obliteration. What this world will look like—figuratively and literally—in a generation or two is anyone's guess.

***

So much for the architecture of democracy. But the continuing process of democratization, and the process of its undoing, has deep implications for actual architecture.

"The victory of liberalism has occurred primarily in the realm of ideas or consciousness and is as yet incomplete in the real or material world," wrote Fukuyama. He didn't mean "material" literally. He meant, rather, that the concept of democracy had matured but that it had not been fully adopted by nations. Fukuyama does not discuss the effect of democracy on the built environment, but to the extent that it inhabits (and indeed creates) the public realm, the system that makes land-use decisions must naturally affect the decisions themselves.

In my travels to places that have fulfilled Fukuyama's vision—often heroically—I cannot help but feel a certain lament. While I would never trade freedom for anything as petty as aesthetics (or for anything else, for that matter), I fear that the free world may never again see the type of greatness that those old kings and bishops wrought.

Cities and their component buildings come about in myriad ways. Traditional architectural styles responded to the natural environment, folk culture, and the historical moment of their inception or revision. Add to these factors the architects who, while themselves a product of their times, impose their own idiosyncratic stamps, otherwise known as style: columns and curlicues, bare pillars of steel, visual puns, ineffable abstraction, and inquiries into the nature of the interstitial. These are the relatively apolitical forces that shape cities. (Meanwhile, the destitute and the oppressed make do with whatever they can, design being the least of their concerns.)

They pale in comparison with political forces. Many of the ancient empires, kingdoms, and dictatorships have faded away, most certainly for the better. But they have left handsome evidence of their glory. Neutered castles, broken-down palaces, and tomblike cathedrals testify silently to former flames of power, now subsumed by modern states. Tourists flock to erstwhile capitals—Krakow, Lviv, Ljubljana, Tikal—that, though they have been subsumed by modern states, preserve environments built by kings. Some of those capitals—such as Riga, Vilnius, and others in the littoral of the Soviet empire—rose, faded, and have risen anew, with their churches, palaces, monuments, triumphal plazas, and administrative offices intact. They have been hurled forward in history and are set on a new, democratic course.

While history has yet to judge their artistic merit, the autocratic design tradition lives on in Dubai, Baku, and the metropolises of China. Those places are building moments that are superficially distinctive, mostly in the form of high-rises and other places so much larger than life that they seem more grotesque than inspiring. Notre Dame invokes awe at a human scale, as rich in detail as it is impressive in its engineering. The bright skyline of Doha, endless superblocks of Beijing, and odd follies of Baku, do no such thing. Even the most fanciful skyscrapers become baubles when lined up one after another like the mountain peaks at Disneyland.

Many ascendant autocracies are enlisting Western architects to build their monuments, in part because they do not have domestic talent capable of slaking their thirst for superlatives. They end up with a sort of cosmopolitan capitalist authoritarianism, in which nations spare no expense to create placelessness. They thus defeat the purpose of national expression that the European kings knew so well. And yet, with those nations reaching skyward, many of their counterparts seem headed for aesthetic dead ends.

Therein lies the paradox for the public arts. Kings, priests, generals, and parties will no longer plan by fiat. The public realm will become truly public and not the plaything of leaders. In the United States, the autocrat Robert Moses was probably the last of his kind. Every aesthetic regulation, zoning law, and planning rule, no matter how obscure, must abide by the public chorus. Its assent is typically voiced by representative entities such as design review boards, planning commissions, and city councils—all of whom must, despite their inevitable preferences, biases, and dalliances, answer to the citizenry in one way or another.

***

At least, that's the way it was supposed to work.

Democracy may promise equality, fairness, and freedom, but in the enterprise of city-building it holds none of the intrigue that monarchs, demagogues, or even ideologies do. The concert halls, museums, courthouses, stadiums, and skylines often say precious little about Dallas, Phoenix, Charlotte, Miami, or Seattle, no matter how handsome they are or how much architects' presentations might protest. They could all be flung around, as if airlifted by a giant trebuchet, with similar results wherever they landed, whether on coast, prairie, or piedmont.

And of course, so many of our public structures bear the names of private individuals or corporations, be they donors or owners. They exalt the individual and his or her wealth, but they reflect little of the society into which they are placed. The result is not necessarily ugliness or irrelevance. Yet the liberal democratic city is just that: a city where most people do what they want and give too little heed to the greater enterprise to which cities, states, and nations are dedicated. While a great many planners, architects, and public officials heed higher callings, cities as a whole seek little more than to be places for "live, work, play," to quote a ubiquitous but deathly uninspiring slogan.

The monumental architecture of the past endures and delights today because it was rooted in vernacular traditions: local styles and local building techniques that distinguished one people and one kingdom from another. But the bright promise of 20th century modernism silenced much of the vernacular tradition in architecture, around the same time the United States and Soviet Union were developing a new sort of building: the missile silo.

That which has emerged since reflects the shallow values of commerce far more so than the indigenous traditions of the past. In the coming decades, ethnic diversity, greater urban density, and the forces of environmental catastrophe will tug at American style. (Someday historians may unearth houses built for families with two dads and factories for businesses that favor clean air over commercial gain.)

Absent design, we get structures that are so banal that they elude public scrutiny: gas stations, big boxes, tract houses and office parks and all the other expediencies that arise by combination of economics and law. Think of it: what's more democratic than a parking structure? Even as genius guides high architecture, its pleasantries are largely academic; expediency rules all else. As the sands overtop Ozymandias, the strip malls rise.

Two of the most interesting things in American cities are the bollards and cameras that supposedly protect us from terrorism. These tools—not spires nor battlements—are the trappings of today's empire.

The similarity between hegemony and homogeneity is not merely phonic. America's sameness is a direct result of the permanence of democracy and of its lack of imagination, its tendency to rush to expedient mediocrity and sameness rather than truly strive, question, or rebel.

So, as what passes for democracy spreads across the globe, meaningless buildings will accompany it. Democracy is a fine way to secure peace, but with peace comes static borders and entrenched capitals. Cities become mere staging areas for commerce where profits flow invisibly into banks and where buildings serve largely as human storage. There are no soaring spires to inspire awe or menacing walls to climb atop and then tear down.

None of this, of course, means that we should ever want to return to anything other than democracy. But it does mean that those of us who care about the public realm must fight for it. Benefactors and enlightened despots will not arise to create the spaces that we may want. Planners and architects have to rally our fellow citizens to our cause and provide a vision that everyone and anyone in a free society should want to embrace.

I suppose, then, that the future of architecture is no less certain than the future of the world itself. The trouble with taking 10 years to write an essay about history is that history keeps happening. As the introduction implies, I wrote this before the fall of Aleppo and before the nuclearization of North Korea. I wrote it when a Donald Trump presidency was somewhere between implausible and a practical joke. We can only hope that he does not inflict his aesthetic on the American landscape.

I first wrote it when I still had hope that the world could recover from September 11—that event being one of the most cataclysmic political and architectural events in modern history—and rediscover the path that Fukuyama blazed for us, strip malls and all. In short, I wrote it when I was certain that, despite the world's stumbles, Fukuyama would still turn out to be right and that aesthetic banality would be the worst of our fears. Now, under the shadow of Trump Tower, I am not so sure.

MATTERS OF TASTE

Corbusian Dream Lives On in Beijing
2009

Chinese state media looms over Beijing, with an assist from Rem Koolhas.

As an avowed urbanist, I would venture that, with apologies to Will Rogers, I never met a city I didn't like. I can usually find something captivating in the most crooked medieval alleys, most absurd strip malls, and most squat skylines. I've been to Paris, Berlin, Dallas, and Des Moines, and I've loved each in their own ways. Then I rediscovered Beijing.

I had visited Beijing in 2002 and liked it well enough, wandering among the requisite icons: Tiananmen Square, Buddhist temples, the Forbidden City, old Mao in repose. They present an odd mix of tourist attraction and historical artifact. Whether capitalist, communist, or imperial, they consume just enough time to draw attention away from the unspeakable sprawl that surrounds them.

Marco Polo visited Beijing only once, but I went back, seven years later. There on business, I had neither time nor desire to dally with that which the Party would have preferred I see. I could have toured China's new collection of modern architecture, gathered for the pleasure of NBC's Olympic cameras, but I cannot fathom why I would travel 6,000 miles only to see buildings designed by Europeans. I'm certain that Herzog and de Meuron's Bird's Nest is astounding, but it would be no less so in any other city—preferably one less politically fraught.

What they didn't tell you on TV or even in the design magazines—in those endless articles about those dozen or so Olympic buildings—is that Beijing trades on starchitecture because too much else in it is gray, lifeless, and oppressive. Beijing's new cityscape focuses single-mindedly on commerce and not on anything so genteel as pedestrian life or culture. Identical apartment towers stretch across the skyline. Thoroughfares that would qualify as minor freeways pass as everyday boulevards. I didn't ride the subway, not because of the language barrier (of which there is none—signs and announcements are in English) but because I knew that upon emerging from the portal I would have no way of knowing whether I was facing Tibet or Mongolia.

At a glance, most blocks in Beijing look the same: massive boulevard, pedestrian tunnel, towers. There isn't a suitable point of reference (assuming you could see one through the smog, which is more like smoke than haze), and they're not the sort of quaint, friendly blocks that you want to get lost in like in Paris, Bangkok, or Tokyo. There's not even a downtown. Since the emperors built Beijing around the Forbidden City, the center is a void, meaning that everything is an edge city, with no meeting place or anchor.

I did not dare go jogging, so I was limited to my daily walk from my hotel to the office where I was working. I passed through a resilient alleyway that had not yet been demolished in favor of something taller and uglier. There, in the lee of buildings with grandiose names like "World International Financial Tower," old China kept watch over grills, crepe ovens, and oil pots full of egg, dough, and onions. There, handfuls of few pedestrians might stop for a bite and a brief word.

Beijing's towers, the tiresome results of even more tiresome jokes about the "crane" being China's national bird, look like a Corbusian fantasy come to life, but with none of the optimism that Corbu at least pretended to ascribe to his towers and gardens. Beijing's quarters are more like public housing projects, with crime and deterioration held at bay by edict and martial law.

Amid autocratic rule and the reported dismissal of civil liberties, Rem Koolhaas's CCTV Tower, for all its European pedigree, is perhaps the most honest thing in sight. It's the black glass structure that, though nearly indescribable, looks like a cross between a desk chair and an upside-down U. In a Western city, the design would appear a ghastly attempt at irony, ultimately too serious and terrifying. But in China, it is appropriately, candidly totalitarian; with a facade that shifts with every new vantage point and a shadow as wide as it is long, it is menacingly inscrutable. As inscrutable as CCTV—run by the state and, by extension, by the Party—itself. While Rem may chuckle at the double irony of a postmodern monolith that seems poised to trample the proletariat in order to save it, I am certain that Mao is as stoic as ever.

Thanks in part to global media outlets like CCTV, the whole world has become one neighborhood now, so what difference does it make for 15 million people to live in such dull surroundings? Quite a bit, if the media and touring public have bought into the notion that Beijing is a great world capital. If greatness requires only a big event and some fancy buildings, then so be it. I would hope, however, that we would not be so taken by China's "progress."

We must look beyond the superstars and starchitects and accept that even if China is not as red as it once was, it has become all the more drab.

The Dark Side of Environmental Quality
2014

A particularly terrible place for star-gazing in Los Angeles.

You think this is going to be another piece about the shortcomings and backfires of the California Environmental Quality Act. It's not.

The most affecting moment in Paul Bogard's book *The End of Night* describes a Cherokee ritual called "opening the night." Participants sit in a quiet place—forest, desert, front lawn, mountaintop—and listen to the sounds within an arm's span. Then the radius doubles. It doubles again. It keeps doubling until the listener has beheld the entire spectrum of perceptible sounds, taking in the landscape with an intimacy that those of us in busy, bright places can only imagine.

The marriage of silence and darkness is an utterly appropriate bit of synesthesia: they are two sides of the same globe. Both are in woefully short supply in California.

Almost everyone reading *CP&DR* spends half their lives in a crepuscular third space created by artificial light. Without it, we would see brilliant darkness, unknown stars, meteors, the ballet of the heavens, and a Milky Way true to its name. Bogard, a professor of creative writing at James Madison University, describes the sublimity of the true night sky first and foremost in aesthetic terms. It is a beauty that all people deserve to enjoy. He explains why Van Gogh's *Starry Night* might have been more the product of observation than of madness. Crazy or not, that's what a real night is supposed to look like.

The trillions of points of light in the true night sky are no match for the mere billions on the ground. You know the culprits: streetlights, parking lots, gas stations, billboards, preening McMansions, "security" lighting, athletic fields, headlights, and on and on. Parking lots alone can account for up to 50 percent of a city's outdoor lighting. It all piles up in icteritious "domes" that hover above every urban area in the country.

Just as Americans in the 1950s gleefully inhaled smog in the name of progress, Americans now surrender the night for much the same reason. Tablets and smart phones are today's cigarettes, enabling us to further disrupt our eyesight, hormone production, and circadian rhythms. Nocturnal animals don't fare so well either. Bogard is particularly protective of bats, which, he writes, consume insects, rarely carry disease, and are way too good at flying to get tangled in anyone's hair.

The Bortle Scale measures the night sky on a scale from 9 (Times Square, the Vegas Strip) to 1 (antediluvian void). If you're reading this at night, a Bortle 9 is probably seeping through your curtains this very moment. Bogard numbers his chapters backwards, from 9 to 1, in a march through time and space that begins with the spotlight atop the Luxor Hotel and ends in an empty Moroccan desert. Under a Bortle 1 sky, he writes, even your first glance is revelatory. Then give your eyes an hour or two to adjust. Then you'll see what's really going on up there.

California features prominently in *The End of Night*. Los Angeles's light pollution is described as second only to that of Las Vegas. At the same time, one of Bogard's many lyrical descriptions of a real night sky (they never get tedious, I promise)—of which there is little in the western United States and next to none in the east—comes from the still back roads of Death Valley. It's amazing to think that California was once so dark that some of the world's most important telescopes were here. (They're still here, of course. They're just not important anymore.)

It's worth reading *The End of Night* just to reach his most inspiring quotation, from the gonzo naturalist Edward Abbey. Referring to nowhere in particular: "This is the most beautiful place on earth. There are many such places." Unlike so many other environmental ravages, light pollution's effects are not necessarily permanent. The depths of Vernon wear the same crown as does Half Dome. The stars are all up there, waiting like cut diamonds to be disinterred.

The End of Night is not a book of urban planning, but the role that planners can play is clear as, well, day.

A few cities around the world, primarily in Europe, are already trying to get their light under control. Flagstaff, Arizona is the only U.S. city that has implemented a comprehensive program to combat light pollution. It has been a modest success. Even Walmart and Target conform to the city's regulations without, apparently, going out of business. Bogard reports that between 2000 and 2010, the city's brightness increased only 17 percent, with a 25 percent increase in population. He isn't thrilled with achieving merely a lower rate of increase, but it's better than nothing.

Ordinances regulating light pollution could be integrated into a general plan, replete with Bortle ratings to set goals and track progress. The International Dark-Sky Association, an admittedly quirky organization to which Bogard makes repeated reference, has model programs that can help cities reconnect their citizens to the sublime. It invites cities to join its International Dark Skies Communities, taking a vow if not of darkness than of less brightness. A few cities in California have taken this vow. But, in my many years of discussing environmental issues with planners, the topic has never come up. It's nowhere on the agenda at the California APA conference, going on right now.

Of course, the dimming of lights could be an invitation for mayhem. But maybe not. Bogard notes that dark places do not necessarily have more crime than bright places do. As in architecture so in public safety: well lit doesn't have to mean brightly lit. Without lights, the would-be burglars can't see either. Shadows give assailants places in which to lurk. Someone who has adjusted to the darkness is keener than someone assaulted by glare. Eyes on the stars can also be eyes on the street.

It takes generations to construct a built environment. It could take months to retrofit a neighborhood with more sensible lighting, especially in the age of sensors and LEDs. Cities could transfer the funds to policing to calm the paranoid. And yes, there's an argument to be made that atmospheric light pollution should be covered under the California Environmental Quality Act. CEQA does refer to light pollution, but that typically refers to nuisances in an immediate area (like this). The entire skyscape might be a tough one for public officials to regulate: it is either immutable or, at a few light years' remove, too far out of their jurisdiction. But surely the health risks of artificial light to 39 million people might justify action?

Why, ultimately, should cities try to put something as amorphous as darkness into their finely tuned plans? Bogard's finest chapter is Chapter 4, midway between light and dark on the Bortle Scale and a far piece into the human psyche. In it, he addresses not just literal darkness but metaphorical darkness. He cities English professor Eric Wilson who, in his book *Against Happiness: In Praise of Melancholy*, insists that sorrow, darkness, and contemplation are all crucial elements of, if not happiness per se, then at least of satisfaction— of the fullness of being human. This ethos runs contrary to the superficial happiness that is ascribed to Californians. And yet, to banish, ignore, or devalue darkness is to lose authenticity, forsake ambiguity, and stunt our souls.

But we can get it back. We just have to extend an arm, and flip the switch.

MATTERS OF TASTE

The Curious Anonymity of Architecture
2014

We know who owns it. But who designed it?

If Donald Trump built so much as a birdhouse, I'd expect him to put his name on it.

That's why I'm not the least bit surprised that The Donald affixed T-R-U-M-P in 20-foot-high letters, for all of Chicago to see, to his new Trump International Hotel and Tower. Somehow, one of the world's most monumental bloviators caught Mayor Rahm Emanuel, the city council, and the entire staff of the Chicago Department of Planning and Development unawares. *Chicago Tribune* architecture critic Blair Kamin, who is no fan of the sign, blames "a lack of sophisticated design guidelines as well as the teeth to enforce them."

They're now annoyed that Trump's name gets to compete with the spires of the Wrigley building and the curves of Marina City Towers.

Too bad. To paraphrase Jon Stewart: it's Donald Trump. What did they expect?

While Trump may be a particularly predictable example, the fact is that developers put names and signs all over their buildings. Some go the egotism route and name buildings after themselves. Others contrive heroic names, as if their buildings are bit characters in *Game of Thrones*. And of course, plenty simply sell their crowns to the highest bidder. That's an old game, and it's all well and good as long as a city deems the signs to be in good taste.

The kerfuffle in Chicago indirectly raises what should be a far more benign question about signage and identity, not about the funders of buildings, but about the designers of buildings.

Let's consider other creative fields:

- Painters sign their canvases.
- Writers, actors, and directors (among others) get their names in movie credits.
- Bands are synonymous with their songs, just as composers are with their symphonies.
- Every theatergoer gets a Playbill identifying playwrights, directors, and choreographers.
- Authors' names often appear bigger than their respective titles on book covers.
- Photographers get credits. Even journalists get bylines.
- And yet, to the naive viewer, the world's most famous architect could be more anonymous than some cub photographer on his second day at work.

Why don't architects get to put their names on buildings? Say what you will about egoism, but it's hard to deny that architects (and architecture firms) deserve as least as much recognition as any other artist or craftsperson does. I've visited countless buildings that I found interesting or attractive (or ghastly) and could do nothing but wonder about the minds from which they sprung.

Of course, some buildings' masterminds are obvious. But forget about starchitects. Everyone who's remotely inclined to care about Frank Gehry knows a Gehry building when they see one. I'm not particularly interested in inflating his reputation. (It's all the more baffling that some of the biggest egos in the field don't insist on even the most modest acknowledgment.)

I'm not suggesting that architects put their names in lights or that they have to hang over the Chicago River. But how about a nice plaque in the lobby, or to the side of the front door? Maybe an inscribed cornerstone or paver? Or even a cool video-art display?

Such "signatures" might not delight the masses, either, but they'd gratify architecture nerds, give architects a point of pride (and, possibly, new business), and give due credit to a noble profession. We might even get better designs: wouldn't you try a little bit harder if your name was going to be on display? To developers' sure delight, these would cost next to nothing and would offend no one.

For the record, the Trump project was designed by a team led by Adrian Smith (he being most famous for Dubai's Burj Khalifa). Maybe Trump will give him a plaque?

A Rowhouse Reverie
2016

The City of Brotherly Love is a cozy place indeed.

As attendees of the 2016 Democratic National Convention surely discovered, Philadelphia is no San Francisco. It's not New York, Boston, or D.C. either. It's not even Cleveland. But delegates who are stuck in traffic getting out of the Wells Fargo Center would do well to take a peek down the side streets as they drive up Broad Street to their hotels and discover some of the delights of the host city.

That goes double for the California delegation.

Most Californians have probably never seen a rowhouse. For the uninitiated, they are a form of town house (or terrace house in Europe), of two or three stories, often with basements. They share side walls with their neighbors. Rear walls overlook small yards or patios, and front walls face the street. They're taller than they are wide, and they're about as deep as they are tall.

They basically look like boxes of instant oatmeal aligned on a grocery shelf.

Rowhouses superficially resemble typologies like Brooklyn brownstones and San Francisco Victorians, insofar as they too are packed tightly and share side walls. But the beauty of true rowhouses is that they have none of the trappings of those fancier cousins. No gingerbread flourishes or imposing stoops, and no dumbwaiters or maids' quarters.

Rowhouses typically have flat brick facades and, at most, occasional details like cornices or porches, and an utterly functional design. They are blue-collar shelters that came of age when East Coast cities were industrial powerhouses. Workers made decent wages—enough to enable them to escape from tenements, but not enough to move into anything fancy. They are the Model T of urban shelter. Unlike a 100-year-old car, though, 100-year-old houses still run just fine.

While rowhouses are popular throughout the East Coast, particularly in Baltimore, Washington, D.C., Virginia Beach, and parts of New York City, Philadelphia probably has more of them than any other city in the world. A full 60 percent of the 600,000 dwelling units in Philadelphia are rowhouses. It has row upon row of rowhouses.

As California cities agonize over how to house everyone, they are missing out on a typology with countless reasons to recommend it. Fundamentally, no typology so exquisitely balances the urban virtue of efficiency with the American virtue of individualism.

Efficiency lies in the massing and use of space. Even two-story versions have floor-to-area ratios greater than one. Shared walls mean that blocks are compact (and that heat dissipates slowly in the winter). A block that houses 10 families in tract homes can house 100 in rowhouses.

Unlike typical multifamily units, every rowhouse comes with its own address, advertising themselves as "home" to the people who live there. Rowhouses dispense with the gratuitousness of front yards, but their exteriors can express as much individualism as any lawn or feat of topiary. Some rowhouse residents plant tubs of flowers or even vegetables that put any lawn to shame. Some paint their shutters, doors, and other trim in imaginative colors. Some paint their entire facades. Others let their facades stand unadorned, in quiet conformity with their neighbors.

Suburban residents might protest that families need four walls to call their own and a freestanding structure to fawn over. Families in New York City and Los Angeles, among others, counter that two walls are better than zero. That's essentially what you get in the multifamily dingbats and mid-rises of L.A., the miniresorts of San Diego, and the walk-ups and high-rises of New York.

Rowhouses promote a special kind of urbanism. The chance to walk out your front door and step immediately onto a sidewalk—in view of every other house on the block—creates a neighborliness that no apartment building ever could. Just like in the suburbs, residents are associated with their buildings and buildings with their residents. But rowhouse neighbors aren't just fuzzy dots that scramble from front doors and into SUVs. Residents live close enough to be recognizable, but not so close that they feel obligated to one another. In very poor neighborhoods—of which there are too many in Philadelphia—squalor is contained on a house-by-house basis. It does not consume entire apartment buildings as it can in places like high-rise public housing complexes.

Far from being monotonous or oppressive with their continuous facades and uniform roof heights, rowhouse streets are cozy—European, even. Streets are well framed and often lively, with subtle design flourishes that appeal to pedestrians, not to speeding drivers. There are no curb cuts to mar the sidewalks. There are few streetscapes as pleasant as a rowhouse street with a canopy of mature trees.

Appropriately, in the city where the United States liberated itself from England, rowhouses liberate their owners from another form of tyranny and taxation: homeowners' associations. Rowhouses confer all the communal benefits of condominium living with none of the expense of HOA dues or headaches of creating and conforming with HOA regulations. Of course, if your roof leaks, you have to fix it yourself.

If entire East Coast cities are built on rowhouses, why does California have, essentially, zero? Surely culture is one reason. City founders in California weren't about to emulate the tired, oppressive old East Coast. But those attitudes are changing. Many California cities are embracing density. Rowhouses might be perfect for low-density urban neighborhoods that really should be medium density.

Except for those darn regulations.

Rowhouses are basically what you get when a city wants to provide single-family homes and goes full-on libertarian. If you get rid of setback requirements, floor-to-area ratio maximums, buffer zones between structures, and height restrictions, you almost inevitably end up with rowhouses. California isn't quite there yet.

You need one more thing: no parking requirements.

When you live side by side in houses no wider than a car is long, there's no room for a garage (unless you have generous alleyways). There's also little need for a car. Rowhouse neighborhoods are generally dense enough to maximize the use of public transit, and because they're dense, they're usually not afraid of neighborhood-serving commercial, like restaurants, bars, and convenience stores. So they're walkable and bikeable. If rail transit is nearby, so much the better.

For all the fleeting political proclamations that came out of Philadelphia that week, we also know that the city is capable of spawning universal, enduring institutions. We could do worse than to add a certain modest, functional, and efficient housing type to that list.

Goodness knows, we all could use some modesty these days.

Paradise Reconsidered
2018

Concrete towers nearly outnumber palm trees in Honolulu.

Mercifully, the most complete realization of Le Corbusier's Plan Voisin in the western hemisphere took the form of Brasilia, Brazil. I say "mercifully" because, for all of Brasilia's failures, at least Costa and Niemeyer did not have to obliterate an existing city—such as Paris, which was Corbu's choice—to bring his monstrous vision to life. As deliberately Corbusian as Brasilia may be, I submit that a runner-up, albeit a distant and perhaps inadvertent one, can be found in a similarly tropical location, hiding in plain sight.

I've never pegged Le Corbusier for much of a beach guy, but he would have loved Honolulu.

I recently visited Honolulu for the first time in 20 years. Last time I was there, I was with college friends for a volleyball game, a year after my own graduation, so you can imagine that attention was not paid to architecture. I knew essentially nothing of high modernism and even less about New Urbanism. The term "vernacular" had not entered my vernacular.

I might not have noticed Honolulu's Corbusian elements, regardless of whether I would have described them as such. I would not have noticed the needlessly wide boulevards. I would not have noticed the parking garages. I would not have noticed the chain stores. Most of all, I would not even have noticed that, though Waikiki's forest of high-rise towers makes it probably the densest neighborhood west of Manhattan, it has virtually no life at street level, save for the tourist shops and luxury stores of Kalakaua Avenue. I would not have noticed any of that because, in 1998, all of it would have seemed normal, or at least acceptable, by urbanist standards of the time. We were in the throes of postwar urbanism, and Honolulu was just another typical specimen.

Times have changed in many other American cities, which are unearthing their historic cores and attempting to create more human-scale neighborhoods. But not so much in Honolulu. The Corbusian connection struck me most acutely when I realized on my recent trip that many of Honolulu's towers, both in Waikiki and throughout the rest of the city, sit atop open-air lobbies, of the very sort that Corbu said would bring healthy breezes to the masses. I suppose it makes sense in Hawaii, with the trade winds and all, but the effect is still deadening. Ground floors are given to parking areas. Towers are surrounded by pointless greenery and setbacks, making them mutually hostile toward each other. Curb cuts interrupt the sidewalk and, in many neighborhoods, there's really nowhere to walk to.

Honolulu has notoriously bad traffic that, as far as I can tell, results from a terrible combination of density and dispersion. Density comes in the form of high-rise residences, and dispersion comes in the form of segregated land uses that ensure all the people who live in high-rises have to get in their cars to get so much as a quart of milk.

I drove around on a Wednesday evening trying to find a neighborhood where I could park, walk around, and have a drink—anyplace that wasn't Waikiki. After a few false starts, I gave up and drove back to my hotel.

We're not supposed to criticize Hawaii. It's paradise, after all. And the legacy of imperialism, I think, leads to a certain deference: the Hawaiians are entitled to do whatever the Hawaiians want to do.

Honolulu also defies criticism, and theorizing, because of its uniqueness. It's too far away and too iconoclastic to have anything to do with mainstream American urbanism, and it relates to no other place. Boston is like Philadelphia in some ways. Dallas and Phoenix are kindred spirits, as are Cleveland and St. Louis. Los Angeles and New York City wield cultural influence, even if their built forms diverge. Maybe Miami is like Honolulu. But, whereas Miami embraces immigrant culture (Latin), in Honolulu, it's the immigrants who are the oppressors.

Honolulu should be the most distinctive city in the country. It is literally an island unto itself. In fact, it's the most isolated big city in the world. I would have thought that a city on an island would embrace efficiency and create dense, lively places in order to conserve scarce land, the way Hong Kong or San Francisco does. Instead, Honolulu looks like Houston with volcanoes.

To anyone who hasn't overdosed on mai tais, it should be obvious that Oahu's disappointing urban environment correlates directly with some pretty grievous sins. The capital city we know today was once the capital of an independent state. I'm sure the Hawaiian people and its royal government were far from saintly, but they laid legitimate claim to their own territory and, like so many other cultures whose lives were cut short by Western abandon, would have developed their own distinctive style of cities and architecture had history afforded them the chance. Then came imperialist conquest, first by the British and then by the United States.

Of course, this is the history of the entire American hemisphere. Honolulu strikes me, though, because imperialism is so evident. The American urban form, however generic, is more out of place in Honolulu than anywhere else. The militarism that won the islands in the first place is on full display, not just with Pearl Harbor but with the dozen or so other active military facilities that dot Oahu.

To add to this hideous concoction of militarism, imperialism, and cultural oppression, we have a third influence that is so often fatal to urbanism in the West: a striking natural environment.

I've always felt that Chicago is the city that got it right. Built on a flat, featureless plain, its builders came up with a striking city that has, for the most part, aged and evolved nicely. Chicago has both a breathtaking skyline and human-scale neighborhoods. Contrast that with Los Angeles (my hometown), which is blessed with mountains, canyons, beaches, and bays and responded with freeways, parking lots, ticky-tacky, segregation, and sprawl. While Los Angeles has spectacular individual works of architecture, many of them are rendered irrelevant because they are trapped in the city's foreboding landscape. Many people don't even notice the environmental wonders of the Los Angeles basin because they are too distracted by the dingbats, strip malls, and car lots. The same could be said of San Diego.

I digress to Los Angeles because, of course, Oahu puts the Los Angeles basin to shame—as it does almost every other natural landscape on Earth. Honolulu's blandness, and Los Angeles's, stem, I think, from a perverse compensatory instinct. If the place is beautiful, we can be lazy about the architecture. If a place is barren, we must work harder. (The same principle applies to Las Vegas, Reno, and Phoenix, among others.)

Of course, all of these places reflect their historical eras and the prevailing fashions when they were built. That's another reason I'm sad about Honolulu. It was invaded too soon, before the native culture had a chance to make a lasting architectural impact. It was built too late, without much of an old compact downtown to provide refuge from the auto-oriented, suburban form that just happened to dominate at the very moment that Hawaii became a state and its (non-native) population boomed.

All of this is, I suppose, evident to anyone who explores Honolulu. But that's the thing: most visitors probably don't explore it. Waikiki does its level best to contain the tourists. No one goes to Hawaii for an urban experience. They go for a tropical experience. The trouble is, the two shouldn't be mutually exclusive. If you're going to pave over paradise, you should try to do it well.

I write this not just to gripe and not to reopen old wounds. Many of the offenses committed in and against Hawaii are unforgivable. But, fortunately, Honolulu can still become a better city.

The City and County of Honolulu Planning Department is currently revising the island's general plan. The 2011 kickoff document lists 11 major issues that the new plan will address. Not a single one of them refers to local character or even such standard planning premises as walkability. The planning firm overseeing the general plan update refers to compact and mixed-use development, so maybe the city's thinking has evolved. No matter what, the plan is moving slowly, as most general plans do, and who knows when its impacts will be felt. This is one of those times when you wish a monarch could swoop in and issue a decree. Then all the planners could go surfing and the architects could get to work.

Then again, perhaps the sins committed against Hawaii, its people, and its capital, are beyond absolution. Yes, Honolulu can, and should, implement smart growth policies, consider different design standards, capitalize on its in-progress (and costly) light rail system, and, in short, try to become a better version of the Western city that it is. But we will probably never know what a truly Hawaiian city would have looked like. Among all the cultural treasures that have survived since the last Hawaiian queen sat on the throne, architecture and urbanism are perhaps the least recoverable.

And so we beat on, outrigger canoes against the current....

The Work of Architecture in the Age of Mechanical Reproduction
2017

Each on a masterpiece.

I attended graduate school, studying geography, in Tucson, Arizona, in the late 1990s. Tucson draws fame from a number of things, including its Mexican heritage, its chimichangas, its sky islands, and its abundant population of saguaro cacti.

Plenty of things about Tucson, though, are perfectly, achingly ordinary.

Perhaps the most ordinary thing about Tucson led me to develop something halfway between a hobby and an academic pursuit. On occasion, whether for sport or research, friends and I used to go "sprawl-watching." We were not exactly, say, Walter Benjamin strolling through the arcades, embracing the human pageantry of Paris. But we did our best to plumb Tucson's depths.

Needless to say, sprawl-watching is not an action sport. It does not happen before one's eyes the way trains pass (for trainspotters, to cite another essential '90s reference) or planes land. And yet, there it was, bright as day, churning ever so slowly across priceless desert habitat.

I grew up in a place that had once engaged in the action of sprawling but had solidified long before I came along. West Los Angeles of the 1970s and 1980s was, if not urban, at least built-out. But in the tract housing developments on Tucson's outskirts, or whatever the outskirts were at the time, sprawl was indeed a verb.

Naturally, you don't gobble up desert by the acre with anything resembling original architecture. The offenses of tract-home design have been cataloged prodigiously, and I won't belabor them here. I'll simply say that the uniformity dazzled me. A half century after the heyday of Levittown, the business model was thriving.

If you spend any time around saguaro cacti, before long you can't help but marvel at the conditions that enable a tiny seed to take root, bubble up into a pup, and climb slowly skyward. The process requires just the right conditions, and it yields mighty succulents that are each mighty in their own way. Like snowflakes and fingerprints, no two are alike.

We cannot say the same for their neighbors, the tract homes, with their identical floor plans, identical façades, and identical amenities.

***

As modernity advanced, mass-produced housing arrived relatively late. The British manufactured ceramics and textiles by the late 1700s. Carnegie's furnaces were on full blast by the early 1900s, and Ford developed the assembly line soon thereafter. During World War II, Douglas and Lockheed produced fighter planes by the tens of thousands. Craftsmanship and artisanal skill had been on the wane for a long time. In fact, by 1936, not much was unique anymore.

That's the year Walter Benjamin published "The Work of Art in the Age of Mechanical Reproduction." I prefer the more literal translation of its title: "The Work of Art in the Age of Its Mechanical Reproducibility," implying that art does not merely accompany mechanical reproduction but it is, in many ways, superseded and changed by mechanical reproduction. Benjamin argued that art—which is supposedly the apotheosis of uniqueness, originality, and human imaginativeness—was not merely a bystander in the industrial revolution, as the common title implies, but was, or could be, itself a product of technological production.

Even in the 1930s, it wasn't hard to imagine that the same mechanical processes that were producing cars and phones and chemicals could be trained to produce art as well. Or, rather, reproduce it. Benjamin does not discount the importance of the artist in the creation of original work. But he implies that human mastery of chemistry and materials science, paired with the precision of the assembly line, could essentially produce copies indistinguishable from their originals and do so in limitless numbers.

Mechanical arms could create brushstrokes in oil to mimic those of Da Vinci and Van Gogh, while mechanical chisels would turn fresh blocks of marble into new *David*s and *Birds in Space*. They would not be forgeries but rather true reproductions. Originals would retain their importance only through their "auras"—that ineffable contact with their respective creators, however arbitrary and immaterial that connection may be.

Benjamin probably overstepped. Even today, the originality of artwork—its imperfectness—provides one of our few steadfast links to our own humanity, even as technology eclipses anything Benjamin could have imagined. And yet, his thesis remains haunting, nihilistic even: what if the mechanical can obliterate the artistic?

This question vexed me from the moment I read Benjamin as an undergraduate all the way up to the moment I visited my first Tucson tract home development. There, in the most unassuming, offensive landscape, I discovered that architecture may yet preserve our sense of humanity.

What struck me then as I strolled those expectant streets (possibly in ways that the residents never will) was that, for all the sameness of the homes, each one retained an essential uniqueness. Those developments, like most such developments, offered a few designs, each with lame, disembodied names like "The Nantucket" or whatever. They weren't so much designs as they were collections of amenities and necessities united under roofs. And yet, each occupied its own special, if not necessarily distinctive, plot of desert.

Sure, machines can reproduce structures. But architecture is more than just structures. The one and only thing that we cannot reproduce, be it in a chugging factory, a humming 3D printer, or a laboratory staffed by autodidactic nanobots, is landscape. I say "landscape" deliberately. We can absolutely produce and reproduce land. Many cities sit on landfill of some sort, from Manhattan's Battery to Boston's Back Bay to Venice's Murano Island and Dubai's Palm Jumeirah. But what every piece of land can claim—whether created by man or plate tectonics—is its uniqueness. We have one Earth, and every piece of it differs from every other piece. The totality of architecture encompasses structures, setting, relationships, uses, and even ideas that, in combination, create a landscape.

Let's consider extreme exemplars: the Golden Gate Bridge, the Sydney Opera House, the monasteries of Tibet, the five-star bungalows of Tahiti, the Houses of Parliament, the Getty Center, Notre Dame, and the Casa Malaparte, and, yes, the Guggenheim Bilbao. (Esoteric though they may be, let's also add works of land art, like Spiral Jetty and The Lightning Field.) A great many architectural masterpieces owe their acclaim not just to their design—the part that lives on paper and could be constructed almost anywhere—but from their relationship with the land. Each of these structures looks the way it does because of its site and situation; from inside, they each look upon different views and, therefore, are capable of inspiring their own unique versions of awe. It's in these landscapes where humanism, if not humanity itself, may make its last stand.

My own home is not a masterpiece because it enjoys a slightly different view and slightly different elevation from the one across the street. But the uniqueness of landscape ensures that architecture can be unique. And, just as Benjamin's point about reproducibility was subtle yet powerful, so is the importance of landscape.

***

Benjamin was a weird one. On the one hand, he celebrated the extreme humanity of the city and the elemental activity of walking. On the other hand, he helped usher in not just the modern age—characterized by mechanical production—but indeed the postmodern age, characterized by reproduction and simulacrum. As intellectually interesting as postmodern ideas may be, they remain distressing. Nothing is special when everything is fake. Taken to its extreme, postmodernism presages the day when artificial intelligence does all our work for us and when no human relationship is unmediated by technology.

That's why I take solace in special places and nonspecial places alike. And it's why I put a degree of faith in architecture, even when so many other human endeavors have slid into banality and self-reference. Of course, not every architect can, or should, be another Utzon or Meier. The world will always need far more workaday structures than it does masterpieces. The more we must strain to see our auras amid the banality of postmodern life, the more we may need to tighten our grip on the incredible places humanity has created.

Nearly two decades later, I hope that plenty of happy families are living in those Nantuckets and Saratogas and whatevers. By now, many have raised children and perhaps sent them off to graduate school. They may or may not appreciate their unique places in the world. Indeed, placelessness is more prevalent than we ever could have imagined, with so much of life taking place online and in the cloud. But while desert sands may shift and buildings may topple, the fundamental facts of the land persist.

MATTERS OF TASTE

On Skylines and Snapshots
2017

Welcome to.... everywhere!

Early in the 19th century, an invention arrived that would change the form and function of cities for generations.

Like all new technologies, it started out rudimentary, expensive, and nearly ineffectual. But it caught many imaginations and developed dramatically, eventually reaching the point of mass accessibility. Soon enough, it took aim at the public realm, with consequences that were indirect and unintended yet profound.

It reconfigured streets. It influenced the height of buildings. It altered foot traffic. It recast the relationship between buildings and streets. It changed how people felt about their cities and changed their points of reference. It turned cities into abstractions and, in some ways, turned city-dwellers against one another. Its influence nearly complete by the close of World War I, the invention has remained fundamentally unchanged, and is still universally celebrated to this day.

All this with the press of a button.

***

Needless to say, the gas pedal played its part too. But for all the primacy of the way we move through cities, we must also consider how photography changed the way we saw cities and, by extension, the ways we build and experience them.

Before the invention of the camera, we could behold the world only through our own eyes. That which pleased us and functioned for us took place in fine detail. There was no distinction between sight, touch, and presence. Anything we could see, we could probably touch. Anything we could touch was by definition within our presence, ours to behold, control, and, cherish.

The detailed cityscapes of antiquity present feasts for the eyes. A Parisian side street, Beijing hutong, or Philadelphia alley, no matter how cramped, unsanitary, or inequitable, could contain entire universes of visual detail and human activity. There is no way to pull back and pan out; no way to rise above the fray.

Wide-angle views with the naked eye, such as the revelatory vista afforded by the Pont Neuf when it opened in 1607, were exceptional and special. Life was close. It took place at ground level. And that's where beauty was found. Even in rough cities, human interaction—pairs of eyes catching other pairs of eyes—gives cities their allure. Appreciation of urban beauty found its apotheosis in the Parisian flâneur, for whom strolling and observing was its own reward.

Interestingly, the very first photo was of buildings: a heliograph called "View from the Window at Le Gras," taken from a second-story vantage point on the photographer's estate in the mid-1820s. An auspicious start.

Because the earliest photographic technology measured exposure times in minutes, it was good mainly for still lifes and portraits of very patient (and very wealthy) subjects. A notable successor to the Le Gras photo came in 1838 when Louis Daguerre, the pioneer behind the technology that bears his name, shot a Paris street scene from a handful of stories above the Boulevard du Temple. Whether intended or not, Daguerre caught two apparitional figures in his frame, doing what people used to do in cities: idling.

In both of these early photographs, technology provides a new way of seeing the landscape. The street becomes an object to behold rather than a place to occupy.

The photography of Henri Cartier-Bresson marked a decisive moment in the history of photography and, indirectly, in the history of cities. "Decisive moment" was Cartier-Bresson's own description of the challenge that photographers face. Knowing when to press the button matters every bit as much as knowing where to point the camera. A crucial, fleeting gesture can leap from banality to intrigue in the blink of a shutter.

Cartier-Bresson haunted the streets of Paris and other cities searching constantly for those moments. He found them in abundance, anonymous, intimate images that celebrate faceless humanity and urban minutiae.

Think of a Bresson image. Even a puddle or a cobblestone becomes the quintessence of Paris, because Paris is in the details. Though Bresson wielded the camera, he did not destroy Paris. He saw Paris through new technology but with an old eye. Paris formed before the camera, and so did Bresson's sensibilities, like a grandparent who still writes longhand letters even though she could send a text message just as easily. The photographers and views that came after clung to no such quaint notions. In our reproducible age, Bresson is the exception that proves the rule.

***

Consider the postcard.

However you spin it, the rack at the drug store holds all sorts of images: barnyard animals, points of interest, thinly veiled advertisements for tourist traps. But if the rack is in a city, one type of image is bound to dominate: that of the skyline. From Manhattan and Los Angeles to Wichita and Toledo, there is essentially no American city that is not defined by its skyline—that is to say, by a photograph of its skyline.

Skylines appear on nearly every city's website and adorn the backdrop of nearly every local newscast. They accompany promotional materials and magazine articles. Their synecdochical power is nearly limitless. The Midwestern massif that culminates in the Willis Tower is to Chicago what the telephone booth is to London. Peachtree Plaza and its fellow Portmans are to Atlanta what the sushi bar is to Tokyo. Even the most unremarkable skylines—Des Moines, Fresno, Rochester, whatever—represent their respective cities for lack of imagination or of anything more distinctive to portray.

But, iconic and photogenic as they are, skylines belie what cities are. And they betray what cities should be.

The skyline is the image of recession. It comes into view not as you approach it but as you pull away. On foot at street level, there is no "skyline." The eye and camera strain to capture it. Only from afar—from automobile-scale distances—does its full silhouette come into view. You cannot, by definition, behold a skyline and experience it at the same time.

The primacy of the skyline is, of course, a deception. Yes, downtowns are crucial components of their respective cities. But they rarely house the souls of their cities. For better or worse, American cities expand into vast orbitals, within which the downtown is often just a tiny nucleus. By lavishing attention on them, photographs elevate bureaucracy and business above all other urban virtues.

In the Emerald City, not only do we not know what is behind the curtain, but we also do not know what lies on the ground. What are the sidewalks paved with, exactly?

But city life is overwhelmingly experienced at the street level. That's where residents emerge from their front doors every morning. It's where the smell of baking bread wafts out and where lines extend out the door at coffee shops. It's where strolling takes place, and where strangers bump into one another in the first step toward becoming friends. It's where humanity and design intersect to create culture. That's the ideal, at least.

Secondhand images don't eliminate these possibilities. But they routinely fail to celebrate them. They enable residents to take them for granted and, as a result, allow them to disappear or degrade. The activity, intimacy, greenery, artistry, and details that appeal to pedestrians are of no concern when we define cities according to those long-distance views. Consider how, as long as we have a skyline we can be proud of, we instinctively tolerate the Starbucks in the lobby of the office tower; with a little imagination, we could just as easily have Café Schwarzenberg on one corner and Café Landtmann on the other. Thoughtless photographs create thoughtless attitudes.

In the 1960s and '70s, when cities were hemorrhaging, literally and demographically, a clean, distant skyline—such as that seen from a faraway suburb—was about all a city might have to recommend it. These images bred a vicious cycle, masking urban renewal and other forms of neglect. A stately bank building or old-time department store not tall enough to get into the frame might as well be a parking lot. And so they become parking lots. As long as the requisite towers stand high enough, and as long as they are viewed from far enough away, the voids below them do not matter.

It's worth remembering that photography was also a mass-produced, mass-marketed American product.

***

The world has plenty of impressive skylines: Dubai, Kuala Lumpur, Shanghai, Shenzhen, Toronto, and so on. Even London now has a skyline, with the addition of the Shard. But most are impressive only superficially, more for the capital that went into them than for their aesthetic merit. Many of these skyscrapers seem to be competing with one another for some unnamed award for garishness.

The more midair spires, cornices, cutouts, and light shows I see, the more inured I become. Every preening new tower belittles those that preceded it while instantly proclaiming its own ridiculousness. As Alex Marshall put recently in *Governing*, "When you go from the view of the skyline down to the ground, you find that these big skyscrapers sit on giant superblocks, on roads that are more highway than street." They are usually surrounded, I might add, by pointless landscaping.

Photos make cities a purely visual experience, rather than the spiritual, emotional, and sensory experience that they should be. They absolve planners and designers from creating environments that comport with what humans, at all of five or six feet tall, actually enjoy.

Of course, no single technology is causal or catalytic. The automobile, elevator, I beam, smartphone, and many others crucial to the development of cities arose in tandem with the hubristic supernova of modernity. But to assume that photography merely reflects the environment and does not shape it would be shortsighted. As John Stilgoe teaches, locations do not become landscapes until they are seen. It's the same reason why photographers refer to "making" photos rather than "taking" photos. Photography is active, not passive.

The image doesn't supplant the city, but it says what's important. It says what the city is supposed to be. We build cities the way we view cities. When we don't value streets and don't value humans, we get the cities we deserve. We pay little attention to detail.

Bresson knew that. His images make the city intimate. The postcard makes it impersonal, eliminating people entirely from the city. It renders the city static, antiseptic, asocial, and atomized. It reduces the city to an abstraction: an object to behold in a single view, hold in the palm of the hand, and manipulate, rather than a place to be shared and enjoyed. Like the mountains that they mimic, these "objects" can be beautiful, but at great cost.

***

Think of the great modern American photographers: Charles Sheeler with lifeless factories; Weegee with the bright spirit of socializing; Cindy Sherman with portraits; Robert Mapplethorpe turning bodies into sculptures. Few besides Robert Frank approach life at street level. And yet, Frank's masterpiece, *The Americans*, laments suburbia and homogeneity. He captures the aftermath of de-urbanization, not the distinctive magic that used to make cities great.

Among amateurs and tourists, the most photographed street in America is brick-paved Acorn Street on Beacon Hill, dating back 400 years. Otherwise, the pedestrian's image of America thrives far from its great cities. It thrives on main streets of small towns and in gems like Charleston, Santa Fe, and Santa Barbara: our most distinctive, pleasant cities. Think of those postcards: none has glass towers to distract from their charms. The best cities are always ready for their close-ups.

The old Boy Scout saying goes, "Take only photographs, leave only footprints." I wish it was that easy.

The photographs of which I write have made it harder to leave footprints. The cities that photography, along with its modern brethren, has wrought cannot change in the blink of a shutter. They certainly cannot change as quickly as photography is changing. We now can capture every moment—not just the decisive ones—if we want to. But let us hope that new perspectives, and heretofore unfathomable technologies, can help the old, analog world stroll back into the past.

6 Everywhere Is Florida

Urban Economics in the Age of the "Creative Class"

Aside from professional Bitcoin miners and Reiki therapists who treat patients by FaceTime, every economic activity still takes place in a real place. I like to view urban commerce, from businesses that sell to the world to those that sell to folks around the corner, the way Jane Jacobs did.

As much as I'm on board with *Death and Life*, I've always highly regarded *The Economy of Cities* and *Cities and the Wealth of Nations*, companion pieces that eloquently discuss what cities actually do. We live in strange economic times, for global corporate juggernauts and corner stores alike. The former make California the world's fifth-largest economy, but they withstand scorn—sometimes deservedly so—for making the state unaffordable and for ignoring the well-being of their employees and their local communities. The latter, while they reap some of the windfall of California's prosperity, continue to backslide as increases in rent often outpace whatever new business they get from the coders, financiers, and Lyft drivers.

With his theory of the "creative class," scholar Richard Florida made the economic case for the revitalization and, to an extent, "hipster-fication" of cities. Florida has gotten a lot of flak for being too flippant, too narrowly focused, and too blithesome about the real challenges that cities face. I think, though, he got a lot of it right. He saw the bright side of de-industrialization and the knowledge economy. He saw that cities could be fun again—not just for the proverbial artists and coders but for everyone who uses the public realm. He never encouraged gentrification or displacement. Those problems, among many others associated with the new urban economy, are hardly of his making.

As they often are, planners are stuck in the middle of this debate over the creative class and over urban revitalization in general. They sometimes must decide whether great places lead to economic prosperity or whether economic prosperity demands great places. The best plan in the world doesn't ensure that developers will build or that tenants will sign leases. Sometimes, even, they are compelled to oppose conventional wisdom and wonder whether economic prosperity is a good thing at all, lest it overwhelm vulnerable stakeholders.

Planners must also consider the scale of the economies in which they are working. They might be able to reasonably assess, say, the wider traffic impacts of a development, but the economic impacts—of something colossal, like an NFL stadium—require more imagination than the typical economic impact analysis might contain.

Richard Florida's Reckoning
2017

The creatives have run amok.

Richard Florida's forthcoming book, *The New Urban Crisis*, will likely elicit one of two responses. It will be viewed as either a tardy, richly ironic attempt to undo damage for which Florida himself deserves partial blame—or as a timely, if lamentable, analysis of unintended consequences and plausible solutions accompanied by an appropriate mea culpa.

Your feelings about Florida may depend in part on your feelings about the new U.S. presidential administration. More on that later.

Florida built his career on advocacy for the "creative class." Back in 2003, he noticed that creative industries—which he defined broadly as anything from fine arts and fashion to programming and pharmaceuticals—did not need suburban office parks or noxious factories. Their "products" are based on ideas. Ideas thrive on collaboration. Collaboration requires congregation—i.e. cities.

Creatives didn't want just any cities. They wanted nice cities. They wanted nice bars, nice restaurants, nice parks, nice transit, and most importantly, nice people. Florida encouraged cities to become the cities that the creative class wanted them to be.

But today, many cities, and perhaps Florida himself, have become victims of their own success.

In his introduction, Florida writes soberly, "I realized I had been overly optimistic .... I entered into a period of rethinking and introspection, of personal and intellectual transformation, of which this book is the result."

We all needed a good think, really. The last great urban crisis—back in the 1960s and 1970s—took place in plain sight. The Cuyahoga River caught fire. So did the Bronx. Downtown neighborhoods emptied out and then got torn down. What Florida realized is that the current crisis, while not nearly as grave as the last one, is profound in its own way. But it's relatively invisible, hidden behind, and not nearly as exciting as, the prosperity of the past decade. He realized that "the very same clustering force that drives economic and social progress also ... generates a lopsided, extremely unequal kind of urbanism. A relative handful of superstar cities ... benefit while many other places stagnate."

Florida invents a statistical index to quantify what a "superstar city" is. Globally, New York and London rank at the very top, followed by Tokyo, Hong Kong, Paris, Singapore, Los Angeles, Seoul, Vienna, Stockholm, and Toronto.

Florida's index, like all indices, is semiarbitrary—Vienna is a "superstar" but Shanghai isn't?—but the point is well taken: talent, cultural influence, and capital converge in what Florida describes as "winner-take-all" situations. Cleveland and Liverpool suffer (relatively) while Chicago and London thrive. And why shouldn't they? Mobility is a hallmark of the creative class. If you're free to move anywhere, why move to the "second-best" city as opposed to the "best"?

The consequence of increasing wealth is increasing hardships for many residents—those who don't make it big, and those who don't want to make it big but instead just want to make a living. But cities are microcosms of global patterns: "Superstar cities fall victim to winner-take-all urbanism of their own, as they, too, are divided into a small number of extremely advanced superstar districts and much larger numbers of less advantaged neighborhoods." Some cities experience trickle-down effects whereby the poor benefit from the spending of the wealthy, but even poor neighborhoods still suffer from inflated costs for housing.

Florida defines these intra-urban problems as inequality, segregation, and sorting. He offers a slew of data to describe these patterns, some of it almost comical in its precision. He offers data sets to rank cities according to different types of segregation: segregation of the wealthy; segregation of the less educated; segregation of college grads; educational segregation; creative class segregation; service class segregation, etc.

With few exceptions, these rankings work out ironically but predictably: very prosperous cities look awful while more middling cities look OK.

(In almost every case, the major California metros rank atrociously, playing a game of musical chairs to see which can be the worst in a given category. Los Angeles has the worst working-class segregation and educational segregation. San Jose and San Francisco are Nos. 1 and 2 in overall occupational segregation. Conversely, four of the top six cities globally for venture capital investment are in California.)

Florida fuses this data into what he calls the "New Urban Crisis Index," consisting of "economic segregation, wage inequality, income inequality, and housing unaffordability." The big winners/losers, are, in order: Los Angeles, New York City, San Francisco, San Diego, and Chicago.

He reserves choice words for political interests that have exacerbated the crisis.

Opponents of growth "not only preserve their own housing values but also put a brake on the very clustering that drives innovation and economic growth." NIMBY activism has produced a "thicket of zoning laws and other land use regulations that restrict the supply of housing." The aggregate result: an estimated loss of $1.4 trillion to $2 trillion in economic gains between 1964 and 2009.

Florida chides activists at the other end of the socioeconomic spectrum too. While low-income residents are understandably wary of displacement, Florida contends that the tendency to oppose new housing in low-income areas is counterproductive. "The media's obsession with gentrification deflects attention from the far more serious problem of chronic and concentrated urban poverty," he writes.

Unlike in generations past, the suburbs provide little relief. "Instead of pushing people toward the American Dream, suburbia today actually hinders upward economic mobility," especially for the poor, who have to shoulder the cost of transportation. Florida's description of the suburbs partly echoes what many people said about cities themselves 60 years ago: "With their enormous physical footprints, shoddy construction, and hastily put up infrastructure, many of our suburbs are visibly crumbling."

The hyperdense, rapidly growing cities of the developing world are even worse off. Across Africa and Asia, rural migrants seek out cities not to realize their dreams but merely to survive. Many countries have only one major city, so migrants can go in only one direction—the ultimate example of winner-take-all urbanism. "Massive inflows of people can easily overwhelm a city's ability to effectively absorb them," Florida writes, "so tremendous numbers of new migrants end up being packed into rudimentary settlements in mega-slums."

For all the gloom, make no mistake: Florida still believes in the power of the creative class—and he's still himself. (You know it's a Richard Florida book when it includes references to "Byrne, Smith, and Moby"—i.e. David, Patti, and, well, Moby.) He just wants cities to take a more nuanced approach.

The New Urban Crisis lacks much of the dazzle that characterizes Florida's earlier work—he's like a Taylor Swift fan who just discovered Morrissey. Previously, Florida presaged, and encouraged, ebullient trends that hadn't happened yet. This time, he's describing depressing things of which many urbanites are all too aware. Whether Florida should have been aware of them—ahead of time—is the question that hangs over the book.

Indeed, Mike Davis, among others, has been warning about this stuff for years, with full Marxist indignation. In 2008, he and coeditor Daniel Monk gave "superstar cities" a far more sinister name: "Evil Paradises." Florida is less shrill than Davis and more optimistic. Whereas Davis sees class struggle and capitalistic exploitation in every penthouse and gated driveway, Florida sees more of a garden-variety mess.

The scholar seemingly most at odds with Florida is Joel Kotkin. In Kotkin's *The Human City*, published in 2016, he presents a passel of self-contradictory recommendations to a) lower their costs of living and be friendlier to young families by b) turning away from dense urbanism and readopting the suburban model that families "like." How less density in San Francisco or New York would lead to lower costs of living, Kotkin does not explain.

Florida's approach is far more realistic and intellectually consistent than Kotkin's: "The way out of the New Urban Crisis is more, not less, urbanism."

Florida has concluded that urban success depends on balance. Balance among cities. Balance within cities. Even balance on the level of a city block. "Urban economics are powered not by extreme residential density and huge towers, but by the mid-rise, mixed-density that promotes mixing and interaction," writes Florida.

Florida prescribes a mix of pragmatic physical and policy solutions. He calls for the reform of zoning codes to support infill development; provision of infrastructure, including transit, to enable dense cities to do what they do best; and development of "affordable" rental housing. On the policy front, he wants cities to get serious about alleviating concentrated poverty and supporting low-wage workers. He even proposes a guaranteed minimum wage for workers and, at the other end of the spectrum, a land-value tax to encourage property owners to develop property intensively rather than let them languish as, say, mini-malls and parking lots.

Florida wants national officials to get with the program too. He proposes a "Department of Cities and Urban Development" to set urban policy and, importantly, maximize federal funds that go to cities. He notes, "the federal government is already spending a lot of money on cities and urban development through a wide range of initiatives, ranging from transportation and housing to education, crime, and economic development—none of them coordinated in any meaningful way."

"We must put cities and urbanism at the very center of our agenda for economic prosperity," he writes.

Uh oh.

Had I read *The New Urban Crisis* on November 7, 2016, I'd have placed it somewhere between obvious and inspiring. The latter is certainly how Florida felt about it. Today, who knows?

Florida wrote the preview draft before the November election, with the assumption that Hillary Clinton would win the presidential election. And he assumed—as did many of us—that a Clinton presidency would respect and support cities, especially since city-dwellers voted for her overwhelmingly. Trump's win, which came largely from rural areas that are culturally and temperamentally suspicious of cities, compelled him to write a late revision, changing the introduction and conclusion.

Trump's election rattled Florida, and not just because he had to write a few more paragraphs. He seems genuinely to fear that Trump will neglect and abuse cities like no other president in recent memory. He puts on a brave face, though, writing in his update, "Now more than ever, mayors and local officials will have to take the lead on transit, affordable housing, poverty, and other pressing urban issues." (Kotkin actually agrees with this, promoting something he calls "localism.") But Florida knows that Trump's presidency transcends specific issues. With chilling certainty, Florida writes, "The geographical and cultural divides that the New Urban Crisis has etched into our landscape are deep .... our newly elected government will only make them worse."

Perhaps what Florida really did by promoting and branding

the creative class was to unwittingly give the forces of stasis and conservatism a target at which to shoot. It's one thing for a city to go about its business, gradually adding residents and jobs by the grace of the free market. It's another thing to be invaded by "the creative class." The invasion is all the more threatening when it consists of young, weird people who work at new, unfathomable jobs.

(Encouragingly, Florida and Kotkin are drafting a joint op-ed about how cities can address the Trump administration. Strange times lead to strange bedfellows.)

Until President Trump's urban policies come to bear, *The New Urban Crisis* provides a tidy, timely summary of the current urban problem in all its enormity. Florida's statistics and graphs may not stir the soul the way stories about evictions, gang wars, galleries, and gastropubs do. But they testify to the seriousness of the trend and its long reach.

Notwithstanding President Trump, I find myself sympathizing with Florida. Sure, he's a target because he's a celebrity academic and he may have marketed his theory of the creative class too exuberantly. But he's not Mayor of the World.

Even as Florida encouraged cities to develop seemingly frivolous amenities and cosmetic improvements, he wasn't telling them not to build housing. He wasn't telling them not to build schools. He wasn't telling them to vest political power in homeowners' associations and not in their new residents. He never told them to cling to outdated zoning regulations or counterproductive tax schemes.

Whatever fantasies Florida foisted upon cities, he never told them to do it *badly*.

If anything, the biggest mistake of Florida and other city boosters was to sell cities to creatives (and vice versa) without fully impressing on creatives their obligation to be citizens. Creative class residents can build awesome iPhone apps, drop dope tracks, and throw great parties. But creativity doesn't inherently lend itself to civic participation. But civic participation—from everyone, not just the NIMBYs—is exactly what's required to create equity, civic prosperity, and urbanism that serves everyone.

Too many members of the creative class have stood by, immersed in their own worlds, while their cities have become more expensive, more segregated, and less accessible. What Florida probably should have advised is that every newcomer should treat their new cities not like playgrounds but rather like projects—projects that require every bit as much attention as do the tech startups, underground theater companies, and urban planning newsletters that keep the creative class busy.

Now we may need to get busier than ever.

Creative Class Gets Priced Out
2015

Plenty of people have been accused of ruining cities in the 20th century. Henry Ford, Le Corbusier, Robert Moses, and Gerald Ford come to mind. Add to that list Roland Barthes.

Barthes is not a planner, of course, nor is he American. He is a philosopher from Paris. His work has nonetheless devastated a certain class of people who live in cities. As Scott Timberg writes in *Culture Crash: The Killing of the Creative Class*, Barthes and other post-structuralist scholars set in motion a vicious cycle that devalued the creative arts and now threatens to undermine one of the most endearing approaches to 21st century urban development.

Richard Florida has built a hefty brand name with his "theory of the creative class," encouraging cities to attract young creative types, whom he defines broadly as everyone from the bassist in your garage band to the person who comes up with names for pharmaceuticals. These "creatives" enjoy lively downtowns (Brooklyn, San Francisco, Austin), dense development and attractive multiunit housing, public transit and cycling, active public spaces, and bars, restaurants, and other amenities. Galleries, studios, and music venues are crucial too.

Florida argues that this approach makes cities not only fun but also wealthy, since creatives are, if not the backbone, then the face of the 21st century knowledge economy. Someone has to design all those web pages and film all of those YouTube videos. USC geographer Elizabeth Currid-Halkett quantified the value of the creative industries to cities in *The Warhol Economy*, with impressive conclusions, particularly for New York.

Timberg tells a less buoyant story.

Even amid the era's profusion of media, writes Timberg, the very same artists, writers, musicians, and architects who used to make decent livings—even if they never became stars—now face grim prospects. Today's pop culture favors a winner-take-all ethos (e.g. Taylor Swift, J. K. Rowling), leaving journeymen and -women with only scraps.

In many ways, he's telling stories that we already know. Symphonies are going silent. Newspapers are getting bought, digitized, and consolidated. Studios focus on dialogue-free blockbusters to please foreign audiences. Novelists don't sell books anymore. Bands don't sell CDs anymore and barely make money on concerts. Architectural renderings get automated or outsourced. Writers endure daily existential crises and create content for free (look at *Girls*, or this review).

Timberg is not a scholar but an arts journalist. He conducted no studies to reach his conclusions, which amount to a clubby, insider-y lament. He bases many of his observations on anecdote and healthy doses of outrage, which is close at hand because Timberg is clearly pals with a lot of people in the arts. It helps if you know your Camper Van Beethoven, The Negro Project, and Patti Smith. As a polemic, though, it's affecting, especially if you think art is a good thing in the first place. And you only have to walk down to where your local bookstore used to be to know that he's at least half right.

Timberg views the consumption of culture as, ideally, a social, place-based practice. Bookstores, record stores, galleries, and even video stores thus played crucial roles in spreading the word about new talent. Those walls, record racks, and stages are the places that house art's aura—making it a communal experience and not just a private delight. The creations may be intangible, but the institutions are brick-and-mortar. They are where art comes alive—not for the artist but for the viewer, listener, and reader.

The "middlemen"—one of several tainted words that Timberg would have us reconsider—who work at these stores are almost as important as the artists themselves. They provide the expertise and the spirit that gets consumers excited about culture. Timberg chides Florida for counting clerks among the mere "service class." Regardless, clerks and their stores are suffering in light of rising rents and what Timberg describes as a "faux-populist disregard for expertise."

Timberg does not focus directly on cities, but that's probably because he considers their role in the creative economy to be a given. Stores are just one aspect of that relationship, albeit an important one. "Strolling, in particular, is something these shops encourage, and, when they close, they often make a neighborhood less walkable," writes Timberg. Removing a beloved store from a city block can ruin the block's appeal, "like knocking out Angelina Jolie's front tooth." The demise of the culture economy leads to "an abandonment of public spaces as well as the notion of a shared culture."

As familiar as these outcomes are, Timberg explains why they are happening now. Technology, corporatism, consolidation, and functional illiteracy are a few of the obvious reasons. Other factors are more subtle.

Fed up with the simplistic binaries of the Cold War and the injustice of the Western canon, critics in the 1960s and onward essentially decided that nothing meant anything anymore. It was Barthes who heralded the "death of the author," meaning that texts are floating signifiers with no connection to artistic intent. These critics insisted that prior notions of artistic greatness depended either on arbitrary aesthetic assumptions such that, as Timberg writes, "'good' is understood to be a suspect term based on the self-interested values of those in power."

By reducing creative works to political implications, poststructuralism strips them of their power to delight and to enlighten. Everything became analyzable—a soup can, or the painting it inspired, became no more or less meaningful than *Moby Dick* or *The Night Watch*. "Fiercely anti-intellectual" film critic Pauline Kael is Timberg's worst villain for celebrating lowbrow culture to the point of obliterating highbrow culture. Andy Warhol may have been an original, but Kael deserves blame for Jeff Koons.

The trouble is, when professors rail about bias and shifting signifiers in books and critics sensationalize works that are truly awful, the result is not that kids read books or watch movies more critically. It's that they resign themselves to blockbusters, and they don't read books at all.

From 1970 to 2003, the percentage of students majoring in humanities at American colleges fell from 30 percent to 16 percent. Today, it's hard to discuss the humanities without referring to "the crisis." Conventional wisdom holds that students shy away from humanities because they won't get career training. Timberg turns this notion on its head. The humanities do not create producers. They create consumers. "One of the things a humanities education has traditionally done," writes Timberg, "is excite young people about books and ideas, preparing them to become dedicated novel-readers, museum-goers, theater-frequenters, and so on."

And while the academy pursued ever more abstruse lines of criticism, arguing about how to unveil and reject expressions of power, the people with actual power—Walmart, Comcast, Verizon, and Fox, to name a few—have carried on.

"Members of the creative class created this mess themselves," concludes Timberg.

Cities can either accept that the creative class will not save them, or they can pursue policies to save it. Timberg prefers the latter strategy. In fact, even as the country becomes more homogenized, cities still have the chance to support diversity. As cities compete with one another in the crass marketplace of intranational competition, so must they distinguish themselves. What better way than through locally sourced literature, architecture, art, and music? The media giants want the same artists to blast out of every station in the country, but that doesn't mean that cities can't put their own bands on stage in the town square or close down the streets for a locals-only music festival. What's good for Clear Channel is not good for cities.

Timberg defines his cultural ideal in urban terms. He writes, "Every decent-sized city would have an array of book and record stores and performance venues as well as a good newspaper that could afford arts coverage and assertive watchdog journalism." It's arguable that these amenities should concern planners just as much as streets, sewers, and affordable housing do.

It's not like cities don't already have enough to do and too little money with which to do it. But so long as some segments of America are turning away from urbanism and art alike, the creative class offers progressive cities yet another opportunity to distinguish themselves and, quite possibly, make themselves more prosperous in the process.

The life of the city, it turns out, may depend on the livelihood of the author.

The City as Factory
2008

Waiting for my man in Soho.

Elizabeth Currid is cooler than you.

Perhaps the only urban planner ever to conduct fieldwork in stilettos, Currid slips past velvet ropes to argue in *The Warhol Economy* that New York City's bounty resides not in the office tower but rather in the street, where art and creativity propel the city's economy and distinguish it from the overgrown office parks that pass for American cities in the postindustrial age.

A professor of urban planning at the University of Southern California by day, Currid locates herself along a continuum leading roughly from Jacobs (Jane) to Jacobs (Marc), with a stop at Florida (Richard) along the way. Her stylish, sassy account weaves history, sociology, economics, and public policy into a compelling primer on a colorful segment of society wedded to its cityscape but alien to many planners.

Andy Warhol's The Factory provides Currid with a metaphor for New York's "creative economy," in which hanging out, getting high, and dancing until dawn supplant board meetings, rounds of golf, and indeed, factories themselves. The city's unique combination of density, diversity, public transit, and distinctive enclaves enables artists, designers, musicians, writers, and other intergalactic visionaries to live, work, and hang out in "the same twenty-five square miles or so." These tight quarters foster chance encounters and the "new combinations" that Jane Jacobs considered the hallmark of healthy economies; in the Warhol economy, they just happen later at night.

Amid descriptions of after-hours clubs, rock shows, gallery openings, street corner jam sessions, and the borderline deviance inherent to the creative process, you can almost taste the cocaine. Yet Currid does not rely on qualitative analysis alone.

She also offers a raft of census data and a decidedly wonky algorithm for determining a city's "location quotient"—the relative ability for different cities to foster different industries. She concludes that "art and culture are New York City's crucial competitive advantage—meaning they form the sector in which New York has a unique lead over any other city." In other words, nowhere else could you call "next" in a pickup basketball game and end up designing album covers for the Beastie Boys.

But this much almost any progressive urban theorist could have told you. Currid's more breathtaking conclusion is not that creativity owes itself to New York, but that New York owes itself to creativity.

No matter how big their Benjamins may be, Currid claims that the brokers, lawyers, and financiers who populate New York's office towers have little to do with the collective enterprise in the semipublic realm. Compared to the real geniuses, New York's businesspeople as mere hangers-on who enjoy the milieu of the creative economy but could otherwise be outsourced to cubicles above Dallas and dream of happy hour at TGI Fridays. "Art and culture are not the little sisters to finance or management," she writes.

Given the traditionally fraternal relationship between cities and big business, Currid's implied planning question is twofold: how can New York's hipsters continue to thrive, and how might other cities get in on the fun and profit? In her final chapter, Currid finally steps out of Candace Bushnell mode to focus less on the sex and more on the city. Her analysis is not encouraging.

The book's greatest failing is, in fact, the scant number of pages that it dedicates to planning per se. Currid pays most of her attention to history and a description of activities that are already going on, but she has relatively little to say about how to cultivate the creative economy. It's as if she's taunting planners and policymakers with images of a world that they can never hope to create.

Currid derides formal civic institutions, such as museums and foundations, and refers to public arts initiatives and city grants as piddling and half-assed. She writes that "public policy frequently misses the mark in terms of what cultural industries and producers really need to sustain and optimize their work." The vagueness of creativity befuddles policymakers and planners, and they can promote it only in oblique ways. However condescending, Currid implies that her colleagues are a bunch of squares.

Not to be sucked into a bureaucratic discussion, Currid offers only a few concrete recommendations: zoning that accommodates live-work spaces, artist lofts, adaptive reuse, strategic tax breaks and other trends associated with urban revitalization. She hearts art schools, wishes that the cops would give nightclubs a break, and encourages dialogue between the art community and the public sector. (She fails, however, to consider whether artists need to play ball and conceive of themselves as a political constituency.)

These ideas may be all well and good for maintaining the status quo in New York, but if dense, vast urban neighborhoods are the art world's true palate, then other cities might have to acknowledge that the Warhol economy may be as unique and enigmatic as its namesake.

Excepting hesitant concessions to Los Angeles, Currid notes that creativity rarely turns a profit elsewhere. Without the critical mass of potential collaborators, promoters, and media outlets, everywhere else amounts to quaint artists' colonies. She says that other cities should focus on sectors that allow them to capitalize on their own strengths, which may or may not include art. "In order to fully participate in the art and culture economy, you pretty much have to be in New York," she writes, without irony. And even in New York, where the art scene flourished amid the decay of the 1970s, gentrification is now taking its toll.

Ultimately, Currid admits that promoting the creative economy in New York, or anywhere else, is an "ambiguous task." You wonder whether Currid should have had fewer martinis and spent a little more time thinking about planning, but at least she is trying. She takes the creative economy seriously and deserves credit for going where policymakers and other scholars have feared to tread. She gives planners plenty of economic reasons to fight for friendly, vaguely chaotic cities and, indeed, to come up with their own creative strategies.

There's also a compelling performative aspect to *The Warhol Economy*. Currid gets a thrill from prancing about, dropping names, and delving into the personalities at the heart of the creative economy. Her exuberance ought to remind us that, regardless of its economic benefit, art is fun. It's fun to produce, and it's fun to live with. And it's a lot more fun to read about than parking requirements, setback restrictions, and floor-to-area ratios.

Battle between Football, Brunch Rages in L.A.
2015

I went to brunch one Sunday morning a while back at Louie's, a place that I will unironically describe as a gastropub. My Sunday rituals usually consist of visits to the farmers market and worrying about deadlines. So I was surprised to find, bellied up to the bar at the ripe hour of 11 a.m., a line of folks dressed in jerseys of the New Orleans Saints.

"Who dat?" indeed.

Louie's is one of many Los Angeles bars that on Sundays look like they've been airlifted from other cities. I'll be damned if I know anyone in L.A. from New Orleans. And yet, if you look hard enough, you'll find a bar for every team. Actually, you don't have to look hard at all. Nearly every NFL team has a local "headquarters;" some teams have more than one.

Such is life in a city that is a) full of transplants; and b) bereft of its own team.

I grew up in the Los Angeles of the Raiders and Rams. My father and I even made a few intrepid journeys to the Coliseum each season to see the Raiders beat up on someone and to watch Raider fans beat up on one another. But then 1995 came and the teams went and, to be honest, I wasn't exactly crushed. Neither were many other people in Los Angeles.

Among Los Angeles's many oddities is its relative indifference to pro sports rivalries. I'd no sooner wear a Ravens jersey in Pittsburgh than I would a meat vest in a wolverine lair. But I'd wager that Los Angeles is the only city in the country where you can stroll down the street unmolested and unnoticed wearing a hat or T-shirt of any major league team in the country (excepting, perhaps, the San Francisco Giants). It's just one (superficial) example of our famed diversity.

Of course, as everyone in Los Angeles knows, many rich and powerful people have been trying to correct our football deficiency for quite some time. At last count, at least five stadium projects—the Coliseum, the Rose Bowl, something in Irwindale, something at Dodger Stadium, and the fictional Farmer's Field at the Los Angeles Convention Center—have been proposed by different developers. No one has yet proposed a floating stadium off Santa Monica, but I wouldn't be surprised if it's in the works.

Shortly after my brunch at Louie's, Los Angeles got the most promising news of all: Stan Kroenke, owner of the St. Louis (née Los Angeles) Rams, bought part of the former Hollywood Park racetrack in Inglewood. He announced a partnership with Stockbridge Capital, the owner of the rest of the former racetrack site, to develop an NFL stadium. Stockbridge is already developing a roughly 200-acre mixed-use master-planned fantasia. The stadium would be, to Kroenke's and Stockbridge's credit, privately funded.

The entire project must be approved via a city ballot measure, for which Kroenke and Stockbridge are gathering signatures. Folks in Inglewood, a blue-collar city whose star is already on the rise, are giddy about it. Adding a football stadium would be a natural fit.

It would be roughly the size of the racetrack and, though the uses would be more intense, it would likely have fewer events than the racetrack did.

This plan seems like a realistic one because, unlike the others, it has the advantage of being attached to an actual football team.

I'm just not sure if I, or Los Angeles, want that. Our city's culture has evolved endearingly in the NFL's absence, embracing all those other teams and becoming very good at yoga. To our collective credit, we have refused to pay the extortionate amounts of money that other cities have paid in order to appease their teams.

I love civic pride and I respect the excitement of football. That's all good. But the people of Inglewood, and football fans around the Los Angeles metro area, need to remember that huge institutions that promise local economic development—think Walmart, which Inglewood voters thwarted in 2007—do not conjure revenues out of thin air. Proponents cite $1 billion in economic development if the Rams move to Inglewood. But these things can easily be zero-sum games, especially when profits ultimately get shipped out of town.

Many of the dollars that would go to the Los Angeles Rams will be dollars that don't go to Louie's, Bru Haus (Steelers), Mom's (Packers), Sonny's (Patriots), and O'Brien's (Giants), to mention just a few places that are a lot cozier than anything that will be built in Inglewood. Even the Rams currently have a watering hole: Malecon. We can do better than to wear the same jerseys and cheer in lockstep so that some person or company, be it Stan Kroenke or AEG, can reap tens of millions of dollars each year. We can have our fun, eat our brunches, and drink our beers in places that seat fewer than 60,000 people. In other words, I'd rather give my money to a local barkeep than to a global brand that pretends to be a nonprofit.

Unfortunately, if the Rams don't come to Los Angeles, Missouri may still lose, fiscally at least. Four days after Kroenke cryptically announced his Inglewood deal, Missouri Governor Jay Nixon conveniently presented a plan for a new 64,000-seat stadium on the banks of the Mississippi. Of the estimated $900-ish million cost, 40 percent would be borne by the state.

Ultimately, I'd rather let St. Louis have its team and its stadium. "Build it and they will come"—one of the most overused clichés in land use—referred to apparitional baseball players, not to football fans or to anyone else. We in Los Angeles have plenty of other places to go and other things to do.

Rams fans, I'll see you at Malecon some Sunday morning.

Amazon and Urbanism
2014

One of many victims.

Sometime in the next few months a bell will ring in New York City and, on the other side of the world, an age-old pattern of urban growth will begin to crumble.

One of the axioms of urban development is that, generally speaking, cities grow according to the mode of transportation predominant at the time of their growth. The layout of Lower Manhattan owes itself to feet and hooves. From the kernel of the Battery, Midtown and Harlem grew because of horse carts and elevated rail. The subway enabled Manhattan to grow higher. Trolleys dropped off commuters at the first streetcar suburbs. Suburbanites fled to Nassau County, Westchester, and New Jersey on parkways and then highways.

You could tell the same story for just about every other urban place, from the Roman Forum to the Ikea in Burbank. Latter-day retrofits like streetcars and long-overdue subways perpetuate this pattern, as streetscapes grow livelier and transit-oriented zones become denser.

Each of these stages engendered their own street patterns, mixes of uses, and building typologies. The life of cities is defined, in large part, by the relationship between the places where people gather and the ways that they arrive at those places. We may soon find out what the post-transportation city looks like.

Among all the behemoths to come out of China over the millennia, only a few have captured the imagination of the business world like that of online retailer Alibaba Group. Founded innocently by a former English teacher, Alibaba's initial public offering, to be listed on NASDAQ, will rank among the top five richest in history. It may generate somewhere between $55 billion and $120 billion.

It's tempting to call Alibaba the Amazon.com of China, but that does a disservice to Alibaba. Its sales are more than twice those of Amazon and are growing far more quickly. A more apt comparison is to Walmart, but it too may be dwarfed by Alibaba. Pretty soon, Alibaba won't have any more companies against which to compete; it rivals those of all but a few sovereign nations.

As a macroeconomic force, Alibaba makes up 80 percent of Chinese e-commerce and more than 2 percent of its GDP, with $295 billion in sales in 2013. That's about the same as the GDP of Switzerland. The upshot is that when Chinese consumers go shopping, they often go nowhere. When Alibaba gets its infusion of new cash, that chunk will, presumably, grow larger.

The first column on urbanism I ever wrote, as a junior in college, compared Walmart to iceberg lettuce (and Whole Foods to arugula—that was prescient stuff in 1995). I've criticized it routinely since then. So, I can't believe I'm saying this: whatever devastation Walmart and the other big boxes have wrought on American cities is nothing compared to that which Alibaba may wreak on China's cities.

My favorite place in Beijing is an alley between 1950s-style buildings that are, in turn, in the shadow of early-2000s luxury apartments. Food carts materialize there every morning, as they do on many corners and alleyways. I found a woman who sells breakfast sandwiches—fried egg, ham, hot sauce, and greens all exploding out of a bun like an English muffin—for the equivalent of 40 cents. That's the side of China that I like.

Otherwise, every day I've spent in Beijing has come with different measures of pollution, traffic, ugliness, and disorientation. Beijing has its charming places, and it has plenty of wonderful people. Sometimes I reunited with old college friends; other times I had business meetings, with locals and expats. No reunion feels right, though, in a city as uncomfortable as Beijing. Beijing is just the most famous of dozens of megacities, some of which were scarcely more than villages a generation or two ago.

What Chinese cities aren't has been well documented and much lamented. They are not the historical hutongs, the tight-knit neighborhoods built around alleyways and smoldering coals. The communists and, later, the capitalists did away with them. Everybody knows about the CCTV Tower and the strato-scrapers of Shanghai's Pudong. We know, at least, what their tops look like. But what of their bases? The Chinese street often isn't even a street. It's freeways and superblocks, with high-rises that recede from one another.

Who knows when my alley and the egg muffin cart too will be replaced by a skyscraper? China has no choice but to build, because the people keep coming—mostly to their and the country's benefit. It's just that this influx, and the building boom, is happening at the worst possible time.

Not only have Chinese cities grown up in the age of the automobile—they've grown fast in the age of the automobile. They've grown with a tension between the informal economy of ephemeral street vendors and the centrally planned economy. Many of them lack, or demolished, the historic cores that redeem even the most sprawling American cities. Mom and Pop tend to their cart while eight lanes' worth of traffic roars by.

Many of those cars aren't headed to the store anymore. Alibaba's entire existence is based on the notion that people in Chinese cities prefer (or have been conditioned to prefer) that their goods arrive on their doorsteps, either because they do not want to go out into the city or because there isn't much of a city to go out into.

In this case, bad urbanism only breeds greater dependency on e-commerce. If Chinese public spaces and retail areas are unpleasant, then residents have less incentive to leave the house, and Alibaba becomes more indispensable. The more indispensable Alibaba becomes, the less incentive there is to improve the Chinese public realm. That's doubly true when so many new urban residents have moved from tiny country towns and therefore may have no conception of what great urbanism—attractive, lively, human, distinctive—can look like. Autocratic rule doesn't help either.

E-commerce has hurt American cities, to be sure. Just look at the demise of the bookstore and record shop. On the other hand, coffee shops are booming, and traditional malls have been devastated, whereas creative merchants and entrepreneurs have whittled old downtown bones into some handsome places. Most American cities had at least a few of their formative years before the automobile came along, so they have something to work with.

In the United States, it seems that Amazon and other online retailers lately have denuded malls far more than they have Main Streets. New Urbanist revitalization of urban cores has been facilitated at least in part by telecommuting and tech jobs that have made young adults more footloose than they were in the landline era.

Alibaba will not single-handedly put the Chinese streetscape out of business. And yet, this is the direction in which the world's largest nation, and now largest urban nation, is headed. Granted, Alibaba's IPO may be symbolic. But so was the assembly of the first Model T. Every yuan that goes into Alibaba will feed a virtual juggernaut that not only affects cities but, indeed, takes the place of cities. Before long, the only strip of brick-and-mortar in China could be the one that is 2,300 years old.

So much for a public offering.

Tech Windfall, Deportation Order Threaten to Snap Los Angeles in Half

2017

When Snap Inc., the parent company of messaging app Snapchat, issues its first round of public stock sometime this year, it will likely raise between $19 billion and $22 billion. That valuation will make it the most valuable tech company in Southern California and one of the most valuable of all Los Angeles.-based companies. Many of its 1,900 employees will make fortunes overnight.

One senior vice president of engineering stands to make $110 million. That's enough to cover rent for 10,000 or so of Los Angeles's working-class residents for a year.

Of course, Snap money probably won't be going into rent. Snap's millionaires-to-be are going to have long wish lists of things to buy. Near the top of those lists will be real estate.

Back when Snapchat was just a sketchy platform for kids to send, um, silly photos to one another, the fledgling company operated out of a cottage in Venice Beach. As it grew into a social media juggernaut, it didn't follow convention by renting space in a high-rise or building a megacampus in the suburbs. Instead, it colonized its own neighborhood, expanding from cottage to cottage, scooping up small office spaces and oozing its way through Venice.

Venice Beach is regarded almost universally as "funky." By Los Angeles standards, Venice has history in spades, with its share of hippies, beach people, drifters, and artists. They fit in well with the early 20th century bungalows and brick. The rise of Snap and its brethren in the so-called Silicon Beach scene has led to a miniature culture war as ambitious millennials have displaced old-timers, forced long-standing businesses to close, and gleefully disrupted the neighborhood.

(In that sense, Snap occupies far different territory than does its counterparts in Silicon Valley. While tech money has driven the cost of living in Mountain View, Palo Alto, and Cupertino to insane levels, there's more history on one block in Venice than in an entire zip code on the Peninsula.)

Despite all pressure to the contrary, coastal cities and neighborhoods have refused to add housing. Los Angeles has done so in places, but housing supply on the Westside is growing at rates somewhere between 0 and negative 22 billion percent. Home prices are already bonkers. We can only imagine what will happen when the Snap folks get real money in their bank accounts.

Real estate agents are salivating. Many longtime Venice locals are terrified.

There is at least one demographic group in the Los Angeles area that's even more terrified. Not necessarily of Snap—though Snap doesn't help.

On the very same day that *The New York Times* reported on Snap's impending riches (Feb. 16, 2017), President Donald Trump announced his intention to fulfill his promise to aggressively deport undocumented immigrants.

Let's estimate the impact of this lunacy on California. Some 2.7

million undocumented immigrants call California home—by far the largest such population in the nation. More than 800,000 live in Los Angeles County alone.

A perverse notion occurs to me as I consider Trump's vile solution to a nonexistent problem. If it succeeds, 800,000 people in Los Angeles County could disappear like so many Snap messages. That's 800,000 lost workers. 800,000 lost customers. 800,000 lost mothers, fathers, siblings, and friends. 800,000 lost taxpayers. It's also 800,000 bedrooms that will open up.

From a purely numerical standpoint, Trump's crusade could put a serious dent in housing costs. After all, demand for rental housing would go down.

The thought gives me chills. I don't want to say any more about it other than that deportation is—to say the least—the most perverse way to solve a housing crisis.

Fortunately, Californians are leading the charge to protect their undocumented neighbors. Indeed, many of us hope marginalized people from around the country will join us, even if we're short on space. Even so, we should be making space. We should be solving the housing crisis the old-fashioned way and the humane way: by building ourselves out of it.

This convergence of wealth, poverty, xenophobia, and exclusivity is no mere coincidence. See, these issues—immigration, housing, gentrification, Trump—are intertwined. Economic booms like that of the early 2010s naturally come with echoes of desperation. Blue-collar workers in the Heartland want to protect their jobs from immigrants. Wealthy homeowners at the beach want to protect their property values from competition.

The Snap IPO completes the process of turning Venice into a superstar neighborhood in a superstar city—which, as Richard Florida describes in *The New Urban Crisis*, is marked by inequality, unaffordability, segregation, and economic dysfunction. It's also marked, I'd argue, by political apathy.

Hillary won 71 percent of the vote in California. The president didn't break double digits in some Venice precincts. I bet you can count on two hands the number of those 1,900 employees who voted for Trump.

And yet, I'd also wager that scarcely more than 10 Snap employees plan on voting in the March 7 Los Angeles election. That's the one with the Neighborhood Integrity Initiative on the ballot. It's a slow-growth initiative that, critics contend, could cripple the city's ability to approve new housing. If that critique is true, then young professionals should vote for it like the second coming of Barack Obama. But they probably won't.

Santa Monica, which constitutes the northern quarter of Silicon Beach, considered a slow-growth measure. Back then, I wrote how the young professionals of Silicon Beach were, as far as I could tell, disengaged from local politics—even though they stood to suffer mightily from further restrictions on housing development in a market already tighter than a noose.

Essentially, the tech crowd has tolerated high rents while hoping that their ships would come in rather than agitate for the type of development and planning policies that would have benefited not only them but also many of their less wealthy, less flashy neighbors.

Now that Snap is going full steam ahead, that's 1,900 more people who can blithely let the other 10 million of us in Los Angeles County fight over the scraps. Or 9.2 million of us, depending how bleak things get.

So, we have two opposing forces. Deportation could lower housing costs. A massive influx of cash may raise housing costs. Clearly Snapchat is doing something right. Good for them. But the other half of that equation threatens to morally bankrupt all of us.

Of course, formerly apathetic citizens are resisting, mobilizing, and donating in record numbers. I'm sure Silicon Beachers are too. And I hope some of them will hold off on an extra bedroom or a Wolf range and instead make some timely donations. America can right itself, and California—with its energy, innovation, and, yes, wealth—can lead the way.

For now, in this tale of one city, it is both the best of times and the worst of times.

Hyperloop and Hyperbole
2016

That's a nice tube. Where are you going to put it?

On December 21, the Falcon 9 rocket launched from Cape Canaveral, deployed a suite of communications satellites, and, in impressive fashion, came back down to Earth. Using its engines to dull the force of gravity, it survived reentry and hit its football field-sized landing pad like a Tesla backing into a garage.

The Falcon 9's return from the heavens was an early Christmas miracle, courtesy of Elon Musk, one of the world's few celebrity engineers. It is a product of SpaceX, Musk's pioneering private space-travel company based in Hawthorne. He can now add space to the list of fields—from electric cars, to battery power, to credit card payments—that his ventures have conquered. (A similar launch on January 17 didn't go quite so well.)

Next, Musk hopes to revolutionize long-distance transit. That one may make rocket science look like child's play.

For the uninitiated: Hyperloop is—depending on whom you ask—either the name brand or the generic concept behind the next generation of magnetic levitation technology. It's envisioned as either a train or as a set of individual pods that, unlike conventional maglev (which never really caught on, except on a 21-mile line in Shanghai), would run through depressurized tubes. Yes, tubes. As in under the ground.

The technology makes intuitive sense. It uses the estimable power of magnetic propulsion while avoiding the mortal enemy of all moving things: air resistance. With potential speeds north of 600 miles per hour, the "hyper" is obvious; whether "loop" refers to the circular tube or to the idea that these things will be encircling us sooner than you can say "California High Speed Rail" is but one of its delightful mysteries.

It's hard to tell whether Hyperloop is a technology, a thought experiment, a company, or just a rumor. Thanks to a mushy public relations campaign and an open-source type of platform, Musk has unleashed yet another visionary idea but, unlike his other companies, he seems to be letting it develop of its own accord.

So far we have Hyperloop Technologies, which is based in downtown Los Angeles and seems to be affiliated with Musk. That's not to be confused with Hyperloop Transportation Technologies (HTT), which is based vaguely in "California," according to its Twitter page, and has plans for a test track in Quay Valley, California. HTT also wants to build one in Nevada. Then there's the SpaceX's own Hyperloop Pod Competition. Who knows what's really going on?

Right now, buzz is overshadowing confusion. And how could it not? Thirty-minute travel times between Los Angeles and San Francisco is the stuff of dreams. And how about Silver Lake to Marina del Rey in 30 seconds?

Hold on a minute. No matter how fast it goes, Hyperloop isn't Uber. You can't push a button and tell it to go wherever you want. And yet, that's what some Hyperloop backers would have us think.

While Los Angeles-to-San Francisco is the holy grail of medium-haul transportation, the mustache-to-mizzenmast commute probably isn't at the top of planners' priorities. But it was one of the selling points that Hyperloop Technologies CEO Rob Lloyd proposed, quite offhandedly, at the 2016 Milken Institute California Summit, which I attended. That kind of speed is a mouthwatering notion for weary urban commuters, just as the Los Angeles-to-San Francisco leg is for tourists and business travelers. But it has little to do with reality.

Hyperloop Technologies claims that "Hyperloop is changing the way we think about transportation." That's not quite right. It's changing the way we think about propulsion. As transportation, Hyperloop runs into the same wearisome challenges that every other project since the Appian Way has faced.

It would be one thing to launch a Falcon 9 from Sunset Junction and land it at Mother's Beach. Where the Falcon 9 goes, they don't need roads. But Hyperloops still need rights of way. If we're in urban Los Angeles, it has to run either on stilts or below ground, lest it plow through your living room.

In fairness, Lloyd was mainly trying to illustrate Hyperloop's speed. But his attempt to illustrate the limitless possibilities of technology still disingenuously elided the drab pragmatism issues that surround land use and transportation policy—the same issues that plague high-speed rail.

Hyperloop seems more exciting than California's halting high-speed rail project for two reasons. First, it has the swagger of Elon Musk rather than the stigma of a public bureaucracy. Second, it's going to be, like, a billion times faster than HSR. That's really fast. There's a lot that we might be willing to sacrifice, financially and otherwise, for the travel times that Hyperloop's backers are promising.

And yet, this combination of enthusiasm and magnetism doesn't buy farmland. It doesn't ease eminent domain takings. It doesn't blast through bedrock or relocate utilities. It doesn't design station area plans. It doesn't write EIRs or dismiss CEQA suits.

Trains, whether propelled by steam, diesel, or a frictionless tube, are still terrestrial things. And what terra we have in California. The very same mountains, cities, canals, farmers, and habitats that complicate HSR also complicate Hyperloop. The more the Hyperloop people drop hints and make innuendoes about zipping this way and that without addressing the monumental public policy challenges that they're going to face, governmental cooperation they're going to need, and money that it's going to cost, the less it's going to sound like Tesla for the masses and the more it's going to sound like a lost chapter of *Atlas Shrugged*.

Shooting for the stars is awesome, of course. Imagine, for instance, if California had dreamed about a high-speed rail system 50 years ago, when Japan was actually building one. Imagine if we decided not to dream about it today, now that the cost is approaching $100 billion. Dreaming big is especially exciting when it involves Elon Musk, who has an uncanny knack for actually getting things done. But pragmatism deserves its day too. Otherwise, Hyperloop may be just another project destined to go off the rails.

Los Angeles's Moral Failing
2016

The center cannot hold.

Whereas a Berkeley resident can cross from the exuberance of Telegraph Avenue into the heart of the Cal campus in a few steps, UCLA is an auto-oriented campus surrounded by a moat of driveways, green space, and city streets. Its neighbors are some of the wealthiest and orneriest an institution could ever have the misfortune to live next to. The university, for all its academic heft, retreats from the city, and the city from it.

UCLA was an ironically illustrative venue for a talk by Michael

Storper, lead author of *The Rise and Fall of Urban Economies*, that I attended recently. Contrary to its expansive title, Storper's study concerns only Los Angeles and San Francisco. Given that both are booming Pacific Rim metropolises, it may be hard to figure out which is the "rise" and which is the "fall."

Until you consider this: in 1970, the San Francisco Bay and Los Angeles areas ranked, respectively, numbers four and one in per capita income in the United States. In 2009, after both areas grew by more than 50 percent in population, they were, respectively, numbers one and twenty-five.

You don't have to have a Ph.D. to wonder: what happened?

***

Some of the reasons for the divergence of Los Angeles and San Francisco, which he defines by their multicounty metro regions, are well known. Los Angeles's aerospace industry crumbled along with the Berlin Wall. Steve Jobs happened to grow up in Cupertino. Et cetera. Hollywood is Los Angeles's superstar, except that it represents only 2.6 percent of the area's economy, compared with tech's 11 percent in the Bay Area, and a hit movie doesn't spin off the returns that a "unicorn" does.

Those factors are just the start. For virtually any given job function, and controlling for all sorts of variables, Storper, who teaches at UCLA's Luskin School of Public Affairs, finds that a worker in the Bay Area makes more money and does more complex work than her counterpart in Los Angeles does. In other words, they're not just making more in the Bay Area. They're making better. This pattern holds for educated and uneducated, immigrants and nonimmigrants, and it trickles down even to unskilled workers.

These are the statistics that back up San Francisco's smugness. Riveting as they are, they describe only the effect but not the cause.

Los Angeles's and the Bay Area's divergence depends largely on what Storper referred to as the "dark matter" of public policy. Lurking behind every data point and every policy are forces like curiosity, relationships, openness, diversity, civic self-image, and values. These factors are often disregarded by shortsighted wonks and bureaucrats not because they're not crucial but because they aren't easily quantified.

Storper argues that people in Los Angeles are lousy collaborators. Scholars in Los Angeles cite one another less often. Patents made in Los Angeles refer less frequently to other L.A.-based innovations. Los Angeles's great research universities—UCLA, USC, and Caltech—are not nearly as entrepreneurial as Stanford, Berkeley, and UCSF. He cites Los Angeles's Amgen as a successful, once-innovative biotech company but says that it's nothing compared to the Bay Area's biotech cluster. And it's all by its lonesome in the suburb of Thousand Oaks—nowhere near a major university.

Storper's analysis indicates that networks of civic leaders in Los Angeles are often mutually ignorant of one another. The Bay Area Council, the region's preeminent civic organization, is three times more "connected" than its closest equivalent in Southern California, the L.A. Area Chamber of Commerce. I know what Storper means. I've been to events at the Chamber, presided over by civic leaders of a certain generation.

Storper said the phrase "new economy" appears in none of Los Angeles's economic development literature in the 1980s. At the same time, San Franciscans were shouting it from the rooftops.

These attitudes are fatal in an era when ideas, and not Fordist production, are the order of the day.

Echoing Enrico Moretti's theories about innovation economies, high-wage jobs generate a multiplier that tends to take care of the workers at the bottom. "If you play to weakness (i.e. poverty) you get a weak economy," Storper said. Interestingly, he said that there's essentially zero good data on the efficacy of any public-sector economic development programs of the last 45 years. He chided Los Angeles's leadership for its obsession with the low-paying logistics industry. A rising tide lifts all boats. Unless the boat is a container ship.

***

If an individual, firm, or government doesn't have the knowledge or the capital to realize their dreams, so be it. But if they fail because they're not open to the wisdom, energy, diversity, ambition, and creativity of other human beings, well, that's something else.

Los Angeles's economic failing is not just a business failing or a policy failing; it is a moral failing.

What else do you call it when 25.7 percent of residents in the biggest county in the richest state in the richest country in the world live in poverty?

Storper didn't say so explicitly, but L.A.'s economic sins arise, in part, from our built environment. The two regions have plenty in common, especially in their outlying counties. But insofar as the center cities set the tone for their regions, the differences are striking. We have dingbats, setbacks, curb cuts, mini-malls, chain stores, McMansions, Pershing Square, streets like freeways, freeways like parking lots, and other elements of our landscape that push Angelenos away from one another.

How can you collaborate with someone when they're in your way, making your drive longer, pouring pollution into your face? How can you feel as optimistic atop an asphalt sheet as you can strolling down a sidewalk lined with Victorians? How can you make friends when you can't walk to a watering hole? Los Angeles is like a party full of beautiful people who have nothing interesting to say to one another.

Atoning for our economic sins must include being a better Los Angeles.

We might not be able to trade Facebook (headquartered in Menlo Park, with 10,000 employees) for Snapchat (headquartered in Venice, with 200 employees). Nor can we trade Google for Disney, or the Transbay Tube for the Sepulveda Pass. But we can emulate some of the Bay Area's urban sensibilities. We can use transit more often. We can build more mixed-use projects. We can embrace public space. We can build to the property line. We can plant trees. We can take advantage of our space rather than squander it. As our city changes, so can its culture.

The great news is that improvement is afoot, with downtown development, new transit, new types of development, and an optimistic corps of young planners. By the time Los Angeles comes into its own, today's tech titans might be old news, just as Northrup

Grumman and McDonnell Douglas are today. Something will have to replace them, and maybe they'll reside in Los Angeles. We just need to give them a better home.

UCLA being what it is, many people who should have attended Storper's talk—captains of industry, thought leaders, and everyday citizens interested in Los Angeles's prosperity—are the ones who are least likely to actually have made the trip. Storper was preaching to a choir, consisting mostly of fellow academics and urban nerds.

***

After the talk there was a reception: hors d'oeuvres, wine, the usual. It provided a chance to do some of that mixing and mingling that eludes us in Los Angeles.

I would have loved to stay. Maybe I'd have developed new ideas or made new connections. But I had to go. My meter was running out.

7 Developer-in-Chief
A different kind of "urban" president

The saddest thing about the presidency of Donald Trump is that, prior to his election, so many things were going so well. Not everything, of course. We still had the Syria crisis, the gun epidemic, Justin Bieber, climate change, and plenty of corruption and nonsense on both sides of the aisle and at every level of government. But let's give cities due credit. Cities across the country, and especially in California, have embraced principles of inclusion, equity, sustainability, and resilience—all amidst phenomenal economic prosperity. Policymaking takes time, and many of those policies that have been implemented so far have not borne fruit yet. But the mood is upbeat, and many policies hold promise. Many Americans are trying to bend the arc of history in the right direction.

California, for instance, adopted its first major policy to curb climate change in 2008, with several important follow-ups. They have the distinct co-benefits of encouraging more compact development and spawning further policies to promote social equity. As USC Professor Manuel Pastor wrote in his recent book *State of Resistance*, California went from being a fairly conservative state as recently as 2003 (the year Democratic Governor Gray Davis was deposed in a recall election won by Republican Arnold Schwarzenegger) to the most proudly and consistently liberal justification this side of the Atlantic Ocean. One recent success: California recently announced that per capita carbon emissions in 2016 were lower than they were in 1990.

And yet, every day since November 2016, we have labored under the putrefaction of Donald Trump and his corrupt, mean-spirited, destructive administration. I confess, I sometimes lose hope. I wonder whether all the planners, mayors, and activists trying to make California (and elsewhere) greener, cleaner, more resilient, less polluting, are wasting their time. Other times, I tell myself that the Trump administration can do only so much and that it's going to last only so long.

(The pieces in this chapter span the years 2010 to 2018. Things have gotten worse since then.)

While Trump doesn't have much of an urban policy to speak of, one of the many ironies surrounding him is that he is an urban creature—a real estate developer, no less. I believe developers can, sometimes, do great things for cities (and have written as such). Yet Trump shows no love for cities beyond their capacities to enrich him and serve as political punching bags. In this chapter, I do my best to punch back.

Deconstructing a Tea Party Muse
2010

Atlas, doing his thing.

For some lucky candidates, the November 2010 election will have a storybook ending. Unluckily for anyone who understands architecture, planning, and land use, the book will, in many cases, turn out to be *The Fountainhead*.

The train wreck of ideologies that is emerging this election season is too ghastly for anyone to categorize. Nevertheless, among the Tea Party candidates, emboldened Republicans, and indefatigable

Libertarians, at least a few of the winners will ascribe to the ersatz-rational, individualistic proclivities of Ayn Rand.

The debate over the value of socialism versus unfettered capitalism is a legitimate one for both the statehouse and the dining room. But Rand's fetishizing of rationality and individual autonomy is no basis for public policy—most obviously because her seminal document, *The Fountainhead*, is neither rational nor objective but is, in fact, pure fantasy. It's a fantasy that strikes at the heart of land-use planning.

Rand's central argument, as embodied by the architect Howard Roark, is that mere mortals should never stand in the way of genius. If political and economic structures would just allow genius to rise to the top (by commissioning Roark or, say, electing Rand Paul), then the world would be better off. It's ironic, though, that she illustrates genius by way of architecture.

Rand would have us believe that Roark's creations overtop those of Wright, Gehry, Meis, and Wren all at once. His soaring edifices delight both tenant and passerby, making bold statements where they meet the ground, where they meet the sky, and through every inch in between. They are sited perfectly, so the rays of the sun will bathe tenants in golden light. Inside their walls, men stand taller and women discover deeper levels of allure. So brilliant are Roark's masterpieces that they cause enlightened financiers to unlock their vaults to ensure their construction and so ennobling that planning commissions invite Roark to rewrite zoning codes. Their lines, materials, proportions, and finishes are perfect. Once built, they stand forever.

Close your eyes. Just picture it. It's breathtaking, isn't it?

Now open your eyes. You're not looking at a building. You're not looking at an aesthetic masterpiece or an aesthetic feat. You're looking at words.

When I read *The Fountainhead* years ago, I too was inspired. For about a week. In that week I felt the same way that many free-market enthusiasts must feel every day as they crusade against tyranny (as if 99 percent of Americans don't support the free market in the first place). But if you wave your hands in front of you and realize that

Rand's images are only air—that they pertain to no city that any planner would recognize—then you can start thinking about serious matters again.

As an entertainer, Rand uses fantasy as it should be used. She replaces the real world with something more appealing, where the usual rules are no longer in play. And yet, in accepting *The Fountainhead* as an actual economic allegory, Rand and her followers fall into a circular argument, using both premises and conclusions that are fictional. The lynchpin in her philosophy is that Roark is a genius, and she "writes" a building to illustrate that genius. The need to realize Roark's artistic vision thus justifies the demolition of the regulations and other obstructions that gum up the free market. To demonstrate the supposed folly of abiding by the common good, Rand picked the worst possible example.

What *The Fountainhead* offers in lieu of argumentation is simply an empty assertion—a demand that we suspend disbelief while coaxing ourselves into wonderment. It is not an analysis of reality, with all of its nuances, but rather an escape from reality. When your building is fake, you don't have to worry about whether it casts a shadow or whether the roof leaks. You don't have to worry that maybe it's so butt-ugly that it diminishes the value of neighboring properties, which might be owned by other Americans just as honest and freedom-loving as Roark is. Moreover, the most common criticism levied at Rand is that her characters are just as two-dimensional as her buildings are. So, in one fell swoop, we have unreal people operating in an unreal world.

Voting for a political candidate according to what Ayn Rand says would be like drafting Roy Hobbs for your baseball team.

(It's worth noting that *Atlas Shrugged* relies on a similar feat of *deus ex machina*: that of a magic metal and limitless energy. Rand would have us believe that these inventions were foiled by corruption, human frailty, and overregulation of markets. But the real reason is much simpler: they don't exist.)

The Fountainhead preys on readers who haven't given much thought to economics—and even less to architecture. Any planner or architect surely appreciates that no matter how astounding Roark's buildings may be on paper, Rand chooses to illustrate the value of individualism via the one arena of human endeavor that, by definition, must heed the collective. In the real world any alteration of the built environment necessarily invites an infinite array of opinions and externalities. Rand fails to understand that Americans can disagree on matters of taste as much as they can on matters of economics.

For instance, we can disagree on whether Rand's own writing exhibits the slightest bit of artistry. Given her stiff characters, contrived, unrealistic plots, and awkward mixing of literalism and fantasy, her own books provide insufficient support for her claims about the nature of genius. In other words, just as a lone egomaniacal architect who is plenty capable of designing a crappy building, so is a lone, egomaniacal author plenty capable of writing a crappy book. Hollering about the triumph of the individual doesn't make the building, or the book, any less crappy.

The self-aggrandizing modernist Le Corbusier was probably just as eccentric as Rand, but at least he had the guts to put something in the ground and see if it would work. Thank goodness Jane Jacobs and her compatriots came along to explain why it didn't. I suspect that Ayn Rand would have hated Jane Jacobs. Rather than create something unreal and irrelevant, Jacobs described the world as she actually saw it.

I almost can't believe I'm writing this, because it all seems so obvious. And yet Election Day approaches on a freight train hewn in part by Rand, with Tea Partiers shoveling the coal. Comical though they may be these days, elections still form the foundation of civil society. But in too many ways the hyperbolic, inspirational abstractions of Rand's fantasy world seep into real-world discourse. Anyone who seeks answers in Rand's stories forgets, however, that fiction is best when posing questions and not being so presumptuous as to try to supply answers.

That's why we still ask whether we ought "to be, or not to be." And it's why, in the voting booth, we should finally stop asking, "Who is John Galt?"

Trump to Cities: You're Already Dead
2016

The Republican campaign went back in time last week. Not to the 1950s Red Scare, to the 1844 Nativist Riots, or to the Great Awakening of the 1740s—though it had elements of all of those. It went back to the 1970s. And it went back to a specific place: the Bronx.

It was in the decade of disco that the Bronx descended into one of the worst epidemics of violence and urban decay that the United States has ever seen. It was the culmination of white flight, corporate flight, disinvestment, racist lending practices, overzealous policing, drug criminalization, poor education, lead poisoning, and many other negligences and offenses that left the borough in ashes and left so many other cities in similar states of decay.

At the same moment that the Bronx was burning, a borough and a world away, a young Donald Trump was plotting his first business deals. His father was reportedly evicting African Americans from his properties in Queens.

In 1975, Gerald Ford proverbially told New York City to drop dead. After four decades of progress, Donald Trump tried to bury it again.

In his acceptance speech at the Republication National Convention, Trump cited a litany of urban horrors that have supposedly festered in the past eight years under an, ahem, urban president:

- "Violence in our streets and the chaos in our communities"
- "Crime, terrorism, and lawlessness that threatens our communities"
- "Homicides last year increased by 17 percent in America's 50 largest cities. That's the largest increase in 25 years."
- "In our nation's capital, killings have risen by 50 percent. They are up nearly 60 percent in nearby Baltimore."
- "In the president's hometown of Chicago, more than 2,000 have been the victims of shootings this year alone. And almost 4,000 have been killed in the Chicago area since he took office."
- "Our roads and bridges are falling apart, our airports are in third-world condition."

Claims and statistics like these are rightfully chilling. Every violent crime that takes place on America's streets affronts our culture and our national spirit. One murder in Chicago, Baltimore, or anywhere else, is one murder too many. Especially when it's committed by a police officer against an innocent citizen. Especially when it's committed by a citizen against an innocent police officer. Especially when it's committed with weapons that should never have been on the streets in the first place.

And yet, for the all the intimate horrors of individual crimes, Trump's carefully chosen statistics—not necessarily false, but certainly incomplete—belie the astonishing progress that America's cities have made.

Justice department data indicate that "the U.S. homicide rate declined by nearly half (49%), from 9.3 homicides per 100,000 U.S. residents in 1992 to 4.7 in 2011, falling to the lowest level since 1963." That trend continued through 2014, meaning that the 17 percent increase that Trump cites is minuscule, in absolute numbers, compared to the averages that prevailed decades ago.

Four-hundred-eighty-eight people were killed in Chicago in 2015. You'd have to go back to the Kennedy administration to find a year with significantly fewer murders (granted, Chicago's population was greater in the 1960s than it is today). In 1983, the year the Trump Tower was completed, New York City had 1,622 homicides. In 2015: 352. That's a triumph by any measure. Surely someone deserves credit for it?

In short: violent crime in America has dropped—steadily and dramatically—for Donald Trump's entire adult life and particularly in the city that he calls home.

He and every other American politician has good reason, of course, to point to dramatic, tragic examples like Orlando, San Bernardino, and Dallas. But they represent a different kind of danger, demanding different kinds of responses, than the broad criminal trends that Trump attempts to cite.

And that refrain about "law and order." When you think of "law and order," you don't think of suburbs or Main Street. You think of the inner city. You think of batons and water cannons and curfews to mute the unruly. You think of militaristic posturing that can be scarier to city residents than crime itself.

Trump can get away with these distortions because he's not trying to appeal to urbanites in the first place. He's not standing in solidarity with the good citizens of Chicago, New York, and Baltimore. Bafflingly, his electorate has made its disdain for "New York elitism" well known. He's creating an image of inner cities that enables the citizens (good and bad) of suburbia and the rural heartland to believe in their own worst visions of the city. These visions may have been semilegitimate reasons for middle class families to flee cities in the 1960s and 1970s. Today, they are fabrications meant only to support their lifestyle choice at the expense of all things bustling and cosmopolitan.

In other words, Trump wants the threat of urban violence to motivate voters who have the least to fear from it.

This would all be typical right-wing pandering were it not so ironic.

The Urban Mystique

Donald Trump is a proud, lifelong resident of New York City. He made his fortune there. He pins his identity to it. He has contributed to it, and he has literally put his name on its skyline—multiple times. He embodies New York elitism—perhaps more so than any New Yorker before or since. Whether the Bronx rioters' crimes will prove greater than Trump's own theft and looting of his fellow New Yorkers will be for history to judge.

Of course, Trump knows what he's doing. If you want to make a fortune, raise your standard of living, enjoy diversity, and rub elbows with humanity—sometimes for worse, but overwhelmingly for better—there is no better place to go than New York City. And if you want to drive a national economy, there is no better engine than New York City.

The metropolitan area's GDP is north of $1.5 trillion, making it the second-wealthiest urban area in the world, after Tokyo. (Los Angeles is a distant third, at $866 billion.) It's six percent of the U.S. population but eight percent of the country's GDP. That doesn't count the economic activity spun off from activities in New York City with benefits realized elsewhere. These are the forces that make the Trump Tower worth many times more than it was when it was completed in 1983.

Indeed, one thing that would make his—and all other urban properties—more valuable would be, as Trump's speech notes, the repair of America's infrastructure. That's a multitrillion-dollar project that the (Republican-led) Congress has scarcely touched and that the current Republican platform neglects yet again.

Of course, none of this is surprising. Despite the need for a coherent, positive urban policy, the federal government, regardless of party leadership, has neglected cities for a great long while. Cities have been dead to the Republican Party for a long time. Trump's rhetoric only makes them—and their inhabitants—seem more forbidding than ever.

And yet, America's cities persevere. Imagine how great they would be if, after weathering so many years of neglect, derision, crime, and, yes, disco, they got the respect, and the national leaders, they deserve.

How California Helped Elect Trump
2017

I haven't had the pleasure of interviewing a president-elect, nor do I ever expect to, unless California actually secedes and I made a trip to the national capital of Sacramento. But I recently spoke with someone who has discussed land use with him.

Paul Petrovich is the developer who is suing the City of Sacramento over what he claims is an improper denial of a conditional use permit for proposed gas pumps at his entitled Curtis Park Village. National politics didn't play directly into what is a hyperlocal story filled with some nasty rivalries. But in my interview with him, Petrovich took a moment to muse on national affairs.

As a self-described fiscal conservative, Petrovich said that he was on Trump's dance card when he visited Sacramento in June. Petrovich shared with Trump a story that California's developers,

Democrat and Republican alike, know all too well: it has taken him the better part of 15 years to pour concrete at Curtis Park Village (notwithstanding his own lawsuit). In that time, he said he held over 200 neighborhood meetings and adapted his project in countless ways to satisfy neighbors. He did so in part to insulate himself against CEQA lawsuits that they surely would have filed had he failed to cross a "t" or dot an "i."

Granted, it's a large project: 72 acres, hundreds of residences, a large retail component, and remediation of a toxic brownfield. It demands careful environmental review. But still, Petrovich's point was that regulations—CEQA included—and community opposition have been egregious.

Not surprisingly, Trump, himself a developer, sympathized with Petrovich's plight. In fact, Trump was "blown away," according to Petrovich. Petrovich said that Trump has cited, with full Trumpian incredulity, a situation like his in interviews, referring to developers who have to wait 10-plus years to win approvals and land clear of the courts.

Petrovich acknowledged that his is hardly the only tale of regulatory woe. And that's the point: stories like his gave Trump, and other conservatives, plenty of material for antiregulation tirades. So, like any number of the microscopic regulations and esoteric court decisions that, collectively, make CEQA a regulatory enormity, it piled on to all the factors, large and small, that inspired Trump voters.

CEQA was not explicitly designed to be an obstructionist law. It was designed to uphold environmental quality, a worthy goal if ever there was one. But there's no doubt that it has, collectively, added eons to the pace of development in California, sometimes with dubious, or nonexistent, benefits to the environment. Pouring molasses on the highway are neighborhood groups—such as Petrovich's nemeses, Councilmember Jay Schenirer and the Sierra Curtis Neighborhood Association—that send plans back to the drawing board, and indeed, file suit even after entitlements are granted.

Many of these groups and many other fans of CEQA are genuine environmentalists. Often their efforts do lead to greener projects, but, with adversarial attitudes toward (and from) developers, they lead to delayed projects. Collectively, these obstructionist tendencies add a supertanker's worth of fuel to the antiregulation fire.

While NIMBYs were tittering about LULUs, the "drill baby drill" crowd was marshaling its forces. The result: President Trump. Secretary of State Tillerson. Energy Secretary Perry.

Now the country's environmentalists are facing what may be the most antienvironment administration since God created the Earth. Whatever localized gains California's environmentalist groups and concerned neighborhood groups have made via CEQA are likely to be undone, and then some, by the policies and projects that Trump will promote.

Petrovich may yet get his gas pumps. And with a pro-petroleum, pro-coal climate change denier in the White House, America may yet burn.

Trump Trades on Geographic Illiteracy
2017

On the first day of my first year teaching Advanced Placement Human Geography at the Archer School for Girls, I naturally started with a map.

I put up a transparency on the overhead projector. It was September 2001. Smart boards and tablets, like African American presidents and women presidential candidates, were many years away.

The most famous map in the country at the time was the electoral map from the previous November. It displayed red and blue jurisdictions not at the crude level of states, with Florida jutting out like a big "screw you" to democracy, but rather at the finer, more fascinating level of counties.

I asked my students to tell me what they saw.

I asked them to consider how counties related to states. I had them inspect the tiny counties of the east coast. Many of them were designed so that county seats were a day's mule ride from any point in the county. Their crooked lines follow organic contours of rivers, hills, and human imprecision. I had my students marvel at the megacounties of the West, with straight lines driving through uninhabited desert and over indifferent mountain ranges.

I told them to look at the red and at the blue. Who were those people? What were those places like? Why did they vote for whomever they voted for? Were they like us? Were they different? How red were they? How blue were they? What did they want? What did *we* want?

That was the map that inspired "One Nation, Slightly Divisible," the *Atlantic Monthly* article that vaulted David Brooks to the big leagues of punditry and made the idea of "Red" and "Blue" Americas the defining idea of national politics. It included the resounding observation, "Everything that Red America does with a motor, Blue America does without a motor." If only that adverb in his headline still applied.

David Brooks had to tell us about the Red and Blue Americas because we did not already know about them. We had been living among each other and yet were unaware of each other, each hiding from the other in plain sight.

And thus, I introduced my students to geography's fundamental axioms: people are different in different places; there are reasons why they are different; those differences have consequences. The next week—the second week of September 2001—we found out just how momentous those consequences can be. This November, we found out again.

We learned a lot that year in AP Geography. I know that not because I'm making assumptions about my students but because I'm stating a fact about myself. I learned a lot that year.

Here's some of what we learned:
- Globalization celebrates the efficiencies of comparative advantage.
- Capitalism, consumerism, and pop culture can obliterate local traditions.
- Cities buy raw materials from their hinterlands and hinterlands

acquire specialty goods and services from cities.
- Most immigrants move for economic opportunity.
- Patriotism means love of country; nationalism means thinking your country is better than others.
- Centripetal and centrifugal forces are always at work in a country.
- The majority of a developed country's wealth comes from services, not industry.
- The geographical advantages of old-style industries have given way in light of communications and transportation technologies.
- The American Dream of suburbia is as much a product of policy as it is of preference.
- The majority of America's economic activity takes place in cities.
- Climate change will wreak havoc and redraw borders.
- A nation and a state are not the same thing.
- De jure boundaries can never fully reflect de facto regions.
- Boundaries can be manipulated for political gain.
- Our notion of a "country" does not begin to express the relationships, or lack thereof, between ethnicity, religion, languages, sovereignty, and statehood.
- Healthy ecosystems are economic assets.
- Racism, ethnic tension, ethnic cleansing, and genocide persist before our very eyes.
- The world is a very, very complex place.

I dare anyone to say that these topics are not fascinating and vital.

The subtitle I assigned to my class was "The Global Condition." I named it so to emphasize the course's natural focus on current events. Amazingly, my class was the only class at the school that explicitly focused on current events. More amazingly, it's one of the only courses in all of high school that focuses on current events.

Even the most accomplished American high school student can graduate knowing more about criminal justice in Puritan New England than about the actual injustices going on every day in the United States. Students can learn every step of the process of photosynthesis and yet have never heard of the Kyoto Accords. They can know how nuclear fission works, and yet they don't know which countries have nuclear weapons and don't understand the (perverse) logic of mutually assured destruction. They know the Five Pillars of Islam but don't know what modern-day country Mecca is in.

My school committed an act of bravery in offering AP Geography. Back then, it was a brand-new AP course with scanty enrollment nationwide. AP Geography has gained popularity today, but it's still a fringe topic, sometimes offered as a throwaway AP to students as young as freshman. I'd wager that my school was the only school in the county in which a majority of seniors took it. Many schools try to fit it and its account of the entire world into a single semester.

In short, the typical high school curriculum renders Americans geographically illiterate. That's partly because our three million square miles of continent mean that we don't have to care about geography. By contrast, it's a core subject in many European countries, both in high school and at the university level.

Our ignorance about the world and about one another has finally taken its toll in the unlikely form of Donald Trump. Trump represents the most simplistic answers to the questions that we explored in geography, and he preys on the unfamiliarity—and indeed, mistrust—that divides Red places from Blue.

I do not claim that AP Geography, or any other course, can cure all that ails America—or that geographic knowledge would have, or should have, dissuaded Americans from voting for him. We should have been learning it to address the very real challenges that concern him and his voters. The study of geography takes seriously the very issues that most vex our nation, regardless of who is president.

Back in 2001, if I mentioned Donald Trump at all, he'd have been in the chapter on urban development. (Why do people build skyscrapers? Usually to maximize the use of land that is expensive by virtue of its centrality. Sometimes to inflate one's ego.) From today onward, he'll be in every history textbook. They're probably rewriting them as we speak.

As for that map? It looks much the same today as it did under that big harvest moon. The colors just run deeper.

Calexit in Reverse
2016

You can check in any time you like, but you can never find a room.

A New Yorker, one whose favorite pastime was building skyscrapers before he turned to statecraft, has bewilderingly captured the hearts of the American suburbs, exurbs, and small towns. Yes, this election hinged on race. But it also hinged on geography. While traffic of all sorts—foot, pedal, taxi, subway—rumbles along below the window of his penthouse, the nation's wide-open spaces and moribund towns cheer for the change they have wrought.

And what of California? What of mid-rise urbanism, midrange density, the blue ocean, and the 900 miles of blue coastline against which it crashes? What of the 60 percent of us who envisioned a different four years?

A California secession movement arose within hours of Trump's victory. It even has a cute, hashtaggable name: Calexit. As much as this prospect may appeal, we all know it's an emotional salve and not a solution. If I knew how to navigate the Constitution well enough to permit secession, there are probably a few other changes I'd make first. A certain Electoral College system comes to mind.

A far more powerful and far more realistic option occurs to me. We should not leave the United States. We should do what we have always done: invite the United States to come to us.

Donald Trump's election reveals that a long-developing trend has now become an axiom: the "sorting" of Americans is essentially complete. America's open interstate borders have enabled like-minded citizens to group together in places of their choosing. Broadly speaking, liberals have moved to cities and coastal states while conservatives have remained in the heartland—effectively gobbling up electoral votes (and House districts) in the process. Structurally, "sorting" gave us the discrepancy between Trump's electoral victory and Clinton's popular victory. Culturally, it leads to the gross misunderstandings between so-called Red and Blue America.

One strategy for a Democratic resurgence is for Blue voters to move to swing states. It's a clever idea for the adventurous. Anyone who wants to wave the flag of progressivism in Columbus, Durham, or Des Moines has my respect. But I don't think anyone should have to uproot themselves for the sake of a political strategy in a free country. And it doesn't solve the clear and present discomfort, disenfranchisement, and, possibly, danger that many Blue voters now feel.

If Donald Trump threatens to pull the nation back into the past, I suggest that California remains—as ever—its future.

The vast majority of my 40 million neighbors are diverse, embracing, industrious, and progressive. (Some of them are undocumented—so what?) As is often cited, California has assets most countries—possibly all countries—can only dream of, foremost being its $2.5 trillion economy. While the presidential campaign lamented the demise of old-school factory jobs in the Midwest, California has developed companies that make 20th century steel concerns look like lemonade stands. California grows artichokes like Iowa grows corn.

From Apple, Google, and Tesla on down, California's future seems pretty secure. (Though, terrifyingly, Trump's victory could undercut the tech industry, which is the economic triumph of our time.) I happen to think that Hyperloop is silly, but if it takes off, I'll be the first one to cheer. We have media, science, medicine, finance, and yes, good old-fashioned manufacturing. What's the country's No. 1 manufacturing county? Oh yeah, it's Los Angeles.

Nobody "took" America. It's been right here all along. And there is no superlative that can fully describe California's opportunities to whoever wants to enjoy this version of the American Dream.

We have the wealth and the economic might. We have the human resources. We have the commercial infrastructure. We have the food and the landscape. We have the ports and the airports. We have global clout. We have some of the finest universities in the world. We have a political class that is not perfect but knows how to make incremental strides. We have the best kind of diversity.

We have all of this and more. Except for two complications.

First, California cannot currently house all the people it has. Residents and businesses alike are paying exorbitant rents, especially in coastal cities. Rents eat into our economic power, limit companies' hiring options, decimate local multiplier effects, and essentially pit neighbor against neighbor in the search for shelter.

Second, California has traffic.

Fortunately, while the rest of the nation was electing Donald Trump, Californians took strides—some small, some large—to address at least one of these problems. In local elections, Los Angeles County passed Measure M, which, at $120 billion, is probably the largest transportation funding package in the history of the free world. The Bay Area voted for sorely needed funds for BART. Sacramento's transportation measure failed, and so did San Diego's. It's worth noting, though, that all of these measures required two-thirds majorities. They will be reconfigured and they will find their voters (as Los Angeles did after the 2012 defeat of Measure R).

As for housing, that's where California's planners come in. The cause of smart infill development—replete with all the urban amenities and efficiencies that should accompany it—is possibly the only thing that lies between California and its full potential. On that front, the votes of November 2016 were mixed. Santa Monica rejected the restrictive Measure LV, and affordable housing measures passed throughout the Bay Area. And yet many cities adopted or strengthened urban growth boundaries—without necessarily embracing the infill development to go along with it. Whatever voters say in a given election, planners need to keep fighting for the cause of density. And they need to promote their work. If nothing else, that is the lesson they can learn from Donald Trump.

And what of the environmental impact of more Californians and the development to contain them? Well, urban living is inherently more efficient than its alternatives. And we have regulations. Senate Bill 375 in particular directs us to build in such a way that we reduce the state's per capita carbon footprint. CEQA does some good and might yet do more if it's ever reformed. That still leaves the problem of water. Even then, dense infill development consumes less water per capita than old suburban development does.

The day before November 8, 2016, these efforts were just commonsense policies for a vibrant, progressive state. The day after, for everyone out there who seeks the embrace and promise of California, they became morally imperative.

I suspect that the new regime in Washington is not going to make things easy on us. Trump willfully mischaracterized cities (including his own) in the campaign, demonizing them to rural and Rust Belt crowds. And, as *CP&DR* Publisher Bill Fulton notes, Trump will surely betray cities as often as he can with the powers of his office. That's OK. We just have to work harder, accept the occasional sacrifice, and love one another a little bit more.

So, let's not break away from America. Let's make sure California remains the best of America.

Trump Raises Stakes for Urban Journalism
2017

The best bathroom graffiti I encountered while attending the Lincoln Institute of Land Policy's annual Journalists Forum in April 2017 in Cambridge, Massachusetts, was "Donald Trump listens to Nickelback." Sick burn, right?

Plenty of journalists and commentators, myself included, have expressed similar, if less concise sentiments as we have speculated on the fate of cities under the Trump administration. The speculation continued at this weekend's journalists' forum, where colleagues and I discussed the heady theme of "Cities and Equity in the Era of the Trump Presidency."

All indications, from Trump's anti-elite campaign rhetoric to his rural voter base to his bizarre choice of Dr. Ben Carson as HUD secretary, suggest that cities stand to suffer. They'll suffer from both unfriendly policies and stingy funding, of everything from housing to infrastructure to the arts. Cities' best hope lies in the administration's general incompetence and Carson's odd brand of cluelessness.

I think we're all tired of making predictions, though. The Trump administration has set up shop and has had plenty of time to formulate its urban policy, however distressing it may be, right?

This was the promise—however optimistic—of the 2017 edition of the forum. It's an essential topic, of course. The country's 100 largest metropolitan areas may dominate the country demographically, and they may generate the vast majority of the country's wealth, innovation, and culture—accounting for 75 percent of GDP—but they are still tied, for better or worse, to Washington, D.C.

In the course of two days and nearly a dozen sessions—which included everyone from obscure policy wonks to big names like scholar Richard Florida, former Philadelphia mayor Michael Nutter, and—ahem—Carson's predecessor, Julian Castro, not a single representative of, surrogate for or even defender of the Trump administration took to the podium.

Both in sessions and in conversation with me, forum organizer Anthony Flint advised that he and his staff took great pains to invite speakers from the Trump administration. Clearly exasperated, Flint referred to emails, phone calls, and everything short of bribery to get someone authoritative to show up. No dice. We thus ended up with the sort of disclaimer that every journalist knows well, "So-and-so did not respond to repeated requests to comment for this story."

Come to think of it, though, maybe Jared Kushner didn't mean to show up in Iraq looking like a misplaced preppy idiot who confused the firing range for the driving range. Maybe he was supposed to speak to us, where, as a Harvard grad, he'd merely be a preppy idiot. (My own most memorable experience with shy sources was, not coincidentally, an article involving the Tea Party a few years back.)

Had the conference taken place in Washington—as it did in 2016, a mere two blocks from Trump's (occasional) residence—maybe we could have taken a field trip, all donning trench coats and fedoras, to do a stakeout in the bushes in front of Carson's house. Indeed,

Cambridge is probably the last place that a Trump supporter would want to be found.

That goes for speakers and audience members alike.

It turns out that Cambridge isn't so unlike Phoenix, Cleveland, El Paso, Des Moines, or San Diego—to name a few of the two dozen or so cities represented at the forum. Demographically and culturally speaking, urbanism-plus-journalism-plus-Cambridge is a recipe for a room that leans well to the left.

Suffice it to say, Breitbart News did not attend. Though, as was pointed out in one session, alt-right sites like Breitbart and Infowars get more web traffic than do all but the largest daily newspapers. "News" items about Hillary Clinton's prostitution ring probably got more hits than any story any of us have ever written.

We discussed, with abundant anxiety, topics including policies toward sanctuary cities (and the definition thereof); the vaunted $1 trillion infrastructure plan, which may or may not be a Trojan horse for irresponsible privatization; funding for housing programs; support not only for mitigation of climate change but also for adaptation to climate change; and much more.

At every turn, both in official remarks, discussions among panelists, and dinner-table banter, a consistent attitude prevailed. Our collective disdain for Trump was evident and unapologetic. References to the administration's incompetence and incoherence drew chuckles. Dire predictions drew groans. Remarks that sounded like Louis C.K. tweets or quotations from Women's March signs drew outright laughter.

And why shouldn't they? As professionals, we are objective. Many of us in the room—which included full-time land use journalists as well as generalists like real estate reporters and metro beat writers—have covered Trump-related news with the restraint, objectivity, and balance that it deserves. But we're only human. I, for one, am proud of my convictions and proud of my values. I imagine my colleagues are too. If nothing else, even conservative journalists respect the primacy of facts.

It's not that the media is "liberal." We're just thoughtful, probing, and literate. And we're not necessarily pro-urban. It's just that we know firsthand that cities are not cauldrons of crime and carnage. We pay attention to data too.

On the very same day that we were meeting, the *New York Times*' David Brooks wrote, "Trump's greatest achievements are in the field of ignorance .... Trump's ignorance is not just an absence; it is a rich, intricate and entirely separate universe of negative information, a sort of fertile intellectual antimatter with its own gravitational pull." This from someone who casts himself as a professional centrist.

I'm also proud to live in a progressive, urban area (Los Angeles). I reject the derisive, self-flagellating term "bubble." Sure, cities may geographically seem like they are floating in oceans of sincere folksiness. But I'd hardly consider a city with 100 native languages, nonstop flights to 155 destinations, economic ties to probably half the world's free countries, and ready embrace of pretty much every idea and culture you can imagine to be a "bubble." I mean, we're not the ones who want to build a wall.

And yet, I want to have that discussion. As I said during one session, I felt deeply conflicted about being in such a politically homogenous group. I want to hear from thoughtful Trump supporters—at least from those who respect the basic premises of journalism—to feel their concerns. I want to understand—if not endorse—the policy solutions that they favor. I want to know what a Trump supporter understands, and misunderstands, about cities. I want to see what a discussion across ideologies and party lines can sound like.

I also want to discover opportunities for compromise and common ground. I know some of my friends will cringe at that. But again, I'm talking about policy, not personality or ideology. Bear in mind, many, if not all, of the concerns of Trump supporters existed long before Trump anointed himself as their savior.

Barring this bipartisan meeting of the minds, many of us concluded that we need to keep doing what we're doing. In many ways, local urban issues and, therefore, local urban coverage will be more important than ever. We may not be able to institute enlightened immigration policies or create incentives for renewable energy, but we can, through objective coverage and thoughtful commentary, exhort and encourage cities to maintain their cultural, economic, and moral leadership. As ever, local issues affect Americans most directly, and so far, local leaders haven't lost their minds. Good journalists and good readers can help keep it that way.

The moral of the story is that we journalists must be vigilant and our cities must assert their own powers, make their own plans, and stick together. If we're lucky, the Donald will turn up the Nickelback and leave cities alone.

California's Nastiest Urban-Rural Rivalry
2017

What doesn't end up in the ocean ends up in Kern County.

While President-elect Donald Trump ignited culture wars across the land in the days following his election, a new development arose in an old story that I thought had been dead and, well, buried a long time ago.

Needless to say, the City of Los Angeles generates its fair share of sewage. I don't think any of us want to imagine just how much that is. The people who least want to imagine it are the folks of Kern County. That's where, for many years, the Los Angeles Department of Sanitation has shipped treated "biosolids" from its Hyperion Sewage Treatment Plant. The department owns a euphemistically named Green Acres Farms, where it puts 450,000 annual tons of waste to use as fertilizer.

In 2006 some of those Kern folks decided that these shipments were both insulting and unhealthy. They launched a countywide voter initiative to ban the shipments. The campaign used slogans such as "Measure E will stop L.A. from dumping on Kern," and "We got the bully next door flinging garbage over his fence into our yard." Sensationalist headlines have read, "L.A. Dumps 500 Tons of Human Excrement on to Kern County Daily"—as if every day a monsoon of sewage rains down on the entire county.

The ban passed.

Meanwhile, Los Angeles kept on flushing and kept on trucking. The city filed lawsuits to oppose the ban and was allowed to maintain its practice. In December 2016, a Superior Court judge struck down the ban, possibly for good. We'll see whether the antisludge forces turn up their noses yet again or whether they learn to live with indignity.

(A similar protest has arisen over the arrival of high-speed rail. Whereas Fresno has largely embraced the train, Bakersfield is ground zero for protests over eminent domain takings. Some aren't even sure that they want a station.)

This spat has long fascinated me. It is possibly the most petty example of intrastate rivalry in California, and certainly the most pungent. It's a rivalry that's become even more poignant in the wake of Donald Trump's presidential victory, which put the nationwide divide between urban and rural areas on full display.

As the Trump vote suggests, rural areas often revile urban areas just as much as urban areas ignore rural areas. The implication is that cities somehow exploit rural areas and that rural areas are irrelevant to cities. Of course, neither case is true—but rivalries are not always rational. Kern County voters took personal offense. Los Angeles became a menacing invader that literally craps on rural folk. Unfortunately, these stereotypes belie the benefits that both places derive from each other.

Whereas the antisludge campaign implied that every Kern resident lives within a whiff of Los Angeles's shipments, that's not exactly the case. Kern County is 8,100 square miles. It's one of the biggest counties in the country. Green Acres Farm covers 4,600 acres, in a nondescript quadrant between Taft, Buttonwillow, Mettler, and Bakersfield.

It's the sanitation equivalent of "The Princess and the Pea."

There's no reason why the average resident of Kern County would be any more aware of Green Acres than the average Los Angeles resident is of Hyperion Water Reclamation Plant.

In reality, there's no reason to think that Los Angeles's trash isn't Kern County's treasure. All that manure isn't going to tend to itself.

In fact, nasty as it sounds, Green Acres is an apt symbol of the symbiosis between rural and urban areas. For every bale of cotton, head of lettuce, and handful of almonds that comes out of the Kern soil, there's someone in Los Angeles ready to buy it at Whole Foods. Solid waste is part of the cycle of life. Farming itself is hardly a pristine industry.

And indeed, the relationship between the counties is much more complex than trees and turds. Los Angeles has, by some measure, been sending entire people to Kern County for decades. Places like Bakersfield, which have always been skeptical of dense urbanism (and, incidentally, supportive of property rights), have become bedroom communities for places like Los Angeles, thanks in part to planning regulations that push development out farther and farther from center cities (that trend is even more acute in communities like Tracy, farther up the Central Valley).

Kern farmers probably don't like competition for their land, but surely everyone else—from the shopkeepers to county supervisors—is glad to have more residents. In other words, the age-old exchange of material goods for cold, hard cash persists. The odd reversal of Green Acres Farm is but an anomaly in an otherwise healthy, vigorous economy. The lawsuit suggests that the only thing unhealthy is the relationship between places and the images that we have of one another.

And in case sewage sludge still makes you cringe, don't forget that Kern County exports to willing consumers in Los Angeles, and elsewhere, something far more disgusting than human waste: oil.

A Missed Lesson in the Heart of California
2017

When urban and rural areas don't communicate, everyone loses.

Many years ago, I rode on a team bus through the agricultural heart of California. Up far too late for a school night, we didn't get on the road until past 10 p.m. and weren't getting back to Los Angeles before 2 a.m.

Strange things happen when you qualify for the California state volleyball playoffs. In California, athletic regions are larger than most states. I was an assistant coach at my alma mater. I didn't have to attend the match, but I enjoy a good road trip.

We took State Route 145 southbound, an empty two-lane highway through cotton fields and almond groves, to get to I-5. Amid the dark and quiet—the kind of quiet that you hear only after a team's season has ended—one of our more whimsical players bolted upright and asked of the entire bus, "Is that the real moon?"

She can be forgiven for her incredulity. The moon rising ahead of us that November night was a reddish freak of refraction known only to the flattest of landscapes. It looked little like the modest disk she'd seen over west Los Angeles a million times before. As far as the players and I were concerned, we were traveling through a foreign land—California's own version of flyover country. For all we knew, maybe it did have its own moon.

Back then, Donald Trump was just an inflated real estate developer. The town of Kerman probably would have voted for him. A typical farm town of 8,500 at the time, 20 miles west of Fresno, Kerman floats amid the politically red ocean surrounding America's archipelago of blue. It is precisely the type of place in which urbane city-dwellers are unfamiliar, just as cities are unfamiliar to many people in places like Kerman.

For all of Kerman's Red State trappings, the facts suggest that politically we were, if not in friendly territory, at least in territory that wasn't hostile. In 2000, 53 percent of Fresno County favored George W. Bush over Al Gore. In the 2016 election, Fresno County favored Hillary Clinton 49 percent to 43 percent. Of the four precincts within Kerman's city limits, only one favored Trump. In neighboring precincts, that number reached 82 percent.

Though Kerman superficially resembles many of the places where Donald Trump dominated—beating Hillary two- and threefold—it was actually one of the few places in California that was relatively evenly split. Kerman teeters on the edge of Red and Blue, making it, paradoxically, an electoral microcosm of the country. And yet, with polarization and geographic sorting, it is near unique among American places.

Kerman's brand of rural America differs from that in places like Oklahoma or Nebraska. As in communities in those states, many jobs—24 percent in Kerman's case—are in agriculture. With a median family income of just over $34,000, it's poor. But it looks different from its heartland America counterparts. One explanation for Kerman's political allegiance with urban America lies in demographics. Today,

Kerman has 13,500 residents and is 71 percent Hispanic, up from 65 percent in 2000. How its volleyball team reflected its demographics, I honestly can't recall.

Until November 9, I hadn't thought about Kerman for a very long time. Come to think of it, Donald Trump probably never paid it, or its thousands of counterparts, much mind either. There's not much of a market for skyscrapers on the prairie. And yet in the course of his campaign, Trump saw his own moonrise the moment he left his tower and met with adoration in the unlikeliest of places. Hillary Clinton didn't figure it out until the moment she lost Michigan.

As I think about the way Trump's America views my America, I can't help but think about what Kerman thought of us or what we thought of Kerman. Some of our players probably didn't think of Kerman at all—it was a team and a gym, and nothing more. Some may have been enchanted by the idea of a small town, so dissimilar from our metropolis. Some may have been less charitable.

And our opponents, the Lions of Kerman High? I hope they didn't think of us at all. If they had, they might have been appalled. My school embodied every private school stereotype: wealthy, worldly, fashionable, probably a little spoiled. The children of what came to be known, soon thereafter, as the 1 percent. The girl so perplexed by the moon? She was the daughter of a celebrity, a rock star known in part for Vietnam-era protest songs. How awful must we have seemed to them. How backwards must they have seemed to us.

We've all developed notions of the noble struggles of the heartland, the Rust Belt, Coal Country, and the rest. But until November 9, I think few of us realized just how badly the fuzziness of these notions could hurt us. What has become abundantly clear is that the hurt goes both ways: rural America, no matter how it votes, feels isolated from and therefore threatened by the cosmopolitan America of the cities and coasts. Cosmopolitan America does not recognize these threats and therefore ignores them. It probably believed that rural areas appreciated the urbanity and economic, intellectual, culturally creative power of cities—looking to them admiringly.

I understand the Trump phenomenon better when I consider what his rallies must have meant to people in towns like Kerman—and in towns far more isolated and far more desperate. In those places, a volleyball playoff game might be the highlight of the year. A win in the state playoffs over a fancy private school might be the highlight of the decade. A Trump visit—one of those rallies where he pledged his allegiance to them and pledged inexplicably to stick it to the "elites"—might have been the highlight of a lifetime.

The beauty and tragedy of athletic contests is that they take place on the court. There's a handshake and a coin toss and then the game comes into being. It is bounded by rules. Schools become teams. People become players. Places become venues. Participants relate to one another through the prism of the game. Then one of us goes home.

I wish we'd done more than just play volleyball that night. We could have gotten to know one another. Coaches could have chatted with coaches. Players could have made friends with their opponents. We could have had dinner beforehand or gone for ice cream afterwards. We could have gotten to know their names and found out what their lives were like. They could have done the same.

This is the type of encounter that, multiplied millions of times, may have prevented our national fracture. It's the type that may be required for national healing. Gentle conversations, free of accusations and bitterness, may lead to empathy on both sides. That's one school of thought, simplistic though it may be. The other school holds that the time for reconciliation is past and that the left must battle like never before. Of course, the right will do the same.

A little friendliness might not have saved the world. But I can't help thinking of the power of small gestures of communion. Those kids grew up four hours from Los Angeles and four hours from the Bay Area. And yet, there's a chance that none of them ever visited either or even met anyone from either. Their impressions would have been rightfully left to their own imaginations. Even a single encounter is memorable if it's distinctive enough. We both could have come away with warm feelings rather than with the coldness of our assumptions. We could have reminded one another that we all live in the same state, in the same country, under the same moon. Maybe, seventeen years later, we'd have thought about one another, if only briefly, when we went to the polls.

To their credit, Kerman fielded a hell of a team. They whupped us fair and square. That's one reason why that bus ride was so somber, celestial oddities notwithstanding. But still, it was just a volleyball game. I wish all losses were so easy to take.

8   The Culture of Planning
Ideas, trends, and personalities behind the profession

I tread gingerly around planners. While I have hung around planning for years, I myself am not a planner. I've never drafted a zoning ordinance, evaluated a project for compliance, or—god forbid—read an environmental impact report. I have tremendous respect for the rigor of planning and for the people who do it, and I have many friends who are planners.

It's fair to say that I'm a fan. But, like any true fan, I reserve the right to analyze, criticize, and poke fun on occasion. Indeed, I think every field can tend toward insularity and groupthink. I like to believe that the occasional outsider's perspective can be healthy and valuable. And, just as planners are great with maps (to name one example), I like to think I'm OK with words. We each have our strengths.

Planning's greatest weakness is that it often divides people with ruthless effectiveness but does a terrible job of uniting them. This tendency played out shamefully in the segregationist urban policies of the 20th century, to which California – though ostensibly a forward-thinking, welcoming state – was far from immune, as Richard Rothstein vividly describes in *The Color of Law*. Today's generation of planners do not bear responsibility for these injustices but they, and every other Californian, bear responsibility for correcting them.

I don't tend to comment much on the technical sides of planning.

But I do comment on the political and public sides of planning. Every planner must ultimately answer to stakeholders and to elected officials. A big part of the job of planning is to listen to stakeholders but also to present to them and, on occasion, promote projects and policies to them. In many ways, I feel like these public roles are at odds with what many planners sign up for. It's hard to be an expert at GPS and public speaking at the same time. Unfortunately, when planners do not present themselves well, entire cities can suffer for it.

Oddly, many of the pieces in this chapter focus on women. This was not by design, though I suppose it wasn't entirely by coincidence either. I didn't set out to pick a fight with Janette Sadik-Kahn, and I didn't even know what *If/Then* was about before I accepted free tickets. On the other hand, two of these pieces, one of which is the longest in this book, focus on Jane Jacobs. That was no accident.

Jacobs's prominence in the field of urban planning is well known and yet can hardly be understated. She was brilliant. Not perfect, and probably not a saint, but she left her mark on planning like no one else. In fact, I can't imagine any other figures—male, female, or otherwise—who have influenced their respective professions the way Jacobs has planning. (Then again, her contemporaries Rachel Carson and Betty Friedan come close, the latter being the inspiration for the title of this book.) From her stoop in the West Village, Jane set an admirable example for all of us—even way over here in Los Angeles.

The Wisdom and the Hysteria
2014

New Yorkers enjoy the fruits of JS-K's labor.

Janette Sadik-Khan reads cities like few others do. She may not, though, have read her Plutarch.

At the recent Lincoln Institute/Harvard GSD Journalists Forum on Land and the Built Environment, I asked Sadik-Khan a question straight out of Cato the Younger: "Was there any wisdom in the hysteria?"

Let's back up and discuss why hysteria might be so familiar to a former commissioner of the New York City Department of Transportation. (As if hysteria wouldn't be familiar to anyone holding that position.)

In her six years serving under then-mayor Michael Bloomberg, Sadik-Khan famously updated New York City's streetscape in ways unlike any of her predecessors. I'm sure I'm not the first to compare her to an enlightened Robert Moses, who built much of the city's mid-20th century infrastructure seemingly by force of will, but it's still an apt equivalence.

Whereas Moses built bridges and sometimes bulldozed neighborhoods, Sadik-Khan took a lighter approach. She brought pedestrian plazas and green-striped bike lanes to the urban jungle, often using little more than some sawhorses and paint.

Moses's nemesis, the late, great Jane Jacobs, likely would have approved.

Sadik-Khan is not merely "progressive." While she fawns over pleasant photos of art students cheerily sketching in a temporary plaza, her progressivism is also based on data, metrics, and an expansive notion of what metrics to follow. She has the metrics about the benefits of bike lanes and the angle of public opinion. And she embraces formerly radical ideas that, though they have been adopted by the younger generation of planners, often have trouble rising through petrified bureaucracies.

She also has a commanding personality.

Sadik-Khan's presentation at the journalists' forum focused not just on her accomplishments but also, to her credit, on her detractors. Time and again a vocal minority of New Yorkers challenged Sadik-Khan, often in harebrained ways. She showed headlines and videos describing some of the more vehement and ludicrous accusations about her improvements. Opponents likened bike lanes to the Gaza Strip. They insisted that the city would crumble.

Dorothy Rabinowitz, a member of *The Wall Street Journal*'s editorial board, famously warned that bike lanes were "totalitarian." She told *New York Magazine* that the Citi Bike bike-sharing program "is the stuff of your darkest aesthetic dreams. There is nothing human about the racks." (As if the city's two million or so cars and trucks are nothing but Rembrandt paintings on wheels. And don't get me started on Donald Trump's buildings.)

As Rabinowitz proves, you clearly don't need a backyard to be a NIMBY.

It's not hard to imagine that Sadik-Khan shrugged off the criticism, knowing that the correctness of her views and the support of the silent majority (and of Mayor Mike) would win the day. She's been able to dismiss naysayers in ways that other planners have not. She's been so dismissive, it seems, that she hasn't even had to formulate a response to them.

As I tried to explain to Sadik-Khan at the journalists' forum, I was wondering—despite her convictions—if any of those activists had ever given her pause or caused her team to alter a project. I was hoping for insight into the mind of someone who has stared down NIMBYism and caused it to turn tail. I suppose I got a firsthand demonstration of just that.

Sadik-Khan couldn't even verbalize a response. Literally throwing up her hands and quivering with what I can describe only as condescension, she made it clear that she resented the question, as if I was the one who was hysterical.

A simple "no" would have sufficed.

I asked my question for two reasons: first, regardless of their personal sympathies, journalists have to at least give passing credence to opposing views; second, as Sadik-Khan knows full well, the opponents whom she brushed aside would have stopped many of her counterparts dead in their tracks. It's not unreasonable to try to give her the chance to explain how she prevailed if only so that others could learn to follow her lead.

Poor responses to NIMBYs and other conservatives—most notably those of Tea Party supporters, many of whom are taking aim at smart growth—have undermined plans into which many fine planners have put their life's work. The ability to calmly and empathetically acknowledge, consider, and respond to opposition—no matter how unreasonable it may seem—can be a planner's greatest asset.

I figured that Sadik-Khan would know how to do this—I know she does. I wanted to see that asset in full force, especially since she is one of our greatest planners. I wanted to be able to write a blog with insight that I could have conveyed from her to the rest of the planning world. I was hoping that Sadik-Khan might be an ambassador for tough but thoughtful planning and would demonstrate that she could be both eminent and sympathetic. Instead, I found myself intimidated and belittled. This from the planner who, some years later, wrote a memoir entitled *Street Fight*.

That's one way, I suppose, to get things done. Make some plans, run some numbers, answer only the questions you like, and give your opponents the occasional icy stare. For what it's worth, the cyclists of New York are definitely better off for Sadik-Khan's efforts—and so is (almost) everyone else.

Undoing the Legacy of Segregation
2018

The average price of a home in Lakewood, a stereotypical middle-class suburb in south Los Angeles County, is $567,000. Richard Rothstein says that African-Americans should be eligible to pay something closer to $75,000. That's the inflation-adjusted cost of what homes sold for when they were new in the 1950s—and when African Americans were legally forbidden from buying them.

Rothstein offers this provocation—which he admits to being unrealistic—in his 2017 book *The Color of Law* to illustrate the profound, enduring financial hardships that African-Americans have suffered as a result of deliberate, widespread, and utterly legal (at the time) residential segregation.

Rothstein, who spoke to a roomful of planners at the 2018 UCLA Extension Land Use Law and Planning Conference, argues that many of the de facto reasons for residential segregation in the United States were in fact de jure reasons. Actual laws and policies passed and implemented by cities, states, and the federal government, not to mention homeowners' association bylaws that were often legally sanctioned, prevented African-Americans from living among whites in cities across the country, California included.

Rothstein, a research associate at the Economic Policy Institute, cites potent illustrations of legal segregation, reaching into the Civil Rights Era and beyond. The East Bay city of Richmond was a small, racially integrated bedroom community before it became a center of shipbuilding in World War II. The federal government built public housing units by the tens of thousands, but it built separate developments for whites and blacks. Richmond has never been the same. Master-planned communities like Lakewood often included anti-African American covenants.

Several Los Angeles communities refused to accept new federally supported development designated for (mostly black) workers at the McDonnell Douglas factory in Santa Monica. Eventually, the housing was built in Watts, which was then diverse and integrated. Not long after, Watts went up in flames in one of the country's most devastating examples of black urban strife. Meanwhile, banks refused to lend to African-American homeowners in neighborhoods that were "redlined."

All of this happened not in Jim Crow Alabama or Georgia, but in liberal, diverse, prosperous California. And it happened not that long ago. There may still be people living in those houses in Lakewood and Richmond who bought them when African-Americans could not. All these examples, Rothstein notes, are meant to debunk the perversely salubrious myth that today's segregation derives simply from personal preferences and economic constraints.

As if.

However integrated the United States may be today, Rothstein pointed out a damning truism: the country cannot desegregate just because laws have changed. When a society finds its conscience and decides to let everyone drink at the same water fountains or attend the same schools, those changes can happen overnight, by fiat. But millions of people—including the white residents who enjoyed privileged opportunities to buy homes and black residents who were shut out—cannot simply switch places, even if such a thing were just. That's because, in part, while African-Americans earn, on average, 60 percent of what white Americans make, their net worth is roughly 10 percent of that of white Americans.

Rothstein attributes this discrepancy largely to African-Americans' former inability to buy homes (or at least to buy homes that appreciated as much as those of their white counterparts). Beyond family economics, Rothstein said that segregation is "the cause of most of our serious social problems," including low educational attainment by African-American children forced into segregated, low-quality schools.

These wounds will take generations to heal.

None of the above is anything new. All of it appears in Rothstein's book. I recount these injustices and their relevance to California because, in his talk, Rothstein issued what amounts to a moral call to arms.

If Rothstein is justifiably disgusted by urban America's history of racism, he's only mildly less disgusted by the efforts to cover it up. He notes that mainstream U.S. history textbooks refer to urban segregation only in passing, and they typically perpetuate the myth of "de facto" segregation rather than implicate the government as they should. As such, Rothstein is on a crusade to inform Americans of the truth. He shared that truth with everyone at the conference, and I am passing it along.

Urban planners are, of course, the ideal audience for Rothstein: they confront the legacy of segregation on a daily basis, and they are in a position to do something about it.

California's planners cannot take $400,000 off the price of a half-million-dollar home. But they can envision diverse communities that offer ranges of dwelling units, commercial opportunities, and amenities—such as parks and access to transit—that can create a more equitable society, benefiting rich and poor, powerful and marginalized alike. (And, of course, marginalized populations include far more than just African-Americans.) On a statewide level, Senate Bill 1000 is being implemented, requiring cities' general plans to include elements on environmental justice. That's a promising step.

Whatever the solutions, today's planners—working amid the wondrous diversity of today's California—now have no excuse not to know about the problem. I leave it to their expertise, and their consciences, to figure out how to undo some of these injustices wrought and tolerated by their predecessors.

Reading, Writing, and Planning
2007

The high school curriculum overlooks a great many subjects, so we could go on at length pointing out its ironies and shortcomings. But the topic at hand is urban planning, so let's stick with that.

I would never want to inflict the intricacies of urban planning on the casual student, slogging through high school or college distribution requirements. Memorizing ordinances and calculating optimal curb heights is no way to inspire young minds to think about their cities and how to make them better. On the other hand, basic understanding of urbanism and planning would seem appropriate, if not essential, for the 90 or so percent of American kids who grow up in the cities and suburbs that have resulted from modern planning principles and whose lives are, by extension, dictated by planners. Let's throw in the 10 percent who live in rural areas too.

There is something unnerving about a curriculum that enables students to remain completely ignorant of the very surroundings in which they live. I'm certain that almost no student understands the forces that colluded to produce their respective culs-de-sac, housing projects, mansions, or homesteads. Nor would it occur to most of them to find out. Laypeople approach the built environment with the patently contradictory attitude that it came about as an act of nature and—despite kids' natural curiosity about the world—that it therefore offers no opportunities for inquiry or betterment.

College is supposed to fill those gaps and nurture the dreams that high school ignores. But running across urban planning in the course catalog is different from, say, running across Slavic literature. You can at least guess at the latter even if you have no firsthand experience with it; the former offers little but mystery. That is to say, the typical college freshman doesn't even know what planning is—so how can he or she be expected to spend precious credits finding out whether it is worthwhile?

If American cities are to heal themselves, and if the planning profession wants to attract the brightest students from the widest possible talent pool, urban planning must find its way into the high school curriculum.

The closest most high schools come to planning consists of passing references to architecture in art history courses. This is a tenuous connection at best. Even so, art history presents architecture only as individual works—often as examples of styles or historical periods—not as elements of a built environment, and never as profound forces that affect everyday life.

But changes are afoot.

In 2001 the College Board brought the often marginalized field of human geography into the mainstream by creating an Advanced Placement course. It came about at the urging of a host of professional geography organizations, including the Geography Education Implementation Project, the National Council for Geographic Education, and the American Association of Geographers. Say what you will about the College Board's powers of arbitration. It has sucked the life out of many subjects. In this case, however, it has done the curriculum a great favor by legitimizing geography and approving it for high schoolers' consumption.

AP Human Geography—which I taught for four years at a private school visionary enough to adopt it as its culminating senior-year history class (and brave enough to let me teach it)—does not, of course, focus solely on urbanism. It runs the gamut of other mysterious, but fascinating, fields such as anthropology, economics, demography, and sociology. These subjects are not only absent from most high school curricula but also are valuable for anyone who will one day flip through a college catalog or otherwise walk this earth. But among those topics, urbanism makes its stand. AP Geo typically includes two solid units of urbanism: one on urban systems and the other on urban structure. That's where planning comes in.

Of course, a high schooler's brief peek at urban structure reveals little of the profession. But it does offer students the chance to contemplate cities and evaluate, in broad strokes, the theories and practices that have made cities what they are. The course treads over ground that the profession has probably long abandoned: Is the Hoyt Sector model useful? Do stores still consider threshold and range in the age of e-commerce? Did redlining happen, or is it a myth propagated by liberals? Does the bid-rent curve reflect land values properly in a multiple-nucleus city? Who cares?

The answers that AP Geo provides are not nearly as important as the questions, or, rather, the opportunity to ask questions. Even simplistic, outdated theories provide invaluable foundations for further inquiry—even if that inquiry proves the original assumption wrong. Moreover, the course can embrace some of the urban canon, many of whose works are as compelling as any nonfiction ever written.

I remember when I first read Jane Jacobs and Kenneth Jackson. I was 25. My life would have been different indeed if I'd read them at 17, as my students have. I don't expect them to become planners, but I do expect that they will at least be better urban citizens than they otherwise would have been.

Despite its potential, AP Geo is not about to challenge AP Physics or AP U.S. History for a place in high school's top shelf. Though the numbers grow every year, it's still less popular than stalwarts like United States history, calculus, and the hard sciences. Back when I taught AP Geography, only about 20,000 students per year were taking it. Many of them hailed from states with mandatory geography requirements. But that's a few thousand more students who graduate high school knowing more about cities than most of their counterparts—which is usually less than zero.

Until Planetizen publishes *Urban Planning for Dummies*, AP Geography is our best hope. And it's not a bad way to spend a couple semesters.

Urban Planning Takes Center Stage
2015

Sometime in the not-too-distant future, the American Planning Association's Burnham Award will go to Dr. Elizabeth Vaughan. She will be recognized for, among other accomplishments, forcing improvements to a megadevelopment on Manhattan's West Side, elegantly creating more affordable housing, and making peace with antigentrification activists.

A former professor of planning, Vaughan is exacting, keeping an entire census's worth of data in her head and crunching numbers on the fly; she analyzes every alternative in her head and sees demographic and social trends long before they take place. She has the toughness, intellect, and resolve of Janette Sadik-Khan. She also has the awkwardness, self-doubt, and nonexistent dancing skills of Elaine Benes.

If Elizabeth sounds like an improbable character, it's because she is. She is fictional. But, whether real or not, as the central character in the Broadway musical *If/Then*, currently on a national tour that begins in California, Elizabeth Vaughan may be the most famous urban planner in the country.

Played by Broadway megastar Idina Menzel, Elizabeth is the quintessential child of the 1990s (she celebrates her 39th birthday onstage). She and her cohort weathered urban decay, stayed healthy through the early AIDS crisis, made the country (or at least New York) a more tolerant place, and survived life before iPhones. She and her friends are spirited, liberal, and diverse to a fault. Matrices of gay couples, straight couples, and biracial couples portray a color-blind and gender-neutral culture. It's a sanitized version of the cosmopolitanism that flourishes in many American cities even as intolerance and fear rises in the hinterlands. Their world is chaotic yet comfortable; they are not quite yuppies, but they're doing OK. They enjoy New York City for all it's worth, from strolls in the park to soliloquies on the fire escape to the chance to bump into eight million other fascinating humans in any one of the 525,600 minutes that make up a year.

If *If/Then* sounds like *Rent* all grown up, that's because it is. It shares both cast members (including Menzel) and creative team members with the original 1996 Broadway production of *Rent*. And of course, it shares a city. But, whereas New York was but the backdrop for the *Rent* kids to explore their Bohemian anguish, the city takes center stage in *If/Then*. A literal "sidewalk ballet" is on display in song-and-dance numbers—in parks, on balconies, in offices—that celebrate urban life with full throat.

Menzel has just enough humility to play Elizabeth with humor and self-awareness—perhaps too much self-awareness. Elizabeth constantly enumerates her flaws, chief among them her ability to make "poor choices." Elizabeth is happiest when she is analyzing the tendencies of eight million data points. When she has to decide for herself—work for the city vs. teach college; go to a party or go to a protest; sleep with her boss or marry the handsome Army doctor—

she is nearly paralyzed. She wonders constantly, obsessively about the sidewalk less traveled.

In many cases, the world ends up choosing for her.

If/Then operates on a clever, if overwrought, narrative conceit. Like the 1998 Gwyneth Paltrow movie *Sliding Doors*, it follows two storylines at once, with scenes and their alternatives weaving in and out of each other. The people, places, and relationships remain the same but the choices are different. And, of course, so are the outcomes.

If Elizabeth, who is "Liz" in one storyline and "Beth" in the other, chooses to marry the handsome doctor, then her best friend, Lucas, marries the doctor's best friend David. If she takes the job with the city, Elizabeth doesn't marry the doctor but instead ends up in halting friendship-romance with the same Lucas. Taking cues that date back to Sophocles, *If/Then* wonders, pedantically and entertainingly, whether we are governed by ourselves or our stars. Or by our city.

Whatever choices *If/Then*'s mere mortals make, they take place on the foundation of New York. Whereas *Rent* celebrated urban life, *If/Then* celebrates the city as such. "Urban planner" isn't just a convenient backstory for Elizabeth. It's a focal point of the plot. Amazingly, we see Elizabeth "doing" urban planning in scene after scene. When Elizabeth isn't actively guiding the city's future, she and her friends are out there living in it. One of its best scenes has Elizabeth's irrepressible friend and obsessive matchmaker Kate serenading gentlemen in a subway car, quite unlike the common panhandler.

Menzel has a colorful supporting cast, but the story revolves literally around her. She is the fulcrum between which head and heart balance. Her choices are the ones that determine whether her friends are gay or straight and whether they take one job or another. By the time she becomes director of the Department of City Planning, her choices are also the ones that determine where thousands of New Yorkers will live, how their public spaces will look, and whether Penn Station will finally get exhumed.

If ever a character has romanticized the planning profession, it is Elizabeth. She is the consummate pragmatic idealist. She understands the joy that pulses through a great city while she keeps the numbers all in their rows. Elizabeth and her colleagues speak honestly about gentrification, demographic trends, tensions between developers and stakeholders, political alliances, housing costs, and everyday things like bike lanes and sidewalks. Planning—if we take it in its purest form, serving the masses and making life better on average—is the ideal foil for the messiness and uncertainty of individual existence.

As much as *Rent* romanticized the creative loafing and angst of the 1990s (while its predecessor, *Angels in America*, revealed the horrors of the AIDS crisis), *If/Then* is a celebration of professionalism. It's a little forced, but it's a refreshing change from Broadway's obsession with meta-drama. (Think *A Chorus Line, The Music Man, Cabaret, Gypsy, 42nd Street, Phantom of the Opera*). *If/Then* is not quite dancing about architecture, but it's close, and it works.

Brian Yorkey, who wrote the book and lyrics, did his homework. Though Menzel's black mane would have to go silver before some of her signature projects actually got approved, it's a reasonable portrayal of basic planning. Terminology is used correctly, the issues are genuine, and even the places in Manhattan, right down to a thinly veiled Hudson Yards, are real, illustrated with street maps and images of landmarks. If only all planners were as passionate as Elizabeth is, or as dazzling as Menzel is. Indeed, there seems to be an intentional chasm between Menzel's celebrity and talent—though occasionally nasal, her voice is crisp and powerful—and the anonymity and bureaucratic tendencies of her character's career. Whatever choices we may face, we cannot all be Broadway stars.

As a musical about place, it's hard not to think about *If/Then*'s audiences. When performed in a literal Broadway theater encircled by the city it portrays, the urban themes must have been obvious. On Hollywood Boulevard, *If/Then* reveals urban possibilities about which Angelenos are becoming increasingly aware but from which they still sometimes recoil. San Diegans may have to consider the battles they've waged over regional planning. Folks in Orange County may glimpse a world they'd prefer to experience on stage rather than in real life.

The production must be prepared for a chilly reception when it goes to Tempe from January 12-17. One of Elizabeth's more regrettable choices was spending 12 years in Phoenix with her then-husband. With its sprawl and its air-conditioning, the city bears the brunt of some genuinely unkind jokes in a musical that is otherwise sweet and forgiving. The creative team may have had no problem unloading on the city of Joe Arpiao and the state of SB 1070.

Let us, then, stop for a moment to contemplate that this review is about a major Broadway musical that is about urban planning. It is a first and probably a last. Whether this means that the profession has come into its own or whether it means that a single creative team got a whim and ran with it is anyone's guess. Planners should enjoy the spotlight while it lasts. And maybe they can even learn from it.

Understandably, neither Menzel nor her production won a Tony Award. The clever first act, which sets up the relationships and amply explores Elizabeth's dilemmas, devolves into melodrama in the second act. The music is not memorable enough, and the whole thing stumbles when it goes from light fun to grave seriousness. And yet, if *If/Then* can get audiences to think more deeply about cities and even get planners to discover (or rediscover) their inspirations, maybe Elizabeth will deserve that Burnham Award after all.

50 Years Later, Jacobs Still Leads a Sorority of Dissent
2011

The 'sidewalk ballet' continues in Washington Square Park.

There must have been something in the water affecting women in the early 1960s, and it wasn't just DDT.

Throughout 2011, planners celebrated the fiftieth anniversary of the publication of a great book, but it is not just one book or one author who deserves celebration. While eggshells collapsed, killing new life in the nest, three women—speaking for the countless other women (and men) who had grown weary of the false promises of the 1950s—issued crucial, intertwined dissents through equal parts activism and prose. That the planner is the most obscure among the three is unfortunate, but ultimately, her impact may be no less profound than the other members of her sorority.

Rachel Carson, Betty Friedan, and Jane Jacobs tore at the social fabric of America at the very moment when the country's own global dominance was more assured than ever. They each published their pathbreaking works in such rapid succession that the sequence hardly matters: Jacobs published *Death and Life of Great American Cities* in 1961, having begun writing it in 1958; *Silent Spring* followed in September 1962; and *The Feminine Mystique* completed the cycle—from city to forest to bedroom—five months later.

Though Jacobs's ink was dry by the time *The Feminine Mystique* went to press, it's entirely likely that each was loosing her fury upon her Smith Corona at exactly the same time, bound by common ribbons of outrage and lucidity.

I am not old enough to know whether anybody at the time marveled at this coincidence. But through the distance of 50 years, it seems that they arose at a remarkable moment. So close were their publication dates, and so original was each book, that surely none can be considered an influence on the others: they were, all together, products of both their time and extraordinary contemplation. E. O. Wilson wrote that Carson "delivered a galvanic jolt to public consciousness"; that Friedan did the same is indisputable. Whether many people beyond lower Manhattan knew of Jacobs is less clear.

A casual reading of *The Feminine Mystique*, *Silent Spring*, and *Death and Life* suggests that each relied on what can only be described as an abiding faith in perceptiveness, observation, and simple common sense—the type of common sense that social science often attempts to discredit. Each too spun literature out of dreary subjects: murderous chemicals, urban blight, ennui. All three remained focused not on the esoteric, learned, and complicated but instead on the achingly familiar: baked goods, birdsongs, stoops. They mix analysis with storytelling. Jacobs describes ideal street corners just as Carson invokes a pastoral ideal before burying it in invisible toxins. Friedan reveals the shocking complexity of the kitchen table upon which she herself served those fatal meals.

They reaffirmed the beauty—unquantifiable, nearly indescribable, but eminently palpable—that had been forgotten in the aesthetic cataclysm of the 1950s, and then they painstakingly explained what had happened and what could be done. They exposed the ego of the builder, the thoughtlessness of the industrialist, and the despair of the so-called housewife—things that turn into nonsense if you try to enter them into a spreadsheet. That's why each of their nonfiction tomes qualifies as literature: not because they aren't based on fact (which they are), but rather because they, like any other great work of art, attempt to drive at truth.

Though they chose different images, they all wrote about the same thing. Carson's concern for nature echoes Jacobs's concern for the built environment. The lifestyle that Friedan describes is the almost inevitable result of the urban form that Jacobs laments. Both Jacobs and Carson (not to mention Friedan herself) are shining examples of the types of women that Friedan believed all women could and should be. They are to Friedan what the poet Whitman was to essayist Emerson: the embodiment, in a country that so much enjoys speaking of its greatness, of unspeakably great hopes.

How these particular truths all erupted in the span of two years is as delicious a question as history ever will provoke. As a historical coincidence, the ascendency of Friedan, Carson, and Jacobs ranks up there—in all seriousness—with the question of how Walmart, Kmart, and Target all came into being in the same year, thus exacerbating to this very day the problems that all three women railed against. (That year happened to be 1962.)

The great postwar sigh of relief that blew over the country in the late 1940s brought with it the toxins that would become the problems of the 1960s. The Baby Boom, Levittown, and even the chemical industry all seemed benign in their inception. Prior to 1919, women's most immediate goal had a name—suffrage—and therefore was easier to combat. But not until the end of the 1950s did women's problems, and so many others that arose in the years following World War II, reach critical mass.

What burst forth in the early 1960s was building up throughout the 1950s. It's no wonder that the regimented "Organization Man" ethos of 1950s business culture found foils in independent, iconoclastic, literary women perhaps oppressed yet unbound by the hierarchy.

Moreover, the task of exposing the defects of 1950s America may have fallen to women if only because many men were invested in the status quo, what with their black suits, skinny ties, and slide rules. They were not inclined to incite revolution—they were, in many ways, the ones against whom the revolution was incited.

While corporations hummed along, Friedan, Jacobs, and Carson were simply the first to look around them, realize how deeply the problems had sunk in, and then air their realizations publically. They were quite unlike, for instance, Martin Luther King, Jr., whose own protests of the early 1960s trace their lineage literally to the Old Testament; the injustices that he fought against and died for were manifest equally to all who suffered them and all who did not.

Betty Friedan launched feminism. Rachel Carson launched environmentalism. They tower over their fields like few other leaders—male or female—do. But if you ask plenty of people involved with urban planning, Jacobs's name belongs atop the Empire State Building, the Sears Tower, and the Space Needle all stacked atop one another. In fact, within planning circles, she is more powerful than ever, as her ideas have made that generational trek from radicalism to budding orthodoxy.

In 2009 the urban planning web portal Planetizen.com conducted a poll, albeit an unscientific one, of history's 100 "greatest urban thinkers." Jacobs won with 6,000 votes out of 14,000 cast. Contemporary architect and planner Andres Duany came in runner-up and yet received only one-fifth as many votes. And, even so, a piece of each of his votes belongs to Jacobs, since Duany's New Urbanist movement is derived directly and unapologetically from Jacobs's ideas. Today, nearly every urban plan that makes headlines can trace its lineage back to Jacobs's promotion of pedestrianism, mixed land uses, community cohesion, and local economies.

If Jacobs had been a physicist, her fame would be on par with that of Einstein. If she'd been a basketball player, she'd have taken Michael Jordan to school.

Jacobs's relative obscurity owes itself to several reasons, not the least of which is the obscurity of her field. Nearly four billion humans live in cities entirely unaware of the forces that create those cities. Being the most local of political pursuits, planning is, for the most part, a leaderless profession. It relies on the principle that what is good for San Juan Capistrano is not necessarily good for San Juan Bautista.

There is also the problem of words. Protest though she might, even her impassioned literature cannot in and of itself effect change when the built environment is at stake. A reader can read *The Feminine Mystique*, or even just the first chapter, and join Friedan's movement instantly. Likewise, environmentalism lends itself to individual, and sometimes instant, behavioral changes. In Carson's case, it required the abandonment of DDT: a politically challenging but logistically simple gesture that culminated in its outright ban in the United States in 1972, only 10 years after Carson brought its evils to light.

But what do you do when the enemy is set—literally—in stone?

Like many other revolutionaries, Jacobs wrote sometimes in militaristic terms. With an eye as much toward the cannon ball as the wrecking ball, Jacobs abandons diplomacy by the fifth word of *Death and Life*: "This book is an attack on current city planning and rebuilding." Although Jacobs's real-life conflict with New York's dictatorial "master builder" Robert Moses was a mighty contest and a great story, Jacobs's real enemy was not a person, and anger would have gotten her only so far. She hews to the inspirational in the very next sentence: "It is also, and mostly, an attempt to introduce new principles of city planning and rebuilding, different and even opposite from those now taught in everything from schools of architecture and planning to the Sunday supplements and women's magazines."

Jacobs spoke for a genuinely marginalized group: people who wanted to live in dense, diverse, stimulating, vibrant cities. But because the urban instinct is not an immutable characteristic of either individuals or groups, these people do not define a protected class, and they have no human antagonist or oppressor. Instead, they have a system, so dispersed and purposeful that it seems almost to have no agency or leadership of its own, even as "whole communities are torn apart and sown to the winds with a reaping of cynicism, resentment, and despair that must be seen and heard to be believed."

What Jacobs fought against, in the 1950s and even today, was progress itself: progress as defined by an elite few.

Few concepts yield so many definitions as modernism does, but for the purpose of Jacobs's activism it entailed the use of engineering, technology, and large-scale industry to alter and expand cities to accommodate the automobile; aesthetically it favors formal efficiency, "honest" use of industrial materials, and lack of ornamentation.

Ideologically, modernism is bound up in the curious fixation with "progress" that prevailed in the middle of the 20th century. At the time, progress achieved an untenably narrow definition that loosely correlated with the notion that the human condition could always be improved upon, typically through science, technology, and rationality. Jacobs's objection to modernism was no esoteric academic exercise, of the sort that plays out at conferences, swaddled in obtuse theory and excess syllables. She despised modernism with perfect clarity—the sort of clarity to which modernist design often lays claim.

"Human progress," as Dr. King points out in his "Letter from a Birmingham Jail," "never rolls in on wheels of inevitability." Indeed, if you ask Jacobs, it does not roll in on wheels at all. Just as Carson heard the silence, Jacobs needed little more than the halo of a streetlamp in order to view the failure that was so prevalent in New York City and just about everywhere else. She saw that "all the art and science of city planning is helpless to stem decay—and the spiritlessness that precedes decay—in ever more massive swatches of cities." Jacobs was, perhaps, the first leader in history ever to lead a movement against progress without being branded an anarchist or nihilist. She ascribed, however, to a heretical notion: the old was better than the new.

By the time Moses proposed the evisceration of lower Manhattan, "progress" had long overshot its mark (or missed its exit, if you will).

The rest of the story is history doubling back on itself. Starting in 1968 with the Jacobs-led defeat of the Lower Manhattan Expressway, countless similar instances of would-be urbanicide were also halted. Since then, some highways have been disassembled and many ghastly public housing projects have been demolished. Formalized in the late 1990s, a wholesale movement to promote historically inspired neighborhoods has arisen in the form of New Urbanism and other ideologies, almost all of which openly proclaim their allegiance to Jacobs, who moved to Toronto in 1969 and, until her death in 2006, engaged in virtually no more rabble-rousing as she instead wrote several more excellent books.

For the purpose of today's progressive urbanism, *Death and Life* did all the leading, and it did so anachronistically, drawing planners and architects back in time to a moment when cities were built at a human scale and with human pleasures in mind. Jacobs led first and foremost by reminding readers that rationality—and its coconspirator, paternalism—cannot constantly arrive at better and better answers. A world insane enough to, say, deny black people their basic human rights surely cannot be neatly tamed by freeways, subdivisions, and glass towers.

Though Jacobs's civic activism was based on the ideas that she articulated in *Death and Life*, the book was not a template for how to get what she wanted. Rather, it was a vision of what she wanted. So, while Jacobs's two personas—author and activist—lend credibility to each other, they easily could have existed in each other's absence. New York is probably glad that they did not.

Though Jacobs probably is not a household name even today, she touched the lives of millions of people whose cities have been planned with her ideas in mind, and those numbers are growing. By now her eminence within the field is more than complete, but her veneration followed a slow process—possibly for the better, given the limits of veneration. To this day her goals are realized through countless dispersed, time-consuming, excruciating battles that take place over and over again and are fought by intimates, not by larger-than-life demagogues who sometimes pass for leaders.

Indeed, the revolution that Jacobs incited is condemned to take place at a nearly glacial pace. Building things takes long enough. How long it takes to not build things sounds like a calculation that only a Zen master could perform. Try putting that in your general plan update.

Then again, it's still easier to unbuild a city than to resurrect an extinct species.

Though the American population is rooted in cities, the vast bulk of American literature that speaks of landscape does so of the natural landscape. Cities hardly existed when the early American novelists and short-story writers—Irving, Hawthorne, Cooper—were writing. The primacy of nature in American culture and consciousness was cemented by Thoreau and Emerson. Since their time, everyone from Mark Twain to John Steinbeck to Cormac McCarthy has reveled in the nonurban landscape, thus leading America through road trips, frontier idylls, and suburban disaffection rather than inquiries into back alleys and bursting subway cars.

But for everyone who lives in cities and believes in what they offer—including a way for Americans to achieve Carson's goal of leaving nature alone and a venue in which to achieve Friedan's goal of self-actualization—Jane Jacobs, even 50 years later, remains the leader who, more so than any other American, gave voice to their desires and a nest from which their dreams can take flight.

Jane Jacobs: 100 and Timeless as Ever

2016

Jane Jacobs's favorite urban hangout: the White Horse Tavern.

In most cases, a century provides a round, nostalgic number. It is an arbitrary marker, offering a chance for living generations to contemplate a past beyond their firsthand comprehension.

A century is not just a convenient marker for remembering Jane Jacobs. It is a crucial interval for appreciating the world she grew up in, the urban devastation she witnessed, the forces she fought against, and the future she hoped for. Even as the planning profession has roundly embraced Jacobs's ideas, the resurrection of the American city remains a work in progress.

This is not your grandmother's city. But it may yet be.

Though Jacobs passed away in 2006 and published her masterpiece, *The Death and Life of Great American Cities*, in 1961, urbanists do not celebrate her for some distant, reverenced work. Contemporary movements such as smart growth, pedestrianism, public transit, New Urbanism, tactical urbanism, and the millennial sunburst of enthusiasm for urban living all hearken back to Jacobs.

Even so, the historical moment that gave rise to Jacobs is still happening, with the momentum of a nuclear meltdown still spitting out radiation, half-life after half-life. "Orthodox modernist city planning ... refuses to die," said Robert A. M. Stern, dean of the Yale School of Architecture. "She did a very good job of trying to kill it, by turning attention back to city streets and the people who inhabit them."

When suburbs were swelling and freeways were tearing through cities in the mid-20th century, few planners or architects recognized, or cared, that cities were dying. Planners followed the European model of Le Corbusier and the International Congresses of Modern Architecture (CIAM), which advocated the demolition of neighborhoods and the erection of sterile towers and pointless open spaces. In the United States, this program evolved into highways, tract housing, and "urban renewal."

Jacobs celebrated life, not objects. She was eloquent, rebellious, endearing, and superficially unassuming—in part because she was a woman in a field that was, and remains, dominated by men. A tenacious activist, Jacobs not only lived her ideals but actually prevailed, staring down New York City's infrastructure czar Robert Moses and saving Greenwich Village from the proposed Lower Manhattan Expressway.

Jacobs arrived at her radicalism by looking backwards—and looking around. She uncovered the great things about cities that had been known, if not fully articulated, for millennia. She contended that "scientific" modernist planning and design was little more than a rationalization to justify the enshrinement of (white, male) egotism in the landscape. Jacobs was the real scientist, using powers of observation and deduction to describe what she saw as the natural environment in which urban humans thrived.

"Her only qualifications were her eyes and her social conscience, and she started telling people there is a horrendous gap between your forms and your social ideals," said architect Stefanos Polyzoides, a cofounder of the Congress for the New Urbanism. "The architectural profession was dominated by this idea that modern is good and everything else is rotten."

It's almost impossible to point to specific examples of Jacobs's influence. If anything, Jacobs signifies negation: the absence of a superblock, the highway that was never built. Or she embodies the ephemeral: the evening stroll, the chance encounter, the purchase of a bagel and coffee. "She was really about ways to experience a city rather than what a city was supposed to look like," said Richard Sennett, professor of sociology at the London School of Economics, who knew Jacobs in her heyday.

Today, it is the rare urban designer who gets to develop a city, or even a neighborhood, from scratch. In mature cities, change happens over the course of decades. By working at the level of the discrete parcel or building—for better or worse—and on projects that typically take mere years, architects, rather than planners, face more ample and direct opportunities to realize Jacobs's lessons.

Decades later, architects are still debating what those lessons are.

Short of Lou Reed, perhaps no one is more closely associated with Greenwich Village than Jacobs is. She is often assumed to be both a preservationist and a historicist, forever promoting bricks and brownstones—likely an unexciting prospect for contemporary designers in pursuit of the new. "Because she defended the Village ... by extension she defended the historicity of the city," said Polyzoides. Jacobs did not, however, explicitly promote a certain architectural style. By embracing diversity, she avoided the fate of her modernist nemeses.

"She's against singularity and for diversity, diversity of all kinds: economic, social, physical," said Polyzoides. "In that sense she might be very pleased with a modern or contemporary building in a traditional street." While Jacobs may have been agnostic about how a building looks, she was anything but when it came to how it relates to its surroundings. Jacobs makes architects think about all the elements of cities that aren't buildings.

Lorcan O'Herlihy, founding principal of Los Angeles-based Lorcan O'Herlihy Architects, said that this perspective compels architects to pay attention to how buildings relate to street life and with surrounding buildings. His design process includes literal interaction: extensive community dialogue through which he tries to understand a project's role in the human environment. While nonresidents may never enter a building, its influence still extends, for better or worse, beyond the property line.

"It's not only about buildings, but it's also about engaging edges," said O'Herlihy. "That is something that is missing in an urban context when you turn your back to the sidewalk and street."

That approach calls for a level of creativity that is often considered lacking in American modern design, which Stern calls "a corporate version of the International Style." Jacobs offers an alternative. She gives architects the opportunity—perhaps even the obligation—to perceive and respond to neighborhoods as they are and not to impose placeless design theories on them.

"Jacobs revered the city as the preeminent site of choice and possibility and she saw architecture's duty as enabling, not domineering," said Michael Sorkin, principal of New York-based Michael Sorkin Studio and author of *Twenty Minutes in Manhattan*. "Her gift to designers was the rejection of fixed formulas in favor of an ever-unfolding dialectic of form and life."

Just as Jacobs celebrated city life, so might Jacobs-inspired designs be capable of living many lives. "The best way to honor her would actually be ... systems of building that are accretive rather than rupturing," said Richard Sennett, author and Distinguished Visiting Scholar at Cambridge University's sociology department. Sennett cited Chilean architect Alejandro Aravena, who designs buildings with the intention that they will be altered and added to in time.

For all of Jacobs's focus on the "human scale" of 20th century cities, 21st century cities may be developing at a scale that makes Jacobs seem, if not precious, then at least inadequate. Jacobs has often drawn criticism for not directly addressing social issues such as segregation and poverty, instead referring to them under the broad mantle of diversity.

But contemporary megacities in the developing world are growing at unprecedented rates. Lagos, Mumbai, Jakarta, and the like make New York City look like a sleepy hamlet. In these cities, swelling with urban poor, the "sidewalk ballet" isn't the most pressing issue.

"Of course they're relevant today, but they're not the macro problems," said Thom Mayne, principal of Morphosis. Jacobs's attention to the street and the neighborhood "doesn't have anything to do with the 50 percent of the world that ends up in these urban configurations."

Then again, Saskia Sassen, professor of sociology at Columbia University, suggests that debates over city form and urban details obscure Jacobs's broader contributions about urban economics. Jacobs's 1969 *Economy of Cities* contends that macroscale productivity, and indeed the capitalist ideal itself, depends on the aggregate of activities that take place on blocks and in neighborhoods.

"Jacobs shows the city as an economic machine, a machine that can process all kinds of elements that are often coming from non-urban settings," said Sassen. "[In] a suburb or a private, gated corporate office park, you have density, but you don't have a city."

Debating Jacobs's relevance presents a thorny challenge. In many circles, she has gained as much influence, intellectually at least, as her modernist counterparts ever did. Nonetheless, the environments that they built still endure. Appealing as they are, Jacobs's theories remain largely untested, even as no one has arisen to substantially oppose or eclipse her.

"The longevity of her influence is attributable to the fact she spoke all the truth in a straightforward way," said Stern. "The profession of planning and architecture has not yet caught up with her wisdom because it is still object-fixated and open-space fixated."

If any century promises to be the Jane Jacobs Century, then, it may not be the past one, in which she spent 84 of her 90 years, wrote seminal texts, and took a wrecking ball to modernism. That may have been prelude. Rather, the Jane Jacobs Century promises to be the current one, in which the urban world from which she departed may—slowly—become more like the one into which she was born.

Sources

Chapter 1

"Beating Boston at Its Own Games"; "Searching for Los Angeles in *Blade Runner 2049*"; "The Real Problem with Carmageddon"; and "The Oklahoman Who Figured Out Los Angeles" originally appeared in the *California Planning & Development Report* under the headline "Art Review: Ed Ruscha and the Great American West."

"How Much Is that Joint in the Window?" originally appeared jointly in Common Edge Collaborative (commonedge.org) and the *California Planning & Development Report* under the headline, "Storefront Ethics: Cannabis and Urbanism."

"Shared Hardships and the Souls of Cities" originally appeared in Planetizen.

"Where Nobody Knows Your Name" originally appeared in the *Los Angeles Times*, under the headline, "In Los Angeles, Thirsting for a Decent Bar Culture."

"In the Market for a Supermarket" originally appeared in the *Los Angeles Downtown News*, under the headline, "A Market, A Life."

Chapter 2

"Los Angeles's Slow-Growthers Have Gotten What They Wanted"/"Los Angeles Reaches Capacity"; "Housing Crisis, Meet Transit Crisis"; "Renters vs. Tenants: A Distinction with a Difference"; "Death by Gentrification"; "Radical Left Burns Bridges amid Quest To Build Housing"; and "It's Time to Stop Demonization of Developers" originally appeared in the *California Planning &*

Development Report.

"Dispatches from the Country's Worst Rental Market" originally appeared in Planetizen.

Chapter 3

"Wendell Cox's Version of *Dune*"; "Dumb Objections to Smart Growth"; "Job Creators Need Not Fear Urban Planners"; and "Fetishizing Families" originally appeared in the *California Planning & Development Report.*

"Debunking, and Creating, Myths of Sprawl" originally appeared in Planetizen.

Chapter 4

"Let the Sun Set on Ballot Measures"; "A Lesson in Planning for Beverly Hills"; "Lodi Gets Stuck on Agenda 21"; "Los Angeles Learns to Play Ball"; "Why Cities Should Back Off of Setbacks"; and "The Opposite of Gentrification" originally appeared in the *California Planning & Development Report.*

"Billboards, Big Money, and (Political) Blight" originally appeared in Planetizen.

"Silicon Beach Misses Chance to Curb Rising Rents"/"Silicon Beach Could Use Less Coding, More Voting" originally appeared in *Santa Monica Next.*

Chapter 5

"The Dark Side of Environmental Quality" and "A Rowhouse Reverie" originally appeared in the *California Planning & Development Report.*

"Cities and the End of History"; "Paradise Reconsidered"; "The Work of Architecture in the Age of Mechanical Reproduction"; and "On Skylines and Snapshots" originally appeared in Common Edge Collaborative.

"The Quiet Evils of America's 'Favorite' Buildings" and "The Curious Anonymity of Architecture" originally appeared in Planetizen.

Chapter 6

"Richard Florida's Reckoning"; "California Needs 'Minimum

Housing' to Go Along with Minimum Wage"/"Minimum Wage? How about Minimum Housing?"; "Tech Windfall, Deportation Order Threaten to Snap Los Angeles in Half"; "Hyperloop and Hyperbole"; and "Los Angeles's Moral Failing", and "Battle between Football, Brunch Rages in L.A.", originally appeared in the *California Planning & Development Report*.

"Book Review: *Culture Crash* Creative Class Gets Priced Out"; "The City as Factory"; and "Amazon and Urbanism" originally appeared in Planetizen.

Chapter 7

"How California Helped Elect Trump"; "Calexit in Reverse"; and "California's Nastiest Urban-Rural Rivalry" originally appeared in the *California Planning & Development Report*.

"Trump Trades on Geographic Illiteracy" originally appeared in *The Huffington Post*.

"Deconstructing a Tea Party Muse;" "Trump to Cities: You're Already Dead"; and "Trump Raises Stakes for Urban Journalism" originally appeared in Planetizen.

"A Missed Lesson in the Heart of California" originally appeared in *Boom California*.

Chapter 8

"Urban Planning Takes Center Stage", "Undoing the Legacy of Segregation", and "50 Years Later, Jacobs Still Leads a Sorority of Dissent" originally appeared in the *California Planning & Development Report*.

"The Wisdom and the Hysteria" and "Reading, Writing, and Planning" originally appeared in Planetizen.

"Jane Jacobs: 100 and Timeless as Ever" originally appeared in *The Architect's Newspaper*.

Photo Credits

Chapter 1

Eberhardt, Jared. "Smog Cutter". 15 November 2008. Online image. Flickr. <https://www.flickr.com/photos/jaredeberhardt/3037615274>

Leong, Kit. "Exterior View of the Downtown Ralphs Supermarket". 5 October 2017. Online image. Shutterstock. <https://www.shutterstock.com/image-photo/los-angeles-oct-5-exterior-view-731614621>

Wong, Benny. "At Los Angeles Memorial Coliseum - Section 9". 9 July 2012. Online image. Flickr. <https://www.flickr.com/photos/bwong/7532214848>

Villeneuve, Denis, director. Blade Runner 2049. Warner Bros. Pictures, 2017, <https://bladerunnermovie.com/post/162843153308>

Derr, Brian. "Superstorm Sandy Hoboken, NJ". 30 October 2012. Online image. Shutterstock. <https://www.shutterstock.com/image-photo/hoboken-new-jersey-usa-10302012-superstorm-1144176503>

Everett, Bart. "A Project to Widen the San Diego Freeway, I-405". 17 February 2010. Online image. Shutterstock. <https://www.shutterstock.com/image-photo/los-angeles-feb-17-project-widen-46893931>

Hitt, Katherine. "High Times". 4 July 2008. Online image. Flickr. <https://www.flickr.com/photos/milkwhitegown/4120304790>

Russellstreet. "Honey, I Twisted Through More Damn Traffic

Today". 10 April 2015. Online image. Flickr. <https://www.flickr.com/photos/russellstreet/37872111251>

Chapter 2

Gustafson, Britta. "PICT6524". 6 September 2009. Online image. Flickr. <https://www.flickr.com/photos/dreamyshade/3894862837>

Diaz, Ricardo. "Hollywood Bowl". 25 June 2007. Online image. Flickr. <https://www.flickr.com/photos/ricardodiaz/636516098>

Dennstedt, Frederick. "Blue Line Train at Pico Station". 15 February 2008. Online image. Flickr. <https://www.flickr.com/photos/fredcamino/2273248879>

Didierbuffon. "SANY0010". 27 July 2008. Online image. Flickr. <https://www.flickr.com/photos/28034287@N02/2708892016>

Chapter 3

Worker101. "Exurbs". 11 December 2005. Online image. Flickr. <https://www.flickr.com/photos/worker101/75441066>

Dillon, Matthew. "Guadalupe-Nipomo 'Oceano' Dunes". 25 June 2011. Online image. Flickr. <https://www.flickr.com/photos/ruggybear/5888889173>

Smart_growth. "Pasadena Light Rail Del Mar Station". 4 February 2007. Online image. Flickr. <https://www.flickr.com/photos/smart_growth/2241566711>

Skewes, John. "K5JS9148 - Warrina". 28 August 2014. Online image. Flickr. <https://www.flickr.com/photos/johnske/15058866891>

Chapter 4

Paterson, Jessica. "California Capitol Building". 18 January 2010. Online image. Flickr. <https://www.flickr.com/photos/modernrelics/4461010654>

Hawk, Thomas. "Angelyne". 26 December 2007. Online image. Flickr. <https://www.flickr.com/photos/thomashawk/2199255616>

Yeeblr. "Snapchat-Office". 19 January 2014. Online image. Flickr.

<https://www.flickr.com/photos/92587441@N03/12044498703>

Natarajan, Reg. "City Hall, Beverly Hills, California". 20 March 2005. Online image. Flickr. <https://www.flickr.com/photos/regnatarajan/4287873546>

Fingerhood, Bruce. "Lodi-1". 1 April 2007. Online image. Flickr. <https://www.flickr.com/photos/springfieldhomer/441419182>

McConnell, Josh. "Tour of Dodger Stadium". 18 February 2014. Online image. Flickr. <https://www.flickr.com/photos/joshmcconnell/16334993155>

Nouhailler, Patrick. "Copenhagen". 11 August 2010. Online image. Flickr. <https://www.flickr.com/photos/patrick_nouhailler/5276275939>

Lund, Ken. "Beverly Hills, California". 20 September 2015. Online image. Flickr. <https://www.flickr.com/photos/kenlund/20968232143>

Chapter 5

Herholz, Dave. "Walt Disney Concert Hall". 19 November 2010. Online image. Flickr. <https://www.flickr.com/photos/dherholz/5191198099>

Láscar, Jorge. "St. Mary's Basilica", 7 August 2012. Online image. Flickr. <https://www.flickr.com/photos/jlascar/9156824321>

Grenier, Cory M. "In the CCTV Shadow". 26 October 2008. Online image. Flickr. <https://www.flickr.com/photos/26087974@N05/4180829945>

Banfield, Steve. "Walk of Fame". 9 April 2014. Online image. Flickr. <https://www.flickr.com/photos/sbanfield/13750765845>

Boed, Roman. "Chicago". 30 July 2018. Online image. Flickr. <https://www.flickr.com/photos/romanboed/42396012050>

Pousson, Eli. "Napa Street Facing NE". 4 January 2009. Online image. Flickr. <https://www.flickr.com/photos/elipousson/3181718084>

Sableman, Paul. "Apartment Buildings". 22 April 2012. Online image. Flickr. <https://www.flickr.com/photos/pasa/6866849764>

Spakhrin. "Las Vegas 2014". 16 November 2014. Online image. Flickr. <https://www.flickr.com/photos/kathmandu/16080741955>

Chapter 6

Schipul, Ed. "Richard Florida". 21 October 2010. Online image. Flickr. <https://www.flickr.com/photos/eschipul/5104461577>

Mannix, Nicki. "Soho New York". 24 May 2013. Online image. Flickr. <https://www.flickr.com/photos/nickimm/9033903700>

Frankieleon. "Barnes & Noble Booksellers". 30 December 2010. Online image. Flickr. <https://www.flickr.com/photos/armydre2008/5306430125>

Kennedy, Ian. "Hyperloop". 3 March 2016. Online image. Flickr. <https://www.flickr.com/photos/clankennedy/25490668985>

Chrisinphilly5448. "Los Angeles City Hall". 25 May 2013. Online image. Flickr. <https://www.flickr.com/photos/chrisinphilly5448/9071028521>

Chapter 7

Mgreene. "Atlas 1". 14 September 2007. Online image. Flickr. <https://www.flickr.com/photos/mgreene/2465928567>

Lund, Ken. "Welcome to California". 25 January 2009. Online image. Flickr. <https://www.flickr.com/photos/kenlund/3227633996>

Searls, Doc. "2008_09_21_lav-lax-bos_008". 21 September 2008. Online image. Flickr. <https://www.flickr.com/photos/docsearls/3014105571>

Sparqtraining. "Kerman Pics 019". 18 June 2008. Online image. Flickr. <https://www.flickr.com/photos/90717329@N00/2594906970>

Chapter 8

Littlenystock. "The Public Plaza Outside the Landmark Flatiron Building". 20 April 2012. Online image. Shutterstock.

<https://www.shutterstock.com/image-photo/new-york-city-apr-20-public-136554425>

Phan, David. "The Pianist of Washington Square Park". 10 May 2014. Online image. Flickr. <https://www.flickr.com/photos/davidphan/14304295541>

Edenpictures. "White Horse Tavern". 8 October 2017. Online image. Flickr. <https://www.flickr.com/photos/edenpictures/37579823132>

Acknowledgments

Bill Fulton probably didn't know quite what he was getting when he hired me in 2010 as editor of the *California Planning & Development Report,* in which many of these pieces originated. I've rarely, if ever, pitched an essay to Bill. I usually draft them on a whim and they appear unannounced in his inbox. Often this transaction takes place between endpoints nowhere near California, depending on our respective itineraries.

I thank Bill for embracing these surprises month-in and month-out and for giving me an unparalleled opportunity to learn and write about the state we both love. More immediately, I thank him for suggesting this book and for shepherding it as its editor and publisher. I look forward to great stories, and more surprises, to come.

I thank my predecessor Paul Shigley for accepting my first pitch to *CP&DR* and for handing me the reins to such an important publication.

While about half of these pieces originated in *CP&DR,* I've had the pleasure of contributing to other fantastic publications dedicated to cities. At risk of missing someone, I thank Christian Peralta, Tim Halbur, Jonathan Nettler, and Chris Steins at Planetizen; Martin Petersen at Common Edge Collaborative; Sam Lubell and Mimi Ziegler at *The Architect's Newspaper*; Janine White and Ariella Cohen at Next City; Jason Sexton and John Christiensen at *Boom*; Juliet Lapidos at the *Los Angeles Times*; and Stefanie Sobelle and Jonathan Hahn at the *Los Angeles Review of Books.* Though none of the pieces are in this book, I owe a shout-out to Arnold York at *The Malibu Times*, who gave me my first professional bylines.

I give special thanks to David Abel of *The Planning Report / Metro Investment Report* for welcoming me into his unusual but fantastic fraternity/sorority of Los Angeles planning insiders and to James Brasuell, of TPR/MIR, Planetizen, and legendary NorCal/SoCal punk band The Wrongs, for supporting me and succeeding me with steadfast aplomb.

Kira Walker produced such incredible options for the cover design, I could have used five different covers and been equally thrilled. I thank her for her hard work and excellent design eye.

Thanks to Taber Falconer for her assistance on this project, Elise Brancheau and Alisa Moore for their superb copy editing, and Talon Klipp for layout.

I could not have accepted the job at *CP&DR* without the kind indulgence, however bewildered, of my graduate school advisors Julie Wilson and Jose Gomez-Ibañez. While I'm at it, let's go all the way back to my undergraduate days to thank Andrew Haughwout for teaching The American City, the course that started it all for me.

I thank my family of producers, directors, actors, cinematographers, writers, artists, fashion bloggers, and other creative types for supporting me and for tolerating such earthly matters as those in this book. I especially thank my parents for moving (separately) to Los Angeles so that I did not have to grow up in Boston. I remember my grandmothers: Evelyn, who lived the American suburban dream in New Jersey, and Carol, the consummate Manhattanite. I thank all of my friends near and far for letting me hold forth from time to time and of inspiring many of the ideas in this book.

Finally, I bid a brokenhearted farewell to Jonathan Wellerstein, my comrade in many an urban adventure.

About Solimar Books

Solimar Books publishes and markets books about urban planning and economic development, especially for California.

Talk City, by William Fulton
Talk City is a collection of the remarkable blogs that distinguished urban planner Bill Fulton wrote while serving as a member of the City Council in the California beach town of Ventura. The blog started out as a way to explain what had happened at the weekly council meetings. Before long, however, it turned into an evocative, real-time chronicle of what it was like to serve as an underpaid, overstressed, part-time local elected official during hard times. If you like local government and politics, you'll love how *Talk City* reveals the stresses and strains of serving as an elected official in a typical American city.

Romancing the Smokestack, by William Fulton
How did Federal Express decide to locate at the Memphis Airport? Why is China also losing manufacturing jobs? Do artists really help turn around a struggling neighborhood? What should you do with a declining auto mall - save it or let it die and start over again? What's better - subsidizing an business or subsidizing the infrastructure such a business requires? *Romancing the Smokestack* is a collection of economic development columns from *Governing* magazine that covers these questions - and reveals the good, the bad, and the ugly about how economic development is practiced in the United States.

Guide to California Planning 5th Edition, by William Fulton and Paul Shigley
Since it was first published in 1991, *Guide to California Planning* has served as the authoritative textbook on city and county planning practice throughout the state. The first book ever written that covers all aspects of planning in a single state, *Guide to California Planning* is used as a textbook in virtually every college- and graduate- level planning program in California. Easy to read and understand, *Guide to California Planning* is far more than a textbook. It's an ideal tool for planning professionals, members of allied professions in the planning and development fields, and citizen activists.

The Reluctant Metropolis, by William Fulton
In twelve engaging essays, Bill Fulton chronicles the history of urban planning in the Los Angeles metropolitan area, tracing the legacy of short-sighted political and financial gains that has resulted in a vast urban region on the brink of disaster. Looking at such diverse topics as shady real estate speculations, the construction of the Los Angeles subway, the battle over the future of South Central L.A. after the 1992 riots, and the emergence of Las Vegas as "the new Los Angeles," Fulton offers a fresh perspective on the city's epic sprawl.

www.solimarbooks.com

About Josh Stephens

A writer with a penchant for covering cities, transportation, urban planning, and design, Josh Stephens is contributing editor of the *California Planning & Development Report* (www.cp-dr.com), the state's foremost independent publication dedicated to urban planning. Josh previously edited *The Planning Report and the Metro Investment Report*, monthly publications covering, respectively, land use and infrastructure in Southern California.

Publications to which Josh has contributed include Planetizen, Next City, *The Architect's Newspaper, Architect Magazine, Planning Magazine*, Common Edge Collaborative, *Sierra Magazine, Los Angeles Magazine*, and the *Los Angeles Review of Books*.

Josh is a longtime board member, and board president, of the Westside Urban Forum, a nonprofit dedicated to civic engagement in his native west Los Angeles. Josh earned his bachelor's degree in English from Princeton University and his master's in public policy from the Harvard University Kennedy School of Government.

His work is collected at www.joshrstephens.net.